Closework

Closework

**A story that will change
the way you think about
your life, work, and future**

Adam Lury & Simon Gibson

CYAN

First published in Great Britain in 2004 by

Cyan Communications Limited
79 St John Street, London EC1M 4NR
www.cyancommunications.com

"Full fathom five thy father lies;
Of his bones are coral made;
Those are pearls that were his eyes:
Nothing of him that doth fade,
But doth suffer a sea-change
Into something rich and strange."

Act I, Scene II, *The Tempest,* William Shakespeare

Preface by Jim Bates

I don't scare easily.

Twenty years as CEO of a number of large corporations prepares you for most of the shocks in life. And those you don't see coming you learn to manage.

So when I say that Mat Durer's story frightened me, I suppose that should count for something. At least it tells you that even a CEO is human. Cut me and I bleed so to speak.

At first I was disturbed by a sense that what Mat had related had awoken, or perhaps re-awoken, in me a belief that not all human experience is entirely explainable. The sense that even in a world as tough-skinned as business, fate plays a troubling hand. But I would probably have dismissed such feelings as mere superstition if events had not subsequently overtaken me in such a chilling and tragic manner. It is one thing to have suspicions of a darker force at work, quite another to see them played out before your very eyes.

For many months I have asked myself whether I should make anything of what has happened. I have worried that an account might open old wounds. But, at the same time, I have felt the discoveries that Mat made along the way were just too interesting, and important, to leave buried. It seems to me that as he was driven on by his own demons, Mat discovered something real and true about being in business. So true it sounds simple. So simple you can't think why you never realized it before.

In the end it was the power of these simple ideas that persuaded me to risk telling Mat's story. I continue to hope it was a risk worth taking.

I have reconstructed scenes from conversations with Mat and others concerned. I have also had access to certain papers and files. From these fragments I have pieced together a narrative that presents as complete and, I hope, as accurate a picture as possible of what happened.

Interview at Jim Bates's house,
Up Island, Martha's Vineyard

I first met Mat at my house on Martha's Vineyard, late on a beautiful July afternoon.

After the polite introductions, in which he exchanged a few words with my wife about the nature of his journey, he and I retired to the garden with some iced tea. It was very quiet; there is no traffic at our end of the island.

He was tense and sat on the edge of a white-painted wooden chair, clinking ice cubes against his glass.

"I used to be the original skeptic," Mat said. "I only believed what I saw with my own eyes. I only agreed with what was logical and factual and demonstrable. I thought everything could be controlled – that it was just a question of knowing how. The numbers were what mattered. I was the ultimate product of the rational institutions."

Certainly Mat looked the rational, preppy type. He was tallish, a little over six feet, medium build with dark hair and bright blue eyes. But his manner was anything but restrained.

"Are you a skeptic, Jim?" he asked.

"It's reasonable to assume that I don't believe everything I read in the newspapers," I replied.

He looked up at the branches of the large American oak as the light filtered through the leaves and dappled the ground.

"Suppose I asked you to deny your successes and instead to admit to failure. Suppose I said that fate has brought me here to give you an opportunity to make amends? What would you say to that?" he said, twisting his body toward me, fixing me with a gaze, like he'd been in a road accident and was stumbling toward help and the light.

"I would probably ask you to leave – politely, of course," I said.

I was stung and would no doubt have left matters at that, if what he had said had not contained an uncomfortable grain of truth. So I went on, perhaps hoping to cover my tracks.

"You call me up out of the blue. You use an introduction from Hardings to get you through my front door. You tell me you need my help. You're desperate, you say. Now you want to tell me that I have been wrong for the past 20 years. That I've screwed up my career – a career that, frankly, most other commentators would say was extraordinarily successful. And you want to be sarcastic, too. I think we're getting to the end of the discussion, don't you?"

"Sure, you're right. I was out of line," he said rapidly, almost stretching out his hand to touch me in reassurance, the way you would a frightened child. "It's just I'm so strung out right now and I have got all these thoughts burning through my head. I really need your help, please."

"All right. I am prepared to give you ten minutes. No more," I said.

Mat straightened up, told me about his big idea. Hooked me into his life.

The note

Mat gave me a scrap of paper. It was an old letter, worn at the folds. It was handwritten and brief, although the writing became barely legible in the last few lines.

Mat,

I was sorry that you were unable to come last week. I missed you.

We have so much ground to make up, and now I fear that we have run out of time. I simply wish you to make the most of your life. Don't sell your soul to business; find it there. Put yourself into something that grows and develops, that generates something through others. I worry that your career at Hardings, however successful, might not provide this fulfillment.

Make the most of that free-thinking spirit of yours. Remember that you're original and that I believe in you.

Be there for Anneka — she's going to need you.

love,

Dad

Pittsburgh: The crossing

Six months before we met Mat was working for Hardings & Co., the leading management consultants. He was 32 and was already being touted as a potential future leader of the firm.

Mat had joined Hardings some five years previously, straight from Harvard Business School. Hardings take a mere handful of new MBAs each year; only the brightest and best. Starting salaries are in excess of $100,000. Not bad for young men and women with no experience in business.

But it wasn't difficult to see why Hardings would want Mat Durer. At HBS he'd excelled academically, with the top grades of his year. He was also a popular figure around campus. Not least, one suspects, because of natural good looks. Apparently he was always around the party circuit, cutting a dash, especially in a tux at one of the formal events like the Newport Ball. Contemporaries say he looked great in a tux, the way some men do in formal military uniform.

So Mat was a natural for the fast lane in business and with Hardings he was given every opportunity to excel. He was introduced to senior executives right from his very first days with the firm; working on a whole range of projects, assisting everyone from private equity firms and start-ups right through to *Fortune* 500 corporations to increase their shareholder value and market share. He advised and management listened; he was a Hardings Consultant.

At this particular time, he was part of a Hardings team working for InterSat, the communications business based in Pittsburgh: the place where the rivers meet. It was early December. There was snow on the ground and taped Christmas carols in the air.

That evening he'd been giving a presentation to the executive team at InterSat in the downtown district. It had been a "double act" presentation with his colleague, Brad Johnson. Brad was tall and thin, with tortoise-shell-rimmed glasses and sandy hair. He was senior to Mat at Hardings – he'd joined

11

some three years before Mat – and had just been made up to partner, but the two of them worked more or less as equals. The presentation had been on "Managing the Marketplace," defining how InterSat could identify early the significant new trends among global audiences.

The meeting had broken up around 7.30 with the promise that Mat and Brad would have some recommendations to make on investment patterns by 8.30 the following morning at the breakfast forum. That was typical of the kind of turnaround Hardings consultants worked to. The requirement for such dedication isn't written into the Hardings contract. It doesn't need to be. Real Hardings people get high on being pushed higher and faster. They want it, they need it. They get a buzz out of forcing themselves beyond the acceptable levels of endurance, of committing themselves to ridiculous demands and crazy schedules. They need to prove they can do it, prove that they are different from the crowd. Eventually it just becomes a way of life.

And Mat and Brad were simply more Hardings than most.

"Mat, do you want to go through the figures over dinner, or shall we just carry on now?" Brad asked, zipping his thin, silver Toshiba notebook back into its black holster.

"I'd suggest over dinner," said Mat. He walked over to a couple of large cartons of research papers marked "Hardings & Co.: Highly Confidential." "That way I'll have time to get these papers to Project Support and get a couple of the young associates to number crunch. They can email me the break-downs by around 9.30. Then we'll have them to add to the mix."

"Sounds fine. We need those figures, that's for sure. I just can't see why this damn management team don't get the message we've been giving them over the past weeks: 'It's Asia, stupid…'" said Brad.

"I think they're getting the message, it's just they don't want to move as quickly as we think they should," replied Mat. "They're cautious."

"Well if they wait much longer they're going to miss the strike and Fox will be all over them."

"I agree, but you can't change human nature. If they're cautious we've just got to work them round to our suggestion."

"That would be fine, Mat. But we don't have time. My suggestion is that if this steering committee don't buy in to the strategy tomorrow, we go over their heads. Go straight to Nicholls and the rest of the board."

Brad had been on the project for six weeks. It was time to move on.

"You know we can't do that. It's not how things work here," said Mat.

"Well, it's how they should work. The CEO is the only one who really understands the market right now. If it weren't for him, this whole company would be in a big black hole."

"Could be," said Mat.

"Trust me. I'm right. I've seen it a hundred times. Get to the CEO and you get results. We're wasting time with the steering committee. I'll try one more time tomorrow morning with these new numbers and after that I'm going over their heads."

"Shouldn't that be a 'we'?" asked Mat.

"Sure, we are going over their heads," replied Brad.

"Well, let's see how things turn out tomorrow morning," continued Mat. "But you know what would really help right now is if I took the project car. It will be a whole lot easier than trying to load all these papers into a taxi."

"No problem," said Brad, reaching into his pocket and taking out the car keys. "It's a blue BMW 4-wheel. I parked at the back of the building. All the courtesy parking bays were full up. Just promise me you won't go speeding around town just because you're driving a car I've signed for. I'll track you down in the end you know...."

"Thanks, appreciate it Brad," replied Mat.

"OK, well, if you can manage those boxes, I might as well take a cab and catch you later," said Brad.

"Yeah no problem. And again, I appreciate the car."

Brad left and Mat pulled together his remaining papers and put them into his auburn-colored crocodile skin attaché case.

His girlfriend, Marianne, had given it to him when they moved in together. Outside, the lights of the corporate towers stood out against the night – reassuring signals that others were still working. Over the next few minutes, Mat sorted through the research materials to make sure everything was there. Then he loaded the two boxes into the elevator and took the vertical jump through 16 floors of concrete and glass. The boxes were heavy and awkward to carry. Mat had to balance one on top of the other as he walked through reception.

"Can I help you with those, sir?" the security guard on the front desk asked as Mat passed.

"No thanks, I can manage," replied Mat. "Cold out there."

"Sure is, sir. I heard that the rivers was frozen over. That's cold, sir. But they say that there's a thaw on the way. Just in time for the game this weekend."

"Yeah, should be a great game," said Mat. "The Patriots are really firing right now."

"Sir, if I was a Patriot supporter, I would be very worried. Very worried indeed. Because this is one mean city and we are going to give that team of yours the Big Chill. Frozen out. Like those rivers out there. Know what I mean, sir?"

"Friend, no one has frozen us out all season. We're top of the league or maybe you hadn't noticed."

"The higher they are, the further they shall fall!" recited the security guard in mock preacher style, and the two laughed in a kind of final "have a good evening" manner. Mat pushed his back against the swing doors and walked out into the parking area.

It was snowing outside and Mat pulled the collar of his coat up high to give some protection from the sharp wind. He was hungry and tired. He just wanted to get the papers to his research assistants and get back to the hotel fast. He would take a shower and then go through the numbers over dinner with Brad.

He walked round the back of the building and placed the boxes down carefully on the tarmac. On this side of the building there were no lights and he couldn't see too well. He clicked on the car's remote alarm, so that its lights flashed on and the doors unlocked. As he bent down to pick up the boxes his cell phone fell out of his jacket pocket and he fumbled for it in the dark. Feeling his way along the ground he eventually found it just a few inches from his right foot. He walked over to the dark outline of the BMW and placed the boxes in the boot, along with his attaché case and his coat. Then he got into the front and put the keys in the ignition. The radio came on. Brad had tuned it to some local rock station and a Meat Loaf song was playing – *Like a Bat out of Hell*. Mat switched it off.

"Brad, you dude," Mat whispered to himself.

As he let off the handbrake, there was a scuffling sound in the back of the car. Mat looked up into the mirror. Must be Brad playing a game on him.

"OK Brad. Lousy taste in music, but you're forgiven. You can come out now."

A dark face leaned forward. It wasn't Brad. And what's more Brad wasn't in the habit of carrying an eight-inch Bowie knife.

"Drive, mister."

The dark face had an Hispanic accent.

At first Mat wasn't particularly worried. He was so focused on what he needed to get done that evening that he found himself thinking: "Wouldn't you just believe it. I've got all this work to do by morning and now this guy wants to frisk me for my wallet. Jesus! As if I wasn't tired enough already."

Typical Mat. Dedicated and determined. Perhaps, one might say, dangerously single-minded – for his own good anyway.

So instead of instantly obeying the order that came from behind, Mat turned round and said: "Look if it's money you want, you can take my wallet and cards right now."

Then a gun appeared at Mat's head. Mat remembered thinking that he'd seen guns on TV and in shops many times before, and they never looked like this. This was metal and real and it was pointing at him.

Mat felt a sudden wave of panic wash through him. His body tensed, his heart pounded in his chest. There was a gun pointing at his head. One shot and he could be dead. For no sensible reason. Just because of a random fact like he'd borrowed a fancy car. That wasn't a good enough reason to wind up dead. Damn BMW! The irony was that it wasn't Mat's style of car at all. It was far too obvious. But that didn't matter. Mat was in the driving seat. He was guilty.

"I say drive!" a second voice said, more insistently.

Mat didn't argue or hesitate. Now he did exactly as he was told.

He drove out of the parking lot. It was snowing even harder and he flicked on the wipers to keep the snow off the windscreen. He drove carefully through the city, following the short instructions from the rear: "Take the tunnel...Take a left here...Go right at the lights...."

As they drove, they passed groups of people at the side of the road or gathered at bus stops, hunched against the cold. The temperature meter on the BMW's dashboard read –8°. A city roadsweeper drove in front of them for a while clearing away the snow.

They continued for maybe 20 minutes across town, to streets that were dark and deserted.

"OK drive down there, man," a voice from the back called.

Mat turned the car down a rough track, which led down a slope and then leveled off. One of the men got out of the car, the other remained inside.

"Now you. Out of car."

Mat stepped out into the bitter cold night air. There was a gun pointing at him.

"Against the limo – put your hands on the roof."

Mat obeyed and the man's hands were over him in an instant. His wallet, his phone – gone. The guy could have them.

"OK, move away, man. Face away, man. Go walking."

The point of the gun was used to indicate the direction in which Mat should walk.

Mat turned and faced into the dark. The snow was falling lightly on his head and shoulders. He could see only a few feet in front of him. He started walking into the snow.

"Walk, man. Till we say stop," the voice shouted.

Mat kept walking – not looking back, just walking into the darkness. The darkness closed around him the further he went.

"Keep walking, man."

Mat took a few more steps. Then he heard the muffled sound of the BMW's engine and the high-pitched screech of wheels.

He was alone in the pitch dark.

He turned around, toward where he thought he had come from.

He heard a loud crack, like a tree snapping in half. But it came from the ground beneath his feet. He recognized the sound, but couldn't explain it. Another crack, another tree snapping. Then he knew. The sound wasn't coming from trees. It was ice. He was standing on ice and the ice was cracking up around him. The bastards had made him walk out on the frozen river.

For the second time, he felt that surge of panic. This time it took his breath away and was accompanied by a hollow rush of nausea. For the second time in half an hour, he felt he was about to die.

He felt paralyzed.

He thought of what would happen – if he went through the ice. The cold. The shock. He would be fighting for breath. In that terrible cold. In the dark. And no one would know where he was. Not Anneka his sister, nor Marianne his girlfriend, not the people at Hardings. No one. He would die alone, water filling his lungs.

He couldn't move. He felt the slightest gesture might cause the ice to break around him. He could barely turn his head.

He breathed in the cold air. The panic started to subside. His mind came back. He was alone. No one to help him. This was the ultimate independence. He had to think for himself. His brilliant mind now had a basic human problem to solve: survival.

The sound of cracking had come from the direction in which he'd walked. There was no turning back. He looked forward. Should he get on his front and spread the load? Should he walk? Should he run? Maybe lying on his front was best in theory, but try thinking theories when you're about to go under the ice and drown in a freezing river. He took a step forward. Nothing. Then another step and another. A loud crack.

Mat stopped and took a deep gasp of cold air. It hurt his lungs. He had to keep calm. From now on, he knew that whatever sound he heard he would have to keep on walking. Not fast, but he had to keep on walking.

He went on. The cracks from the ice cut through his nerves and seemed to be right at his side, and he knew that he would not last long. At that moment, he saw a light. A soft light through the snow. A beacon. He moved toward the light and he longed to run. Get there fast. Get there somehow. But he kept his pace and his eyes fixed on the light. Then he stumbled, he had hit uneven ground. Ground. He had reached the bank. He was shaking and nauseous, but he'd made it. He'd survived. The panic gave away to a split second of light-headed euphoria. But then he remembered the sound of the ice cracking. It felt like it was cracking inside of him.

Mat walked up the slope, clapping his arms around his body to try to generate some warmth. He was getting nearer to the light.

Suddenly, from darkness to his left he saw a figure also walking toward the light. It was a man wearing an overcoat and hat. He was walking slowly through the snow, shoulders hunched against the cold.

Mat called out: "Hello."

The man kept on walking.

Mat called out again: "Hello. Hello. Can you hear me?"

The man slowly turned his head. His face… Mat knew the man's face. It was the face of his father. But his father was dead. He'd died five years ago.

Mat gasped for air in the cold. He looked again. It couldn't be him. But it was.

It was his father. He was certain of it. He felt both sick and joyous at the same time.

His father lifted his hand and gestured toward Mat, as though beckoning him toward a pool of light ahead. It was illuminating the falling snow, creating a narrow arc of white flakes, while the rest of the sky, also filled with snow, was dark. Beneath the light there were some iron gates at the entrance to a disused factory.

His father stopped for a moment at the gates and turned once more. He beckoned and then walked through the gates.

"Dad... Dad, wait for me," Mat shouted and started running toward the pool of light.

But in that moment his father was gone.

Mat stood by the iron gates. Alone. He was sobbing. Tears were running down his face.

He started shouting into the night air.

"Dad. Wait! Dad. Dad...."

9.12.2003
Pittsburgh Police Report
Interview with Mat Durer

Subject was picked up at disused Wentworth
Industries site following call from site
janitor, John Christie.

Subject appeared in considerable state of
shock and was transferred to Allegheny General
where he was attended by a physician and
discharged. Subsequent interview revealed
that subject was victim of car hijacking by
two armed men. <u>Vehicle stolen BMW 4x4 Series.
Metallic blue. License Plate DFL 9611.</u>

Also stolen personal effects including wallet,
credits cards, mobile phone, and attaché case
(see list attached).

Subject also claims he was forced out of
vehicle at gunpoint at Curlew Point. Yet he
was found at a site on the other side of the
Ohio River. Interviewing officer expresses
amazement that this could be possible. Even
though parts of the river were frozen over,
such a crossing would be nothing short of
miraculous. No one has ever made it across
the Ohio in these conditions. Subject
maintains veracity of story and there is
no evidence to the contrary.

Subject performing photofit of car hijackers.

<u>Status: Treat with caution. Possible armed
assailants.</u>

<u>All bureau: Stolen vehicle.</u>

Boston, Massachusetts: The offer

The Hardings head office in Boston is just a block from the John Hancock Tower. I have been to the offices on a number of occasions. The interiors are statements of power and the pursuit of power. Take the reception, for instance. There's a long low desk with three young women taking calls and greeting visitors. Actually, these young women are Sirens. They draw you in with their soft voices and perfect complexions. In a matter of seconds you find yourself willingly handing over your coat.

On the wall behind these Sirens is a huge stylized map of the world across the entire length of the low atrium. It's a statement of corporate intent: "This is our territory." As soon as you enter the world of Hardings & Co. you feel in safe hands.

The inside is classic, timeless elegance. The carpets are peach and the desks of maple. Hardings aren't into fads like open plan. But neither are they fusty or reactionary. So while all consultants have their own offices, all offices have glass walls, underlining the transparency that lies at the heart of the Hardings code of conduct.

Of course the offices have superb views across the city. You can see the waters of Massachusetts Bay, glimmering between the darker masses of the coast and the islands, across the Inner Harbor and out to Deer Island, Bass Point, and Galloupes.

But, for all of their superb views, Hardings offices are at the heart of Boston's hard edge – its business community. They are surrounded by companies. There is an undoubted energy on these streets. The sense of business happening. Hardings would claim that they respond to the intellectual side of business. But they are also affected by its adrenaline rush. The excitement of making deals. The excitement of a company in action.

Arguably, the company, this unit of organization, has done more to change the world than all your philosophies. Forget Marx or Leon Trotsky; the firebrands are Inc., or Ltd, or S.A. What we eat, what we wear, in fact just about everything about our daily lives started off as someone's bright idea, which then became a business idea and then a company. Capitalism is just a lazy term applied by those who don't understand how things really work. The true unit of change is the company. It shaped history; ended history. It's a unit that can be one man or several hundred thousand, that can adapt to any activity, that can speak English or Chinese or all languages on earth simultaneously, that can be a single shop or a global enterprise, that can be owned by a close family or by people who will never, ever meet. In fact, it can be owned by machines and frequently is. It's a unit of organization that goes beyond the tribal and yet creates fierce loyalties, that can have a culture without a nationality, that can be run by tyrants or benefactors and with equal success. It seems to be a classic primate organization but often works best when the authority is devolved like you'd find in an ant colony, that you can join for a day or a lifetime, that defines who you are and then changes its name. It's an investment vehicle which happens to have people. It can be just about anything you want it to be including sleeping, that most people in the world will belong to at least once in our lives.

Therein lies the seduction. The endlessly versatile nature of the company offers endless analysis, which is why you need smart people like Hardings to help sort things out.

The senior partner at Hardings & Co. is Anthony Elliott. He's an impressive man, tall, urbane, and silver-haired. In fact he's exactly what you want from the very highest ranks of executive thinking. For a start, he's disarmingly modest. He'll never try to make you look a fool in a meeting. He's direct but never aggressive, charm is his offensive. He wears elegant suits from Huntsman, Savile Row, and his is mind razor sharp. He's the Grand Master, the man with every move in his head.

He's well liked in business and many of the world's top executives who have met him enjoy his easy company. They'd probably also describe him as a bit of an enigma. On the one hand he's the ultra intellectual, on the other he has a beautiful young wife (16 years younger) and he has a passion for ocean yacht racing. *Forbes* magazine just loves that combination. The

Grand Master has hormones. That's cool.

There is a sense of this mix in Anthony's office. First there are great views over the Charles River, he can practically see into Harvard Yard from his desk. Then there are the photographs on the wall. Some taken by Anthony, but most by professionals. There are also images of ocean racing yachts – Anthony owns a yacht that competed in regattas. Next to these are shots of Anthony and his wife, Sagradio. He's fifty, she's thirty-four. He's Ivy League, she's a Brazilian Beauty. She's the Girl from Ipanema. She's Jobim's Muse. Still other photographs show Sagradio and their three-year-old son, Harrison. By the photographs, there's a set of worry beads, made from semi-precious stones. A gift from a grateful client from the Middle East.

Anthony has a broad desk equipped with a cordless phone and an ultra-thin iMac screen. There was rarely any paper on his desk. Right now, there was just one sheet in front of him. It was a letter from Mat Durer. Anthony had read it carefully several times. He had even thought about it over night and now had to take some action.

There was a knock at his door. It opened. Mat Durer walked in.

"Good morning, Anthony," he said.

"Mat, good morning. Do please come in. Take a seat," said Anthony, standing up as Mat entered the room. Mat was sharply dressed in a blue suit and button-down Oxford shirt and red tie. The two of them went over to sit in the armchairs – in the "relaxed conversation area" – arranged around a small coffee table to the side of Anthony's office.

"I was so terribly sorry to hear of this ghastly incident in Pittsburgh. Are you all right after it all?" asked Anthony.

"I was a bit shaken at the time," Mat replied, "but I seem to have recovered OK and the rest of the InterSat team have covered for me while I have been trying to piece my life together. Getting all my cards and papers sorted out. Fortunately the InterSat papers which were stolen in the car weren't originals so we haven't lost too much time."

"Well, yes, we can always sort the papers out. The important thing is that you weren't harmed."

Anthony's concern was in marked contrast to his colleague Brad's panic reaction to the loss of confidential papers; a loss for which he blamed Mat.

"Oh yes, I'm fine, Anthony, really," continued Mat.

"I am delighted to hear it. We wouldn't want to have one of our young stars damaged in any way would we?" said Anthony with that warm, professorial charm of his.

"Actually, that's part of the reason I have called you in. I know that this sort of incident can be very traumatic and that the ripples of its aftershock can go on for quite a while. So I wanted to suggest that you take a few days off. Don't count it as leave. Just take some time with your lovely Marianne and make sure that you're really all in one piece before coming back to projects full time."

"I much appreciate your concern, Anthony, but I want to get back to the InterSat team as soon as possible," Mat said. "Things are at quite a critical stage. And really it was only my pride that was damaged back on that ice."

"Well, I will leave it up to your discretion, of course, Mat. But when it comes to restoring your pride perhaps there is one thing I can do."

Anthony got up from the armchair and walked over to the window and looked out. There was a brief pause as he took in the view and then he turned back to look at Mat.

"I haven't spoken to my partners on this matter, but I am sure that I can say that there is a general goodwill about your career among us and that we would expect you to be made up to partner at the next review meeting. I cannot promise this, but I would be surprised if that were not the case. I wanted to tell you now, because at difficult times it's important to know one is valued. Which you most certainly are."

It was masterly man management from Anthony. He'd read the situation. Mat was a diligent, hard-working member of his consultant team. A few kind words now might ensure absolute loyalty for years to come.

But for Mat the words were like an electric shock, a sudden intense charge that crashed through his whole system. Was he hearing right? Did Anthony Elliott really just offer him partnership? Now? Mat felt flushed, like he was breaking out into a sweat. He wanted to loosen his tie.

The offer of partnership was something he had dreamt about but never actually dared to hope for. This was the moment he'd worked for non-stop for the past five years. This was his pinnacle: partnership at Hardings. It didn't come better than this. And yet he felt sick inside.

He put on a forced smile.

"Well thank you for that great compliment, Anthony. Obviously it's good to know that my contribution is appreciated."

"Absolutely, Mat," Anthony went on. "You're a highly valued member of the team."

Anthony made an almost imperceptible move back to his desk. It was sign enough. The interview had come to an end.

"Thank you, Mat," he said. "And I know it goes without saying, but I would be glad if you would keep this conversation confidential until after the next partners' review meeting."

"Of course."

"Good," said Anthony. He stretched out his hand to Mat.

"Congratulations," he said with a firm shake.

Lunch with Anneka at the Mirage Restaurant, Harvard

"Na, wie geht's, Junge," said Anneka.

"Gut, danke und dir? Du siehst ein bisschen müde aus. Ist alles in Ordnung?" Mat replied.

German was Anneka and Mat's secret language, their familiar language. They had both started to speak German when their father had been posted to a job in Frankfurt. As is frequently the case, children become fluent in the language far faster than their parents and so it had been for Mat and Anneka. Thus, for quite a while they could converse in German without their parents understanding what was going on.

"*Ja, alles klar,*" she said with a smile.

They were seated in one of the side booths at the Mirage Restaurant at the back of Harvard Square. The Mirage is a small friendly place, popular with academics who like home Italian cooking and a quiet place to talk.

Mat looked closely at Anneka. Although she was saying she was fine, she didn't look great to Mat. There were dark shadows below her eyes and she was thinner than he was used to seeing her. Having said that, she was always petite. So perhaps there was nothing to worry about. Mat changed tone and became more upbeat.

"So, Professor, are they overworking you at that asylum for the technologically insane called MIT?" asked Mat.

"Oh no, I get regular meals under the door along with the promise of parole for good behavior – just like any normal academic," said Anneka. "In fact the older I get the better the warders treat me. Strange that, must be they think I'm no danger any more."

Although Mat teased Anneka about her professorial status, he was in fact very proud of his big sister's achievements. She was always the academic, the real intellectual of the two of them, taking after their father. While Mat was a little more like their mother; perhaps you could say a bit more creative as a result.

Now, at age 35, she held a post in psychology and technology at MIT. She specialized in the relationship between the human brain and the computer. She was one of the digerati, that glittering band who were bringing science and technology into a new intellectual dimension, what they described as the "third place."

"Now it's your turn to tell me that you're leading a thoroughly fulfilling lifestyle and are not in the least tired by the demands placed upon you," said Anneka. "Or is there some other reason why we're here?"

"There is," said Mat.

He took a drink of his mineral water. He was uneasy.

"I have never felt so lucid in my life, like every nerve ending is switched on, and yet I think I'm losing the plot. I can't work out what's going on. Some very weird things have been happening to me."

"Like what things?" asked Anneka. "I'm the rational one remember."

"Well for a start I have just been offered partnership at Hardings. Completely out of the blue. This morning. By the senior partner himself."

"Mat that's not weird… It's wonderful news," said Anneka, forgetting her sense of irony for a moment and reaching out to touch Mat's hand across the table.

"You've worked so hard to achieve it. I am so delighted for you. You can certainly pay for lunch on the back of that news."

"Yes, sure I know I should be delighted but instead I'm feeling tight and nervous," he said.

"Well that's only natural, it's a big step in your career," Anneka replied. "Things will never be the same again. But that's a positive change up."

"I know, I know. But it's not that. This huge sense of unease has come over me," he paused and took another sip of mineral water. "Like I don't know who I am or what's right any more."

He looked at Anneka more intently. He wanted her full attention.

"There's something else, too," he said. "I saw Dad the other evening."

A half smile flickered over Anneka's face, which quickly gave way to a look of unease, even panic.

"What do you mean you saw Dad?" she said leaning toward Mat.

"I saw him. Coming toward me through the snow. It really shook me up," said Mat.

"Sure it would, but there's probably a very simple explanation to it. Projection is a well-documented phenomenon. We quite literally see what we want to see," said Anneka.

Then straightening up a little in her chair she said, "Have you been feeling all right recently? You're not on any medication are you?"

Mat pulled his hand away. He was upset.

"No of course I'm not on any medication. I saw him," Mat said tersely.

The couple in the next booth looked up and turned their heads slightly toward Mat and Anneka. People rarely raised their voices in the Mirage.

"All right, all right, *Junge*, calm down. Tell me what happened," said Anneka.

"Well, it's as I say. I saw Dad. It was at the end of a bizarre set of circumstances. I was hijacked in my car and made to drive to some remote part out of Pittsburgh."

"Mat that's dreadful. Why haven't you told me this before?" interrupted Anneka, now really concerned.

"Well I was sorting things out and I didn't want to bother you with it all," he replied.

"It's no bother, you matter to me," she said.

"Yes I know," Mat said, softening once more to her.

"So what happened?"

"It was like I told you, the car I was in had two thugs in the back. When I got in they pulled a gun on me and forced me to drive off."

"Jesus," said Anneka. "How terrifying."

"It all happened so fast I didn't really have time to be terrified," said Mat. "We drove off and they took me to some deserted spot by the river. Forced me out and took my wallet and briefcase and everything – and the car of course. Then they forced me to walk away from the car. I kept walking in the dark and it was snowing lightly and I didn't know where I was going. Then suddenly I realized I was out on the Ohio River. It was frozen over and real cold. But the ice began to crack and I think they expected me to fall through and drown."

"Mat, God I can't believe this. It's a nightmare poor, *Schatzie*," interrupted Anneka again.

"It was getting that way. Anyway, I made it over the river and got to the safety of the far bank and I was just looking for help and I saw this figure coming toward me. I looked and it was Dad. He was wearing that old gray coat and blue Homburg of his. At first he didn't look at me but then he started to beckon me toward him. He was walking toward some gate. I followed. He stopped and beckoned again. I was about to burst into tears, it was so freaky. It wasn't just that I saw someone who looked like Dad. It was him. I could feel him. There's a difference." He was speaking fast, his breath coming in short gasps.

"And I was suddenly overcome with this intense desire to talk to him. To say sorry. To go up and hug him. I started to run toward him and he seemed to wait for me for a moment and then he went through the factory gates and disappeared."

"Poor, *Schatz*, you must have been so upset. I can only imagine," said Anneka.

"Yes, it was awful. He was there and the next moment he was gone. But the thing that really freaked me out was the way he beckoned to me. It was like he was guiding me. I went through the gates to this factory and it all seemed weirdly familiar. Like I had been there before, but I couldn't remember when. Eventually I came across this old janitor and he helped me out, got me into the warm, and called the police. And you know – it turns out that I had been to this site before. It belonged to a company called Wentworth Industries. I had worked there on my first ever assignment for Hardings. Everything had gone great and we had done the work, identified a new strategy for the company, and left. We had even been congratulated on doing such a good job. And now here I was back at the factory five years later and the place had not only closed down, it was half derelict."

"Well, that sort of thing happens all the time. It was just a coincidence you wound up back there," said Anneka.

"No it wasn't a coincidence," said Mat. "It was like Dad was guiding me there. He wanted me to go back. Take a look at what had happened to the place after I had left it."

"Mat, you had just been through a terrible ordeal. But honestly, people can project all kinds of things under such states of shock. You were frozen through, you'd had a gun pointed at you. I mean it's a classic situation."

"You're probably right," said Mat, a little wearied from the emotion of recounting the episode to Anneka. "But I still can't get over it. I've kept asking myself since then: was Dad trying to tell me something? Because it really felt like he wanted me to go back to Wentworth again. To witness what had happened to the company. And then what happens? A few days later the senior partner calls me into his office and offers me partnership! At 32 years old, I'd be the youngest partner on the books. Don't you think that's a bit of a coincidence, Professor?"

"Coincidence, why is it a coincidence? You deserve partnership, Mat," said Anneka.

"Yeah," said Mat, "and it was just the sort of career move that Dad was worried would happen to me. You remember that that big row before he died?"

"Mat, you can't go on torturing yourself about an argument you had with Dad five years ago. It's water under the bridge. And it wasn't much at the time. You both felt passionately about something. End of story."

"But that's just it. It was 'end of story,' end of his story. I never had a chance to put things right between us. I even messed up on seeing him at his birthday because I was still cross with him. So it's end of story, but I still want to change the last lines."

Anneka could see the tears welling up in Mat's eyes. She felt suddenly close to tears herself.

"*Schatz*, take the afternoon off," she said. "Come and have a walk with me along the Charles. We'll have a chat like the old times."

Letter from William Durer to Mat Durer

Dear Mat,

I am writing to congratulate you on your new position at Hardings. They are a major firm and have a tremendous reputation at the most senior levels of business.

Part of me, however, can't help feeling dismayed at the news. As you know from our many conversations over the years, I distrust those parts of the business world who, in my terms, deal in victory without success. Who offer empty solutions which may sound good and even deliver short-term success, but which ultimately fail both commercially and personally. I am worried you're joining these ranks and will become one of what the Ancient Mariner called "the Nightmare Life-in-Death."

For way too long there's been a tacit acceptance that to be in business means suppressing a certain degree of one's human-ness. On one level it's the old maxim that you have to sell your soul to get by; on another, it's simply an acceptance that people are (and should be!) treated differently at work. They have to fit in with work, not the other way round! How absurd. Do you remember visiting Tony Marton's offices together all those years ago. We both asked ourselves whether they were really designed for actual human behavior or were they trying to fit round pegs into square holes. Doesn't the very design and layout of most offices mean the company who operates them wants to deal with a theoretical worker, rather than an actual one?

Hardings and all organizations like them underpin these attitudes, however silently. They believe that they can intellectualize and abstract business life, the way you might study a laboratory experiment. Unfortunately, these smart people have taken over the high ground of business and that's bad news for us all. Because a business isn't a model, it's a human thing.

I believe it's the human dimension we have to concentrate on. Work should fit with people, not vice versa. More importantly, you don't have to stop growing as a person to win in business. I believe personal growth can go hand in hand with both a more humanistic, as well as street-smart approach to business life.

We can have both victory and success, but only if we let the soul have its space too. That's what I have been trying to get across to you all these years. I now realize that it is not something that I can necessarily convince you of by relying on logical argument. It is something you have to experience for yourself. It's an idea you have to feel through, not just think through. One day you will perhaps have a chance to reflect on these words.

I look forward to seeing you on my birthday when we can discuss these matters more.

I remain your loving father, D

The arrival home

Mat got back to his home around 11.30. The lights of the condominium were off, except for a night light outside his and Marianne's bedroom.

He put his bags down quietly in the hall, and walked through to the bedroom.

"Hello darling, how are you?" said Marianne, lying in the bed in semi-darkness. She was wearing a short silk nightgown with thin straps.

"Hi, sweetheart, I'm fine," Mat replied. He reached forward in the half-light and clasped her outstretched hand.

"Thank God you're home darling. I have been worried sick about you all week. What a terrible, terrible time you've had. That nightmare on the ice and the gun. It still makes me feel sick just talking about it," she said.

Mat took off his shoes and lay down beside her. She smelled warm and sexy in the heat of the bedclothes.

He wanted her now. Without talk and the generalities of how the week had gone. He was stressed and tense and his body needed the relief of making love. Not on the profound level of being wanted, but on the plain simple, animal level of physical need. He ran his hand along the sheet covering her thigh. He kissed her mouth.

"It's good to be home," he said, kissing her face and eyes and cheeks.

"I've missed you," she said, "I so wanted to be with you when all that bad stuff happened."

"You're here now," he said. He moved his hand up her thigh, into the angle of her crotch. He felt her tense a little from the touch. It was unlike him to be this instant. He pulled the sheet back from her body. The nightgown she was wearing had ridden up under the sheets. She was naked but for a stretch of silk across her waist and breasts. He pulled the nightdress up and off. She let out a small gasp of surprise or expectation. They did not make love like this. He kissed her right breast, holding it in his hand. His other hand moved back down to the warmth below.

"Mat…" she tried to speak.

He put his fingers to her mouth. He did not want to speak. He wanted to take her now. Whether it was right for her or not. This time he wanted to take her on his terms. Take her as an act of sexual acquisition. Not mutual embrace. Take her for what she offered, the sweet, warm, wet, body.

Florida: Mat and Marianne's condominium

Mat and Marianne lived in one of those desirable condominiums on Blue Key. Inside it was pure minimalist elegance; in other words very little furniture. Mat had left the decoration and furnishing to Marianne as he'd been busy on work projects and anyway she was much more creative than he was. It also helped that she had a friend, Leona, who worked for Glo, Florida's première interior design agency. Leona had helped put a palette together of colors and fabrics. The result was what the interior design magazines might call "restrained," a statement of good taste. Soft lines, stretched fabric on the walls, and lighting by Masarella – they'd spent a whole heap of money on Masarella because as Marianne said, "The one thing that people fail to take proper account of these days is good lighting. They'll spend fortunes on furniture and art and then they'll get the lighting so wrong that it feels like you're standing in some motel reception."

Mat and Marianne had met at a Hardings party in Boston. Marianne co-owned a company called Vernissage which specialized in renting contemporary art to offices. It was a good niche business since most companies end up buying the art they've rented for the past four years and thus pay double for the same picture. Hardings had brought in Vernissage to decorate their new main reception and Marianne had done a wonderful job with some Calder hangings. (Enigmatic seems a popular mood for receptions.)

They had fallen for one another almost immediately. Everyone who knew them thought that they were a delightful young couple and absolutely right for one another. Marianne was very classy, her father had been a successful attorney and Marianne had been brought up in a professional set that took holidays in Europe and went to well-respected, though slightly unfashionable, private schools. She admired Mat for many things, but not least his drive and commitment. She was different from other women Mat had met, more self-contained, even apart. Mat found that very attractive.

As Mat spent much of his time traveling, it didn't really matter where he lived. So they decided that since Marianne was based in Florida and she liked it, and the weather was great down there, that they might as well base themselves there for a while. If Mat took on a really senior position at Hardings they would have to relocate to Boston, but that was in the future.

For now, Mat and Marianne were living in a great condo on Blue Key, with fabulous views of the ocean. And that was another big reason why they had chosen this location: the broad blue sea stretching out to the Bahamas. Marianne loved to go diving, sub aqua, and free diving and she'd managed to get Mat interested in it too. He said it was the best way he'd ever found to relax and switch off. When you were underwater, you entered another world and left all your concerns and stresses behind in the old one. Well it worked for him so who am I to question it? Though in my experience stress follows a person wherever they go. Mat didn't have enough time to get really good at diving, since weekends were always a mix of catching up on unfinished business and phone calls and handling all that email which he hadn't had a chance to respond to during the week. But he had always been a very technical diver. He knew what the manuals said.

The weekend at home together

When she awoke that morning, Marianne was thinking of Mat. The way that they had made love the night before had been different. It was more immediate, more physical, and more intense. As though they had met as strangers, made love and left one another without a name or a note.

She felt almost as if it was a different Mat that had lain with her, touched her in a new way; found her differently.

"Wow, what came over you last night?" said Marianne rolling over and putting her arms around Mat.

"I've been missing you, that's all?" said Mat turning to kiss her. But deep down, he knew the physicality of the way that they had made love last night was connected to all he had just been through. It was a symptom.

"Well let me know when you're missing me that much – and I'll get ready next time," she said.

They held one another. The sunlight filtered through the blinds, making patterns on the ruffled sheets. That weekend they had planned to go diving early on Saturday but that didn't seem right now.

Then Marianne rolled over again, with her back to him, her fingers outlining the patterns of sunlight and shadow on the sheet.

"I know there's something on your mind," she said. "And from what I know about you it's not because you're worrying about the car-jacking. There's something else that you're not telling me. Is it something about us?"

"No, no. It's nothing about you and me," said Mat pulling her over to him and clasping her hand. "But you're right there is some other stuff. It's work. There's something I have to sort out."

"Anything you want to tell me about?" she said, smiling at him.

"Well, actually, I suppose I should tell you. I was called into Anthony Elliott's office on Thursday. It's all still very confidential, but he said that he was going to put me forward for partnership at the next review meeting."

"Hey Mat, that's wonderful," said Marianne, throwing her arms about him. This was what she had been waiting for, too.

"You must be thrilled," she said. "I'm thrilled enough and it's not me who's being made up to partnership of the world's No. 1 management consulting firm."

"Sure, I'm pleased," he said. "It's just maybe that's it all come so fast and on the back of that madness in Pittsburgh that it's taken me by surprise. I don't know what to feel about it."

"Poor darling it has been a bad week hasn't it? But don't let that get you down. Partnership at Hardings! No wonder you were such a stud last night."

They kissed and she pressed her body close to his. She wanted to make him feel right. She sensed that he was feeling vulnerable but couldn't understand why. All she knew was that she wanted to take this feeling away from him.

"Love me," she said. "My clever, talented darling. I need you."

"I need you too you know, now especially," he said.

Going to the Ball

On the Saturday they had tickets for the Continuity Ball (one of those smart charity affairs which raise money for good causes) and although Mat felt tired and hadn't much wanted to go, they'd decided it would be a good idea if they went after all just to get his mind off things for a while.

Like all these society affairs, the Continuity Ball was formal and that meant a formal evening tux. As Mat dressed for the evening he searched for his dress shirt studs. They were old-fashioned pearl studs. They had been a present to him from his father on being accepted to HBS. He looked now but they weren't in their usual place in the top drawer of his cabinet.

"Hey Marianne, have you seen those dress shirt studs of mine? I can't find them anywhere."

"No I haven't touched them," she replied.

Mat searched for them again. He always kept them in the same drawer, ever since he and Marianne had taken on this apartment three years before. He knew because he felt they would always be safe there.

Perhaps Marianne had moved them for some reason.

"Are you sure you haven't seen those studs?" he called out again.

"Yes I'm certain," she said. "Honestly. Besides I never go into your drawer. Those are your things in there."

But Mat wouldn't give up. He spent the next twenty minutes, checking every cufflink box and drawer in the cabinet. He even checked over his dress shirt.

"Come on honey, we're going to be late," Marianne eventually said to him. "Why not wear those black studs I gave you? They're fine for this evening."

"OK, I'll just have one last look," he said "And then I'll give it up. It's driving me mad looking for them."

But the last look also proved fruitless and Mat ended up wearing the black set of studs from Marianne.

In the car, Marianne had promised not to tell anyone about the "incident." Mat didn't want to have to reiterate his ordeal to every second person he met.

Marianne had arranged for the tickets to the ball several weeks before. A lot of the high-rolling local society people would be attending; people with whom you like to be seen. It was an excellent opportunity for Marianne to meet clients. The environment would be perfect: relaxed but exclusive. Mat and Marianne fitted right into this smart set – Marianne particularly. She had friends there that evening and over the first glass of champagne she introduced Mat to a customer of hers called Joel Litbarsky. Joel had a medium-sized software business and seemed to have made a fortune out of it according to Marianne. She had left the two of them talking together.

"So what do you do Mat?" Joel had asked.

"I'm with Hardings," he'd replied.

"Sure I've heard of you guys. I read somewhere, *Forbes* maybe, that your senior partner reckons you're the brightest collection of employees in America. Is that right?" asked Joel with a slight edge to his voice.

"If the senior partner says so, who am I to argue?"

"Not if you want partnership I guess," said Joel with a tongue-in-cheek smile. "I heard this joke once about consultants and how when you join the first thing they do is a surgical removal of all feelings," Joel started to laugh, hoping Mat would come with him. "Is that right?"

"I think we've cut down on the surgery bills by only selecting candidates without feelings in the first place," said Mat but he wasn't laughing.

Soon after that Mat moved away and started talking to someone he knew from the local mayor's office. He felt uncomfortable about the way that he had reacted to Joel's comments. Normally wisecracks like that didn't get through to him. But on this occasion it had struck home.

Just then Marianne came back to join him, and hooked her arm through his. She was just about to lead him away when one of the photographers working for *Florida Society* came up to them and asked if he could do a portrait for the "About Town" page. Marianne said, "Of course." Mat posed but felt uncomfortable. He never liked being part of the limelight.

Feeling a bit uneasy with his situation he put his hand inside his jacket pocket, it was a nervous gesture he often used. As he put his hand into the pocket he felt something sharp. It pricked the end of his finger.

He mumbled "ouch" under his breath and then put his hand back into his pocket and pulled whatever had pricked him.

It was a pearl collar stud; one of the set from his father which he treasured. How did it get into his pocket? They were always kept safely at home. They never left that top drawer in his cabinet, ever.

Mat looked down at the point of his finger. A small pearl of blood was forming.

"Come on, folks, big one for the camera," said the photographer.

Mat sucked the tip of his finger, looked into the camera, and smiled the briefest smile he could.

The stay

At about 12.30 on Sunday, Mat and Marianne went to Jack's Seafoodery for brunch, as they always did on Sundays. Helen and Richard Anderson were there and so were the Jacksons and their cute daughter Schezade.

After brunch, Mat and Marianne took a walk in the sunshine along the harborside and checked out a few of the yachts and talked about how they'd both like to own one and that maybe one day they'd just sail away. After the walk by the harbor, they went into the Ever Glades shopping mall. Marianne wanted to check out something in Louis Vuitton and they spent an hour or so just wandering around with all the other Sunday crowds.

When Marianne went into Versace to try out some shoes she just loved, Mat sat down by the indoor fountain and looked about him. Next to him was a very large, middle-aged black woman, her hair twisted up underneath a large gray cap. Mat guessed this shopping mall was the place she called home and so naturally she was sitting in her front room going through a *Martha Stewart Living* magazine. She flipped through the recipes page, examining the glossy photographs of Christmas tables laden with "fayre:" rack of ribs and joints of beef with all the trimmings. Mat thought if he was feeling sharper he'd have made some comment to himself about the irony of it. But Mat wasn't feeling like irony. He was feeling his feet slip on the ice.

Which probably explains why Mat wasn't thinking as he usually did. He wasn't thinking like the next partner at Hardings. In fact he wasn't thinking like a young turk of 32 at all. He was thinking about his father.

Had he, Mat, really made such a mistake? Had he wasted the last five years of his life? If he was made up to partner, he'd never be able to walk away from it. Not just because of the money, but because accepting partnership would mean buying into the faith, becoming part of the priesthood. Partnership opened some very alluring doors, but it also closed off others that were marked "destination unknown." People changed when they became partners; they stopped doubting. Doubt was bad but it was also good. It meant you were still alive. That's what Mat had realized.

A few moments later Marianne came out of Versace, he stood up and they walked on through the mall pausing at Thomas Pink to look at some new shirts for Mat. The natural order of things had been reinstated.

At home they listened to some light jazz music and the afternoon passed fine. Around five o'clock Mat packed a few things and got ready for his trip to the airport. He had a 7.45 flight to St Louis. He had to go overnight as he had a very early start on Monday with a presentation to the executive board of MidWest Mutual. The cab came for him at just after 6.00. He kissed Marianne and said he would call when he got into his hotel in St Louis.

On the way to the airport, Mat sat in the back reading some papers. He liked to keep his head down on these sorts of journeys, otherwise before he knew it he'd be hauled into some long conversation with the cab driver about his family, or how little he was earning, or his last visit to the hospital, or taxes, or what the President was doing wrong, or whatever else the driver wanted to get off his chest and it could turn out to be terminally boring.

"So you got yourself set for the holidays?" enquired the cab driver. Opening conversation gambit, thought Mat as he bent his head closer to the papers.

"Yes thanks," he said and turned his whole body away from the cab driver so that he was looking out of the side window.

The driver got the hint and turned his attention to the radio instead.

At the airport Mat collected his bag, gave the driver a $20 tip and walked into the departures area. He didn't go the Delta desk. As usual he'd check in at the departure gate, it was quicker that way. He walked through the main departures hall to security. Without his laptop and other devices he made it through the screening quicker than usual.

He went to the news kiosk and bought a copy of *Newsweek*.

He took a seat in the departure lounge and flicked through *Newsweek*. Then he looked out at the tarmac apron of high activity: planes were taxiing in from landing, baggage was being unloaded, and small trucks were moving around the tarmac at speed. The stewardess announced that Delta flight 324 to St Louis was now commencing boarding and extended a pre-boarding courtesy to first class passengers to take their seats.

Mat got up to walk forward onto the plane. Then he saw him. His father, standing squarely at the departures gate. As though he was barring the way.

The Islands: Sacrifice

Mat lay motionless on the sea floor. Above him the thinnest pane of liquid glass, so clear the sky seemed just an arm's reach away. Nothing but the sound of his own breath. Lying on the sea floor at 35 feet. On sand. Not moving, nor thinking, but lying in inner space.

A large grouper swam by, hovered in the stream for a moment to inspect this strange shape on the seabed below, and then moved on. In turn, the spadefish and yellowtails, soldier fish, squirrel fish, and chromis all inspected him and then swam on uninterested. A large hogfish rooted about in the sand with its long snout, searching for a meal, blowing clouds of sand from its gills.

Mat turned his head and looked across a sloping sandy arena toward two coral towers. The towers stood like sentinels at the edge of the vertical coral wall. Just a quarter of a mile from the shore in these crystal clear turquoise waters you come to an edge, a lip. You can stand in waters just 35 feet deep and look down from the lip into the dark abyss – some 7,000 feet below.

Mat turned his head back and looked up at the sky. Four giant eagle rays swam over him in formation. Not swimming but flying, for Mat could not distinguish between the water and the air. Their shadows flew over his body and on across the sandy ocean floor. He felt a silent communion. In a moment, they were gone.

As he lay on the ocean bed, he closed his eyes. It was the ultimate float tank, the place to quieten his inner spirit. A lot had happened in Mat's life over the past weeks and months since the strange events in Pittsburgh and Miami airport.

Most significantly he had left Hardings temporarily. He had decided to ask for a sabbatical. This had been very difficult. Not least because Marianne could not understand him.

"But, no one gives up partnership at Hardings. It's inconceivable," she had said. She'd burst into tears on several occasions and their relationship had suffered in the short term because of his decision. It seemed to her he was putting their future in jeopardy. However now they were on the Turks and Caicos Islands things were going much better. At least they had a shared passion for diving.

His colleagues at Hardings were equally mystified by Mat's decision. They presumed he'd had some kind of breakdown. This had hurt him. It was not true but there was little way he could disprove it. Brad had been heard to say to others in the peer group that Mat was now damaged goods and couldn't be trusted under the pressure of a big account. "It got to him," Brad had said. In an environment where the pressure proves too much for 25 to 30% of young men and women, Brad had had no difficulty in making the accusation stick. For Mat it was the ultimate betrayal. He'd told Brad so. "You know I can take the heat of this job. I just want time out for a while." "Brave decision," was all that Brad was prepared to say. Anthony Elliott had been gracious but disappointed.

Even Anneka had seemed concerned about Mat's decision, though she alone knew the real reason behind it.

When you give something up which others covet you will find yourself completely alone. This was exactly what Mat discovered. He felt more alone than at any time in his life. He was just a figure lying in shallow blue water. He had sacrificed everything. And because of what?

I remember asking Mat about why he had left Hardings at our first interview on Martha's Vineyard. He'd said: "I felt it was the only choice I could make. Other people wanted to take it as a sign of weakness or that I didn't care or that I thought I was better than them. It was none of these things, though I had to endure the accusations. I couldn't get it out my mind: 'He has come back for a reason.' I kept thinking: 'What is Dad trying to tell me?' I didn't know what it meant, but I had to find out. You have to understand that for me seeing a ghost, well it was absurd on one level. I'm not that sort of guy. I am an objective, rational, non-believer so to speak. So far from the kind of person I was, and the way I used to think, that it really shook me up. But here I was having an experience which I couldn't deny and yet which I could not explain. It hit me deep down. For a while I guess I was just plain terrified."

Mat's father had died a few weeks after Mat had joined Hardings. The rows referred to in letters took place just around the time he was first offered a position. William Durer was living on the West Coast at that time, near Santa Monica. No one knew how ill he was. Mat had promised to go and see his father on his birthday and discuss things further. But a project had come up and since Mat was new and very keen, he had decided to work that weekend. He missed out on the trip to his father's birthday. He never saw his father alive again.

Diving with Jean-Claude Daran:
Turks and Caicos Islands

It was February and the temperature on Grand Turk was an idle 78°. Mat and Marianne had just finished a lunch of grilled chicken and salad. They had been on the islands for some weeks now and had got used to the new pace of life. Later they would go diving, but for now they took a walk along the beach beneath the shade of tall Australian pines.

"Happy?" asked Mat kicking his toes into pure white sand.

"Very," said Marianne, taking his arm in hers. "I have no idea what we're doing here or how long we'll stay, but for now I'm not bothered. I just want to spend time with you, give ourselves some shared memories, rather than the 'your day and my day' dinner conversations."

"Yeah, I know. I don't know why we're here exactly either. But then it's as good a place as any to find yourself lost."

"Sure is, Crusoe," said Marianne, kissing him lightly on the temple.

Mat had not told Marianne about the visions of his father. He was still shocked by them. Like a letter you dare not open. A voice you don't dare hear. All of this was going on way down in Mat's being, deep inside his cool and rational mind, far from Marianne's view. As a result, she had no idea of what was driving him. But she did know he was hurting. And he wasn't telling her about it. Part of her worried that the cause was their relationship, but he was always quick to assure her everything was fine. So she did the only thing she could in the circumstances: created the right environment in which Mat might eventually open up to her. She was supportive and loving and the surroundings were idyllic.

The Turks and Caicos Islands are a bit like paradise but without the apple tree. They say Columbus landed here and claimed the New World. You can see why. The climate is just about ideal, warm enough to make your body relax but not so hot that you can't sleep at night. There's little rainfall to concern yourself with. There are achingly white beaches. The water temperature is always good too – rarely out of the 75° to 79° range. And the ocean is crystal clear, particularly in winter when visibility can be as deep as 200 feet.

It had been Marianne's suggestion to come to the islands. She had been visiting them with family and friends since she was a little girl. If Mat was going to take a sabbatical from Hardings and she was going to have to give up working on her business, Vernissage, then at least they should go somewhere exotic while Mat got his head clear. What's more Mat had always wanted to become a better diver and here was a chance just to get away from it all and concentrate on scuba.

The Turks and Caicos Islands have some of the best scuba diving anywhere. Jacques Cousteau rated it one of the top ten destinations in the world. The breathtaking coral wall, sand canyons, and coral reefs are home to manta rays, eagle rays, turtles, sharks, eels, batfish, whales, dolphins, and just about every other type of aquatic life you can think of.

Mat spent as much of his time diving as he could. Learning a new skill, that was a big change for him; at Hardings he had been the instructor. Now he was re-discovering what it was like to acquire a skill. Together he and Marianne had joined a diving school run by Jean-Claude Daran. Daran was one of the father figures of the world of scuba diving and as a young man had worked with Cousteau. In those days scuba was for the very fit and the very brave. Jean-Claude was both and had made his fame from deep diving. For a few months in 1968 Jean-Claude had held the world record for depth diving at 411 feet. Although others subsequently came to take the title from him and although he never managed such an extraordinary depth again, it was superhuman to get beyond 400 feet back in 1968.

Maybe it was his reputation or his forceful character, but Jean-Claude had an aura about him. Now in his sixties, he seemed as fit and hard as ever. Narrow hips, broad shoulders, and a great barrel chest, he was as someone said, "So tough it's surprising he doesn't rust." Still addicted to deep diving, he frequently went down the wall to two hundred feet and beyond. He had opened a diving school on Grand Turk in the late 70s and had been here off and on ever since. Together with his team of diving instructors he could take you to the unforgettable.

Already during the time with Daran, Mat and Marianne had done some of the great dives of the area. For a while they'd been on a live-aboard and had been out to Northwest Point to where the wall plunges for 5,000 feet to the bottom of the Caicos Passage and had spotted wild dolphins. The nearby passages are full of giant stands of lush coral and sponges. They'd been to Shark Hotel running along the shallow edge of the Caicos Bank. Beginning at around 40 feet, it's lined with huge barrel and elephant ear sponges, before dropping into the abyss. For reef sharks and black tips it's a favorite hangout. At the Hole in the Wall, they'd descended into a tunnel cave at 50 feet and emerged at 95 feet, their descent in the dark lit by the luminescence of silversides and tiny fish fry. At Pinnacles, spurs of coral rose up to within 20 feet of the surface. And at Graceland, they'd met one of the diving instructors' local friends, Elvis the barracuda. Off Grand Turk they'd done The Amphitheatre, The Library and The Anchor, and many more.

Each dive was different and illuminated the memory with different shapes and colors: the twisted forms of purple sponges, rounded basket sponges, spreading sea fans, and the towers of precious black coral, silvery clouds of semi-translucent larval fish, the impossible elegance of a turtle, the rich gold and iridescent blue of a golden hamlet. And everywhere, the vertical plunge of the wall. Like a wall of life, linking the abyss to the sky.

Experiencing these sights together, in the light of the liquid world, it's not hard to understand how Mat and Marianne became very close during this period. Strangely, or perhaps not, it was often underwater that their relationship became most intense. In that dimension of no words, just the light touch on a shoulder or a silent gesture, they seemed like one. It felt like they were most in love under the water.

After their walk along the beach, Mat and Marianne went out on one of Jean-Claude's low skiffs to the coral wall at a spot the locals like to call McDonald's. It took its name from the two soaring arches of coral that are large enough for divers to swim through. Turtles are common here and Mat and Marianne spent some wondrous moments watching a loggerhead turtle glide by, the sea transforming its awkward body, conferring on it the magic of a graceful dancer. During the migration season, humpback whales take this route on their way to the Silver Banks for mating and birthing. One morning in early February they had been diving around this area and had heard the whales' songs from a migrating group. It's a sound that enters the soul.

Nothing quite as dramatic on this trip but the loggerhead turtles were marvelous to watch and Mat and Marianne still had many other days ahead.

They came back to their hotel and went to their room.

As they walked in there was a message for Marianne slipped in under the door.

The envelope was marked "Confidential."

She picked it up and walked over to the bed and read it. Mat went through to have a shower. When he came back through a few minutes later, Marianne was lying back on the bed staring at the ceiling, the note folded up and lying beside her. Mat noticed she avoided his look as he came back into the room.

"Everything all right?" he asked.

"Oh, I suppose so. Just a bit of bad news from my office. About Geoff Duncan my partner. Nothing I can't handle."

Mat would have quizzed her further but at that moment the phone rang. Marianne reached for it as though she was determined to be first to the call. It was Jean-Claude.

"Marianne, I want to steal Mat from you for this evening. Maybe we go for a dive together at night. I think it is good for him. A new experience."

"Sure, Jean-Claude, I think that would be a great thing for him to do. What time do you want him?"

"Say at 8.30. At the boat."

"Fine, I'll tell him."

Marianne replaced the receiver and turned to Mat.

"Very privileged, young sir. Jean-Claude wants you to join him on a night dive. Looks like you're accepted."

That evening they ate early. Marianne was rather quiet and still seemed a little out of sorts. Mat left to go to the boat in good time. It was dark on the water with a clear, round moon above.

They took the boat to the edge of the coral wall and kitted up and stood by the transom waiting to dive.

Mat expected Jean-Claude to give him some advice, some directions. He did not.

"You will see many new fishes, night fishes," was all Jean-Claude said. " It will be fun." And with that he lowered himself from the transom and into the dark sea.

Mat felt the fear inside him, felt the taste come back in his mouth. Being there on the ocean at night brought everything back to him: the night on the ice, seeing his father at Wentworth, the sharp prick of the collar stud to his finger, his father at the airport. He was terrified that this strange environment might open things up. Coming to the Turks and Caicos Islands had been also an escape; an escape from the mainland world where Mat's troubles had started and also an escape underwater to a different dimension. But what if this escape was no use? What if the fear returned?

Mat tried to occupy himself with small tasks. Push the fear out of his mind. He put on his mask, adjusted it to the contours of his face and slipped into the water, his flashlight cutting a bright shaft through the gloom. Then he went down into the black ocean.

The water was warm and the dark held him.

He had expected his fear to grow, alone in the dark in this other element where there were no objects to guide oneself by. Instead it was all a deep calm, like he was wrapped in the dark water. Mat could cope with his fear, the sea helped him.

Then something brushed by his leg. A surge of panic gripped his body. He stared down at the dark water beneath him. But there was nothing.

He swam on down, the beam from his flashlight cutting a path through the blackness. He was entering a different world.

The sand comes alive at night. In the freedom of the darkness when the predators have gone to sleep, the sand creatures come out. Within moments Mat had seen a dramatic cushion sea star, a big orange puffy starfish, an octopus perfectly camouflaged against the sea bottom and anemones protruding their tentacles across the sand.

He swam on, drifting along in the guide of his flashlight, letting his mind wander. Being underwater, in that other liquid world frees your mind. That's how Mat saw it. In scuba diving you're balancing between floating and sinking, so you're as near to being weightless as you'll get this side of the earth's atmosphere. No gravity on the body or the mind.

When you're underwater, especially in the dark, the normal boundaries don't apply. You have total freedom of movement and direction, yet you're in an environment that's outside of your usual sphere of survival. Jean-Claude had talked about this several times to him: "It is different here," he had said of the sea, "your mind tells you different things. It talks to you in very simple terms: life and death. Will I die? Will I drown? Get me out of here!"

"Quite simply down there you can't breathe," he went on. "So in other words, underwater you experience very different and very specific questions: where do you get your source of oxygen, how long will it last, and how deep can you go? In an office, you have complete freedom to breathe and so your mind gets locked up on problems. But when you have to think about breathing your mind gets freed up. It's an intriguing reversal: physical chains open the mind."

Some 20 minutes later, Mat re-emerged exhilarated and excited by the new world he had been to. He had survived the dark and the water and his own fear.

Jean-Claude was on the boat, getting out of his gear.

"Fun, yes?" asked Jean-Claude.

"Great fun," said Mat, looking out into the darkness of the sea at night.

Jean-Claude set the boat for the shore. A few lights shone from the houses and bars along the beach. The stars were out above them.

"It was not frightening – the water?" asked Jean-Claude.

"Yes and no. It was only frightening out of the water. Inside it was very calm," replied Mat.

"Yes, it is interesting to experience," Jean-Claude said. "We all have this survival brain in us. Deep inside. It is the basic set of instructions and we build it up over many years. We build it up on land. But it's not so useful in the sea, no. This survival brain says, 'If we do not find air soon we shall die!' When in fact we have a tank of air on our back. This survival brain says 'I cannot see, so I shall be eaten!' when in fact the predators are sleeping. Interesting, no? If we are to be a great diver, we must talk to this survival brain. Give him new memories."

Jean-Claude hung his suit on the back of the cabin door and scooped his mask into the sea, swilled around the water to wash it out.

"If we are going to change ourselves we first have to change the behavior of our survival brain," Jean-Claude continued. "We have to teach him there is no threat. This cannot be done quickly. It cannot be taught. The survival brain must experience for himself and he must build his own memories over time. Through actions. We are human, no? So when the survival brain says, 'I can't do this,' we must gradually replace this by new experiences, little small experiences that build over time, over and over, so that with each step we add to our survival memory and we eventually break through. This cannot be done fast. If you come up from the deep water fast, you will die. It is gradual, hand over hand and repeat. The survival brain only learns from doing and we cannot ask too much in one go. We must have little experiences. Then one day this brain shall say: 'but that is great I have done it.' And when we get through and we have survived then this is a very important moment."

During this coaching session, Jean-Claude had been walking around, tidying away his gear. Now he sat down next to Mat.

"And what is it that your survival brain is telling you now, Mat?"

"What do you mean?" Mat replied.

"You are worried. This fear is with you. It is why you are here. So tell me, what is it that you think so much about?"

"I want to get better at diving that's why I concentrate so hard," Mat replied.

"Yes, I know you are a dedicated person. But I think there is more going on. If you want to talk to me about this fear, I can help. Tell me when you want. It is easy with me because I have no needs from you. No expectations. You are free with me."

Mat smiled at Jean-Claude. He could talk about the things that had brought him here. But it was not right. Not now.

Beach barbecue

Every Thursday night Jean-Claude put on a barbecue on a long stretch of pure white beach just to the south of Cockburn Town. It was an occasion for the whole diving school: instructors and back-up team as well as clients. Jean-Claude presided over the evening like Napoleon at a banquet. The temperature of the barbecue had to be exactly right to make the meat or fish sear at first touch. The beers of course had to be ice cold. Everything for the barbecue was fresh from the markets or the ocean. But the real star of the menu was the island's own favorite food, the conch. Not what most off-islanders would consider their first choice entrée, but in Jean-Claude's hands this pearly-shelled mollusc became a sweet and succulent delicacy. There was either a conch salad prepared with slices of onion, sweet pepper and tomato, or the more exotic conch fritters: conch seasoned with garlic and coconut milk and grilled in foil.

At each barbecue, the diving team would build a small open fire, not for warmth but as a place to gather in the twilight beneath the immensity of stars – the Big Dipper rolling on its nightly round.

Sometime during every evening Jean-Claude would weave a spell around the fire with stories about the old days and deep diving. About those out of body experiences you get below 300 feet and about how it made him believe in some supernatural force at work down there. He'd tell about the heroes who founded the sport, about the dangers, the triumphs and the tragedy of those who did not survive. But mostly his tales were of the good times, of the fun and the parties and of diving into uncharted territories or as he put it, "diving within ourselves." He believed that people were deep down stronger than they knew and rose to most any challenge. "Doing the heroic thing is often just being given the chance to try," he would say with the kind of philosophic assurance that only a man of his charisma could get away with.

Although Jean-Claude would hold court, most of the conversation and the jokes came from his diving instructors: Gregor, Josy, Javier, and Alessandro. Usually they would swap anecdotes about diving around the world, of times on the Seychelles or the Maldives, each one a signal to the rest of the group that they belonged to some holy order of free spirits. I expect for most people who work a nine-to-five job, these guys did have a pretty blessed existence. They go to some of the world's most beautiful resorts and get paid to do so. They were for the most part their own bosses and each day was spent admiring the oceans' mysteries. They worked with the rich and often famous, who were in awe of their skills. And they had ample time to plan their next career move: Would it be the Bahamas or Mauritius? You and I get caught up in the daily chores. But they were like players on the pro circuit of any sport, living for the next tournament. Young, healthy, tanned, and with their hair bleached blonde by the sun and water, they looked like they had discovered the secret of eternal life.

Mat and Marianne knew all of the instructors quite well by now and had been to a number of the beach barbecues. But they still loved the magic of these evenings and the fun of just listening to tales about diving.

"Hey Josy," shouted Gregor across the lick of flames of the fire, "you ever seen ghosts down there in the water?"

Mat felt his body stiffen. Ridiculous but he was even frightened by the very word. Imperceptibly his arm tightened around Marianne.

"No, can't say I have," replied Josy.

"I have," Gregor said. Mat felt another ripple of fear go through him.

"One time I was diving off the coast of New England," Gregor continued. "Green water diving, if you know what I mean. I went down looking for the wreck of this World War Two U-boat. Got down to about 95 feet and the thing started to come into view, like this gray image coming out of the seabed. My buddy and I went on down and came by right near the bow.

I mean it was amazing, this whole great, gray monster shape was down there, just like it was sunk yesterday. We went along the topside and found this gaping hole in the side where the U-boat had been hit by a depth charge, ripped right through the metal. We decided to go on in and have a look."

Gregor paused and then lowered his voice a little.

"Then we're swimming along this passage way and we go into the forward torpedo room and it looks like there are still torpedoes on board and we're just about to swim through to the control room area, when my buddy points to this shape on the floor. We go toward it and the silt moves around then suddenly – out from the gray – this skull comes out…"

Everyone was waiting on Gregor's next words, "…and I swear I saw a face appear over the skull and then it moved forward at us like it wanted to look at us."

Someone in the group gave out a small uncertain laugh. Mat turned his head sharply in their direction. Marianne squeezed his hand.

"And you know what we thought we heard it say?" Gregor went on, looking down at the sand at his feet, moved by the memory. "We thought it said…mine's a Jack Daniels…"

For a moment there was silence and then everybody began to laugh. Mat laughed too. At first uncertainly and then loudly with an intense feeling of relief. His whole body laughed. He was free, he was getting better. If he could laugh then nothing would worry him. He could do whatever he wanted. He could take his life in whichever direction he chose. And the more he realized his new position, the more he laughed.

Marianne pushed him a little and gave a mock look of disapproval as if to say: "It's not that funny, Mat."

He kissed her on the lips.

"You've just spent too much of your life narced up underwater, Gregor," said Josy.

"Well, can't be all bad. Just look what it's done for Jean-Claude."

They all laughed some more and Jean-Claude took a mock

bow at the barbecue.

The food was ready now and they helped themselves to the beef skewers or grilled snapper or, of course, the conch.

The sky grew more immense; the beers and food were good and Mat felt like he was going to be here forever. Meanwhile the instructors were still putting the world to rights, right now discussing the different types of dive buddy.

"Hey, how do you tell whether your dive buddy is a philosopher?"

"Don't know...wears a toga?"

"No, but nice try. He keeps asking himself whether his tank is half empty or half full."

Then Alessandro got into a long discourse on his own diving philosophy, which was interesting mostly because it mixed real insights with spoof ones; definitely not the sort of thing they told you in diving manuals.

"Keep breathing boys and girls that's my first tip to you. Breathing is good for you." he said half closing his eyes in concentration.

"Forget worrying about whether you're going to be eaten by the local life forms. To them you're just a meal. The real troubles you'll experience during your dive are apt to be things that never crossed your nitrogen-soaked mind – the kind that will keep you in a decompression chamber until 4.00 p.m. next Tuesday.

"Don't waste your time on seeking perfect buoyancy," continued Alessandro. "Sometimes your dive slate will sink you like an anchor; sometimes you can't submerge without the aid of a 55 gallon drum full or lead shot. There are five billion variables and you will bleed from your ears if you think about it too much.

"Don't feel bad if you haven't quite mastered your compass. The most interesting dives I have been on were led by dive masters who didn't know how to use one. The most interesting dive masters I know often mistake it for their watch."

Shouts of: "Jean-Claude, are you listening?"

"Get plenty of Dramamine," Alessandro continued, "and

make sure you always keep it somewhere handy.

"If you're enjoying your dive too much, it's probably the nitrogen narcosis setting in.

"Always polish your depth gauge.

"Go gentle with your mask strap; you'll miss it when it breaks.

"One day it could be that you'll come across some sane, human-type dive buddy. Maybe you won't. Life isn't meant to be fair. Whatever, don't wallow in your own self-pity. Who cares if your buddy is insane? So is everybody else's.

"And here's two pieces of advice for all of you rookies out there: first, at all costs stay alive, learn by example. Second, always spit in your mask. Do it as often as possible. Don't be afraid of what other people think. Spit is the best de-fogger you'll ever own.

"Over time you will come to accept certain inalienable truths of diving: you, too, will pee in a rental wetsuit.

"Buying second-hand diving gear is a form of brain sickness.

"And remember keep breathing," said Alessandro. "Breathing is sincerely good for you."

Alessandro's advice went on into the night and others added their own philosophy, so that after a while anyone listening to these exchanges could be forgiven for not knowing which was ham philosophy and which was for real. And if you were as passionate about diving as Mat was, you didn't care.

That sense of freedom

The next day was a shore day, when Mat and Marianne could wander the island, such as it is, and the diving team got to do a complete safety check on all the equipment. Grand Turk is seven miles long by two miles wide, but there is still plenty to do on it. People were always looking for some way to turn a profit on the island. So you could hire a horse and ride along the beaches or take a boat and go out sport fishing. If you didn't want to go ocean fishing, you could even stay on the shallow banks. A couple of local entrepreneurs had organized a boat that would take you out to the Caicos Bank to go look at bonefish. They feed off shrimps, crab, and clams and grow to about four to six pounds and they shoal in their hundreds. You can go after them in waders if you like, or pole fish from the back of the boat. Either way they're ferocious feeders.

But this morning Mat was heading for a different venue. He had been up early going through the local papers. He had phoned a few numbers from his cell phone, scratched a few contenders off the list and eventually settled on a meeting. He was going to look at a boat for sale. It needed work doing on it, but the basics were all there.

The sense of release Mat had gained the previous evening had given him a whole new set of issues to think about.

Should he take the easy route and go back to Hardings, take the line of least resistance? After all he had had a fantastic start to his career there.

Or maybe he should follow this ridiculous notion and start his own consulting firm? After all, Hardings had taught him all there was to know about the traditional model of business: the arena of strategies, big ideas, hero CEOs, and abstract market forces. This business model was supremely successful, so successful that it was the only idea in town.

Yet at the same time, his father was right, it also brought with it unacceptable costs: in wasted human potential, wasted resources, company closures, and the general belief that failures prove the market is working.

But what if there was another way? What if there was another dimension to making business work that went beyond the elegance of pure strategic thinking espoused by Hardings and its kind? What if there was another, more human philosophy, that got the most out of everybody, that did away with wasted potential and made people feel fulfilled at work? As his father used to say to him, "Why not let people experience that success in business isn't about selling your soul, but finding it?"

This idea, though only half formed, like some vague shape seen in the distance, had caught Mat's imagination, the way that an entrepreneur becomes obsessed with a market opportunity he feels in his gut but can't quite find a way to capture. It was there, just out of reach. At that time Mat even struggled to define exactly what he was searching for. It was a sensation. The best way he could describe it was that he was looking for a more complete answer to business. You could make a company more successful by making it more alive.

Of course there were always doubts. Perhaps this was just wish fulfillment, trying to do something to put right his rows with his father? Shouldn't he go the whole way and really escape into some new line of business? If he was looking for freedom and independence, why shouldn't he start up his own small business here on Grand Turk? It was this last idea that most appealed to Mat that morning and he was going to try it on for size.

Mat got a taxi from the hotel up to the Caicos Marina and Shipyard where the boat was moored. His taxi trip was short and often bumpy. Both the length of the trip and its comfort were in large part shaped by the speed at which the driver took the island's roads. She was a woman maybe in her mid-seventies and she drove with great panache, bordering on recklessness it seemed to Mat, for a woman of her age.

Mat got to the Marina and the old lady turned round to him:

"You want me to wait for you, sir?" she asked. Mat took a look at her gray hair and horn-rimmed glasses. He would feel kind of guilty keeping the old lady hanging around.

"No, no. I'll be fine thanks," he said, reaching into his pocket for the fare.

"Well I'll just hang around anyway and look at the boats for a while. If you want a lift back to the hotel, I'll be happy to oblige."

Then it dawned on Mat: "Poor old lady, she must be really

hard up and need the fares." He'd been insensitive.

"Oh, OK," he said. "Fine. I've got to take a look at this boat but I shouldn't be too long. If you could wait that'll be great. Keep a count of the time," he said and left the old lady as she moved the taxi into the shade of a palm tree.

The boat Mat had come to see was an out-of-service 77-ton Sea Ranger. She was out of the water right now, but she had loads of potential as a live-aboard dive boat. Her current owner, Tim, was a tall, likeable Californian who'd spent ten years in the US Navy before finding his niche here on Grand Turk doing the odd deal on boats and running his own small charter operation. Like many Californians, Tim sells dreams.

"She's a beauty," Tim had said, looking over the boat. "Sixty-five foot in length and 20 in beam, three decks, four bedrooms and a 40-foot sundeck. Galley and air conditioning and stereo system come included!"

Mat thought she was a beauty, too. The ideal, ultimate live-aboard.

Of course Mat was not buying a boat here. Nothing so simple. He was buying a wish, a fantasy. So he didn't bother to ask why it was she was out of water. After all, fantasies float.

The boat offered Mat the dream of a new start, a new way of life: running a luxury dive boat. Between them, he and Marianne had all the contacts in the US; with the right boat and the friends they had already made on the island they could make a real go of it. They could start up a business that no one else was catering for properly: top of the range diving. He'd even done a basic spreadsheet on the business back at the hotel and the numbers had worked out real well. With just 30% occupancy he'd be cutting even and anywhere around 50% and he'd be making enough money for his second boat.

Besides, he said to himself, it was the kind of business that needn't be a permanent thing. It was not like he would be committing himself for life (and that appealed right now). He could just do it for a while and then move on if he didn't care for it. Running his own business would cut him free of the past, but in a positive way.

After taking another look round the boat, Mat shook Tim's hand and said that he'd get back to him in a couple of days and maybe ask Marianne to come over and have a look.

Mat walked back to the taxi. The old lady was still waiting in the shade. Why chase after a new customer when she already had a fare?

"Got all your business done, young man?" she's asked.

"Yes thanks, could we go back to the hotel?" he said, settling in the back.

The old lady turned the cab around and the headed out to the coast road. She floored the old vehicle down a short stretch of dirt track and the dust flew up behind them.

Mat hunkered down a little on the back seat, ready for the drive back. If there had been a safety harness he would probably have put it on. He looked forward at the old lady. Mat couldn't help feeling that it was a shame that she still had to work at her age. She should be able to enjoy herself at her time of life, indulge herself a little.

"So are you thinking of buying a boat?" she asked. "That Tim's mighty persuasive."

"Well I'm thinking about it," Mat replied. "It could make a good business venture and we'd be able to set up here on the island for a bit. It seems like it's such a great place to live."

"Sure is," said the old lady. "I've been here for 71 years and I wouldn't leave it now. Got all my family here besides. Two boys. My husband died two years ago, that's when I took up this driving."

Thankfully they had reached the coast road and the ride eased down. The view of the ocean opened up before them like a continual promise.

"Must be tough making a living out of a cab on an island that's only six miles long," said Mat, looking out of the window.

"Would be, I suppose. But I don't do this just for the money, although an income is sure nice when you reach 71 years old like me," she laughed and turned her head a little. Mat would have preferred it if she'd watched the road.

"I do it because I need a purpose," she continued. "Can't just sit at home and re-arrange the photo albums all day. When Joe, my husband, died I needed to get out and talk to people. I could have gone off on some endless cruise I suppose but I thought that would just be running away. I felt I needed to get a job, keep myself occupied. Which is why I took up the driving. It's a great way to meet people. And my boys take care of the money side of things anyhow. One's in real estate and so he can look after our properties and the other's runs a financial company – looking after people's offshore trusts and the like – so he can take care of my investments. That means all I have to do is keep driving."

At Hardings, Mat had been used to applying the "five-second rule." This says that you can tell most things about a person in the first five seconds, from their first five sentences, and their first five steps. First impressions count in business.

Not here. This old lady didn't work because she needed the money. With properties on Grand Turk she was undoubtedly a real estate millionaire. She worked for a purpose. Work was good for the soul.

They arrived back at the hotel and the old lady pulled up to a spectacular stop outside the reception area. Heads turned inside.

"Oh and do let me know if either of my sons can help you out now," she said to Mat. "Just give me a call on the cab number and I can get them to contact you. No problem," she'd said handing over a taxi company card with her number on it.

Mat thanked her and gave the old lady a tip, probably larger than he'd normally do.

Marianne said that she would be waiting for him in the lobby. But she wasn't there. He checked his watch; it was just after 11.00 – he was back a little early. He looked for Marianne around the lobby area, rang the room and the hotel's Spa Lounge, and then walked out onto the lawn by the main pool and bar.

He was making his way over to the bar when Mat saw Marianne seated with two smartly dressed men. They certainly weren't islanders, in white shirts and ties. She was talking to them animatedly and they were nodding. She looked down at her watch on several occasions as if concerned about the time.

Mat held back, watching the group in conversation. Marianne hadn't told him about any meeting and he was unsure whether or not to approach. On balance he decided not to.

The meeting lasted a few more minutes and then the two well-dressed men stood up, put their papers back into their briefcases and shook Marianne's hand. It looked very much like a business meeting to Mat. Instead of approaching Marianne straight away, he went back and took a seat in the lobby. The two men walked through; they had noticeable Boston accents and were dressed in smart suits. They asked for a taxi to the airport and went outside to stand on the steps to the hotel. A few minutes later, Marianne came into the reception, left an envelope at the desk and then walked toward the seating area. She seemed surprised that Mat was already there waiting.

"Hello, darling," she said kissing him on the cheek. "You're back early. Does that mean you had a good or bad trip?"

"Both really. I went to see that boat I mentioned over at the Marina. It needed some work doing to it but it could make a fabulous live-aboard. We'd have our own little diving business and never need to leave Paradise," he said in an ironic tone to cover the truth about the dreams he had for the boat.

In the next breath, he switched the subject: "And how about you?" he asked. "Did you have a good morning?"

"Sure did," she said. "I was over at the Serenity Spa. It was divine."

Killing me softly with her words

Mat and Marianne spent a relaxed day together and later that evening decided to make the trip to a restaurant and club a little way down the coast called Mambo.

Marianne seemed excited to be going out for an evening and having the excuse to dress up. Much as she liked being with the diving gang or spending the evening with Mat around the hotel, she missed the small thrill of going out together. Tonight she looked radiant in a deep red silk strapless dress, with strings of freshwater pearls about her neck.

Mambo was one of the most popular places on the island. The food was excellent. There was no set menu, the head waiter just came up and talked to you, ran through what they had that night and then you sort of came to an agreement on what you would have. But no matter, it was always excellent, especially the seafood. However, the food wasn't the only attraction. The principal draw was Yolanda. Yolanda sang at Mambo six nights a week (she was off on Mondays) and had about the best voice you would hear anywhere. She also had a mesmerizing stage presence. She was tall, very dark, and very beautiful. When she sang her face was like a mask. She left all the emotion to her voice. But because she kept her face so expressionless, there was a stillness about her that brought with it a sense of tragedy. She was a lover who had lost her man and would never recover and all of the songs carried this tragedy somewhere in their delivery. The effect was absolutely electric.

Yolanda was accompanied on the piano by Benny. Benny was everything that Yolanda was not. He was huge and happy and beamed his way through every song. He would normally sweat profusely during a set and would mop his brow carefully with a large white handkerchief he kept in his white tuxedo jacket. He played the piano with complete ease, so that it didn't seem so much an instrument as a voice to match Yolanda's intense and tragic beauty.

There was a small dance floor at Mambo, enough space for a few couples. Marianne and Mat took to the floor while Yolanda sang in her haunting way of love's own story.

"Are you serious about that boat?" asked Marianne as they danced, holding one another in a light embrace.

"I don't know," said Mat. "It seemed like a fun idea and I just thought it would be a complete break from what you and I have been doing all our lives."

"Too right there," said Marianne. "But I thought that this was only a sabbatical from Hardings. That you could and would go back when you liked?"

"It is a sabbatical, but I'm not sure if and when I'll be going back."

Marianne looked at him.

"So how long are we going to be staying here?" Marianne asked with more intensity in her voice than usual.

"As long as it takes to find a future I guess," said Mat drily.

Marianne did not reply.

They danced a few more moments and then Mat asked:

"So who were those men you met with this morning?"

He felt Marianne's body stiffen in his embrace. She turned her head away slightly.

"Oh, they were just some banker friends of Anthony's. He suggested that I meet them. They were passing by so I agreed. That's all. Nothing sinister at all."

Mat was angry that Marianne had obviously been doing some favor for Anthony. He had believed he could leave Anthony and everything that related to Hardings behind on the mainland. Now it was coming back to haunt him through Marianne.

"Why didn't you tell me you were having the meeting?" he asked.

Marianne turned to face him. She had tears in her eyes.

"You're right, darling, I should have told you. I just didn't want to bother with that sort of traffic while we're here on the island. I just wanted you to forget all that."

He looked at her. He felt that she was telling the truth. She hadn't told him because she wanted to protect him in some way. But he was still upset that she had met with friends of Anthony's. It was not like her to lie to him.

At the end of the song, they went back to their seats and the waiter brought over a bottle of white wine and some langoustines grilled in garlic butter.

Yolanda was on set, her face half illuminated by a small spotlight above. Benny would look about from the keyboard every now and again and smile at the room of diners. Mat was still upset and seemed distant as they sat watching the show. Marianne reached out and took hold of his hand.

"I'm sorry, darling, really I am. Let's just forget it happened. It's unimportant anyway."

She smiled at him. He looked up and smiled back.

"How are the langoustines?" asked Mat.

"Divine," she said, dabbing her napkin on a little streak of butter that had seeped from the corner of her mouth. He wanted to lean forward and lick it away.

The Wall

Divers can get addicted to the coral wall. As though it's too beautiful to leave. Sometimes they can become so enraptured by it that they forget to look at simple things like their depth gauges. They forget about depth altogether or maybe they just don't care. Whatever, some don't come back.

Mat loved the wall. He loved that feeling of standing on the edge of it and just letting himself go. Going into free fall, down its sheer cliff face, the wall of life.

Right then, with a clear blue sky above and the dive boat waiting for him, Mat was going down, down below 160 feet. He'd never gone this deep before. But the wall was there and it made him feel like there were mysteries to discover. He was entering a new dimension of magical life. It was like a warm glow inside and it was saying: "Don't worry, be happy."

He floated down in a state of wonder. He didn't know it, but nitrogen narcosis was setting in.

Was this enlightenment? Pretty soon, he'd be so high he'd lose the ability to reason, he'd lose any sense of purpose. The dazzling colors of the reef life, in yellows and oranges, blues and reds shone out at him in a gorgeous palette. Was he seeing these images for real or simply dreaming them?

Now the doubts were starting to fade from his mind. "Did he need to go back to Hardings?" was becoming, "No need to go back, ever. The wall is where you should be. Here is right, here is now."

He thought of Alessandro, making that speech at the barbecue saying: "Who cares if your buddy is insane. So is everybody else's."

At 170 feet he was still floating down. Two angelfish appeared from the wall. Life is so rich down here.

"Why stop now," he thought. "I am on the brink of something beautiful. A few feet more."

He went on down.

He forgot altogether about going back. The wall and its life were all that mattered.

A few more feet, a few more seconds and he would pass out. "Don't worry, be happy…"

Then he heard his father's voice. Clear and simple. Saying the words that Alessandro had used at the barbecue.

"If you're enjoying your dive too much, it's probably the nitrogen narcosis."

It was his father's voice and it was repeating these words over and over again:

"If you're enjoying your dive too much, it's probably the nitrogen narcosis."

Mat shook his head violently, forcing his attention to the depth gauge. It read 172. He shouldn't be here. The survival instinct kicked back in. Get to surface. Get some air. Keep breathing.

Don't rush. Take it smooth. Too fast and you're in that hyperbaric chamber.

He made his way back up the wall, its summit silhouetted above in a cascade of white light. He was no longer flying; his scuba kit was not a pair of wings, it was a cylinder of oxygen and it was all that was keeping him alive. Keep breathing.

Mat made it back slowly to the summit, paused on the reef edge, and pushed up onto the surface.

He was breathing but inside he was gasping for air.

Mat struggled forward and clutched at the transom at the back of the dive boat. His arms felt weak, but he managed to pull himself up slowly on board. He pulled up his mask and breathed in deeply, letting the air tanks rest on the side of the boat. He sat on the deck and loosened his suit, freeing his arms and chest. He looked up at the sky above: he was there and alive.

"That was a long dive Mat," said Jean-Claude approaching him from the far end of the boat.

"Too long, I forgot myself back there," Mat replied, still gasping a little.

"You went too deep, yes?" said Jean-Claude.

"Yes, I suppose so," replied Mat.

"And what happened?"

"I heard my father's voice. My dead father. He was telling me to get out of there. He saved me," said Mat, his head now buried in his chest.

"Is this what you have feared all this time?" Jean-Claude asked.

"Yes," said Mat.

"Why do you fear him?"

Mat lifted his head and looked at Jean-Paul.

"Because I have seen him. Twice. I know it's him. It's not some vision. It's actually him and I feel he wants to tell me something. I came here hoping that this feeling would go away and for a while it did. But now I know it's not going to go away unless I do something."

"You cannot dive so deep that it will go away. It will always be there with you," said Jean-Claude.

"I know that now," said Mat.

"Do not be ashamed to speak of these things," Jean-Claude said after a brief silence. "I have been in the deep many times and I have been touched by something down there, something which I cannot explain and yet which I know to be real. Foolish people laugh because they have not experienced such things. They do not know."

"Thank you Jean-Claude," Mat replied.

"Good," he said. "Then you have no choice but to listen to what your father wishes to tell you."

"Can I stay here?" asked Mat afraid of leaving his island paradise, "Here on Grand Turk?"

"No," said Jean-Claude. "This is not your place. I am a dive master. That is what I do. Diving is the only thing I can do. Since I was a little boy I have only wanted to see what lay beneath the water, to live there in that liquid world. The same is true for Gregor and Alessandro. But you are not the same. This is not your world."

"But I love it here," said Mat. "Marianne and I both do. We both feel free."

"Free," said Jean-Claude, pointing out at the ocean. "This is not free. Freedom is finding your own rules. Besides, you will not feel free until you have found what course you must take. Go back to your life. Start back at the beginning. Follow your soul – your father's voice will not be far away."

The re-emergence

A person gets lost, just as a business gets lost. Although I have to say that over the years I have found it interesting that when a business goes into crisis we describe it in abstract, market terms rather than the human ones. Anyhow, when it happens, both start asking themselves the same question: "Who am I?"

Most people – and companies for that matter – experience some form of identity crisis along their way. Either because of too much failure or too much success, or because they have reached some crossroads which poses such a challenge that they doubt their ability to continue.

Escape is one solution to this perennial problem. For businesses, escapism usually takes the form of bringing in the "ideas" men or women. For individuals, like Mat, it often takes the form of a charter boat on the clear blue waters of the Turks and Caicos Islands. I have to admit the attraction of this option. There's part of me that would like to sail away some days. But I am also bothered by it, too. Escapism has just become, well, so acceptable. What's more, "finding yourself" is always conducted away from mainstream business. It seems you can only "find yourself" running an art gallery, or traveling the world, or helping the needy. And societies reinforce this cliché, praising those who give up their job in the "heartless" arenas of banking or industry for a career in education or pottery classes.

Is pottery really so much closer to the soul? If so, how come?

This situation has led to two things. First, those in professional careers are always talking about what they are going to do "when I get out." They defer, they don't do. Second, all this escapism simply reinforces the image of business as unethical and without values. We only find ourselves in other more "human" pursuits. But why does it have to be that way? Why shouldn't business involve this more human dimension? Why can't business be a world where self-development and fulfillment are natural and integral?

In the light of these questions, I find it interesting that Jean-Claude told Mat to go back to work, rather than escape to a boat and diving. He talked to Mat about the everyday bravery of work. That was one of the main reasons that Mat decided to leave the Islands and return home. Another, of course, was his realization that running was no use. He knew after that near-disastrous dive that he had to confront whatever was going on in his life.

Mat was seeing a ghost. He couldn't explain it. But it was real and true for him. It wasn't something he just saw or heard, he experienced the ghost.

He was being driven by something that he didn't understand, but at the same time he was thinking clearly and rationally. His rational mind was trying to work out why this was happening to him. His irrational mind was telling him he had to listen to his father's presence. For he felt more certain than ever that his father was trying to communicate with him. At this stage, he had no reason to believe that the ghost was anything other than benevolent.

So as he went over and over in his mind the conversations they had had about work and business he felt that he had to know whether his father was right. Was there another way to understand business, which delivered better performance and a more human focus? Was there a more complete picture, where you didn't have to sell your soul to succeed, you had to find it?

To Mat's mind his father was putting that challenge before him: "Leave Hardings. Prove me right or wrong."

So that was exactly what he was going to do. And he was going to do it with every fiber of his being. He could do nothing or think of nothing else until he'd resolved it. It was like he was putting his whole life on the line.

Instead of being a radical by escaping – the typical sixties, Timothy Leary mantra – Mat was going to be radical by staying inside the system of work that he knew. He was going to look for that more complete picture he'd had intimations of when he was on the Islands: a new dimension to business.

His way forward now was to go back to the beginning. He had to experience business for what it is, not how it seems. He would go back to his life as a consultant, but instead of serving the twin gods of strategy and ideas, he would look for a new way to make business work better – either through that consulting firm or by setting up his own.

Of course this decision put even more pressure on his life. His friends and peers couldn't understand. People could accept him leaving Hardings to do something wild, but not something as mundane as "work." Who turns in a Ferrari for a Ford? Furthermore, what was there to admire about his choice? Taking ordinary decisions isn't what one expects from a hero.

Headhunters

Mat walked through the arrivals hall. It was a crowded Wednesday morning, people coming from every corner of the globe, changing planes, taking off to new destinations. Above him, the flight announcement boards clicked over their list of names: Denver, London, Toronto, Los Angeles, Paris, Delhi, Copenhagen, Perth. Such endless possibilities, the sense of going places. I've often wondered if that's why headhunters choose hotels near airports for their meetings. On the one hand, airports are discreet and practical. On the other, the metaphor of travel might just get candidates thinking differently. The suggestion of new destinations, of change and excitement, might prey upon their mind.

But Jason Pearce of McHenry Matzocoulis Fox wouldn't need any such persuasive artistry. He was a smooth enough talker all by himself.

He'd taken up position in an armchair, with a low coffee table in front of him, inside a gray meeting room at the end of a long gray, echoless corridor that had last been cleaned by Germaine at 7.23. You knew because you could see her signature on the form on the wall and you could call her back if necessary. There was water and ice, tea and coffee on the table, and some clean white note pads and blue pencils. The hotel china was white with a somewhat less than confident pink flower pattern; the napkins were double-strength tissue.

Mat had on a dark gray suit. It was very different to the shorts and T-shirts he'd become used to over the past three months. Jason wore a blue suit with a white shirt and blue tie. He never wore anything else.

They greeted one another and spent a few moments talking about their flights. Mat served himself some iced water.

"You've sure got yourself a good tan there, Mat," Jason had commented.

"Thank you," Mat replied. "We had a great break on the Turks and Caicos Islands. I just wanted somewhere to think things through for myself and Marianne loves it there so it seemed like the perfect destination."

"Yes. I understand. It's good to take time out in a career, give yourself the clarity to build from. It can help you plan exactly where you're headed," said Jason.

"I suppose you could say that," Mat replied "I certainly know what I am looking for now."

There was something about the tone in Mat's reply that rang alarm bells for Jason. This wasn't a typical candidate or a typical brief. He was on a mission of his own. Jason might have been a headhunter, but thick skinned he certainly wasn't.

"OK which way do you want to play this meeting, Mat?" said Jason taking on a sudden change-of-direction tactic. "Straight or whacky?"

"What does straight sound like?" asked Mat.

"I have heard a lot of interesting things about your career from a number of sources," started Jason. "And I believe there are many parallels between some of the things you have been doing at Hardings and the role I would like to discuss with you today. I can, of course, understand your reservations about meeting, but can assure you that our discussion is confidential, and will remain so unless – or until – you tell me that you wish to explore matters and take things to the next stage and meet the client."

"And whacky?"

"It's a jungle out there and we all know it's populated by two kinds of animal: herbivores and carnivores," replied Jason with a very straight face.

"OK on reflection, I'd say on the whacky side of straight," said Mat.

"Fine we'll give it a try," said Jason. "You're an extreme candidate. On sabbatical from Hardings, but not because you were pushed like the rest of them I see. I hear you were up for partnership. So we're talking special forces here. Someone I can send into unusual territory.

"That's the fun part over. Here's the advice," he continued. "First, you have to watch that your career doesn't plateau real quick. Six months out of action and you're raising questions about your integrity. Not a good thing.

"Second, if you want to get to CEO, you have to start now. People who get to the top spend an awful lot of time managing their careers. It doesn't just happen on its own."

"Take me out of the CEO race for now," said Mat. "I just want back in, back into consulting."

"You could go mainstream, I can get you into Fane & Co. or other equally mainstream Hardings competitors…."

"From Coke to Pepsi? I don't think so," said Mat.

"OK, then where are we placing you?"

"I want a consulting firm that works on real change activities," said Mat. "At Hardings, I was all senior executive and theory. What I am looking for in my career right now is something more hands on. More involved."

"You're not looking for a pay raise then?" Jason joked ironically.

"No, I am looking for a new direction," replied Mat.

"Hey," said Jason, "What's that you're saying? You want God on a good day!"

Mussel wars and job offers

Two weeks later Mat was on a flight to Brussels. Jason had put him in touch with a management consulting firm called Tactilis who were looking for what they termed "an investigator." Tactilis had a reputation for no-nonsense change management. They were active in Europe and North America with some operations in the Middle East. If you wanted a business to work at the coalface with you, Tactilis was as good a choice as any.

Jason had summed this up in a brief email:

Job offer at Tactilis. It's about as far away from Hardings as you can get and stay a consultant. Hands on. Practical. Real fixers. Oh and the job spec is described as an 'investigator'! Interested?? Regards, Jason.

It was just too enticing for Mat not to at least check out. If the description was right it could be that Tactilis was what he was looking for: a consulting firm that dealt with the fundamental building blocks of a business. Mat, by whatever hand, had been brought face to face with the failure of Hardings to find a solution for a company like Wentworth Industries. He was now wrestling with his father's belief that the clever people were pursuing a flawed business model. As a consequence, Mat felt he had to look for an answer to his quest in the mundane, the everyday. He'd read somewhere that Picasso said the big breakthrough in technique comes from going back to the beginning, returning to the simplest elements of one's art. Mat realized he had to do that for himself.

So he agreed to go to an interview with Tactilis almost immediately. He also ran an online search on Tactilis and discovered that the boss of the company was Max Larsen. Max was Danish and had started his career in the oil business working in oil and gas exploration. It takes a special type of person to do this kind of job; exploration has always been a risky pursuit.

There was one other part of the Tactilis file that intrigued Mat: during his first posting to Colombia, Max had been kidnapped by the local FARC guerrillas. They had stopped his car at a checkpoint on a road between two drilling rigs and had taken Max off into the bush. They cut off the top of his little finger on his left hand and had sent it to his company as proof that they were holding Max. The tip of the finger was accompanied by a ransom demand for $4 million or they would start sending more fingers through the mail.

Fortunately the executives never had to call the kidnappers' bluff, because two weeks later Max turned up in a hotel lobby in some small town. He'd escaped the guerrillas and walked out a free man. He called his office in Bogota just as cool as you like. What's more, instead of getting the hell out of the country, he stayed on. He even set up a negotiation team with the guerrillas and brokered some kind of settlement. You just had to meet somebody with that kind of CV thought Mat.

Mat took a flight to London and then on to Brussels. He had booked in to a small hotel in the center of the city, the Metropole. He checked in with the pretty young receptionist and went upstairs to his room.

The room was small but well-furnished with a writing desk by the window and a single bed down one side of the wall. There was a telephone by the side of the bed. As he walked in he noticed that the red message light was flashing on the phone. He put down his case and picked up the phone, pressing the message button. The line went dead. He phoned down to reception.

"This is Mat Durer in room 325. Is there a message for me?" he asked.

"No sir, there is nothing for you," the receptionist replied.

"Strange, the message light on my phone is flashing," Mat went on.

"There must be some mistake then, sir. I certainly haven't taken any calls for you and I came on duty at lunchtime today."

"Well thank you anyway," said Mat and hung up.

Mat took a quick shower, dressed and read a few pages of *Dangerous D@ta*, a detective story he'd picked up at the airport.

At 7.30 he went downstairs and checked directions for the restaurant, Chez Patrice, with the female receptionist. She knew the restaurant well and told Mat that it was famous for its *moules frites*.

"Like just about every other restaurant in Brussels," Mat had responded, opening up the conversation. She was young and attractive, with medium-length light red hair, a trim figure inside her receptionist's blue suit, and a good, friendly smile.

Mat smiled at her. There was definitely a connection between the two of them.

"Yes that's right, but this one is very good and still not too expensive," she replied. "You know that we have a real problem now with *moules* in Brussels?"

This had to be interesting: mussel wars, thought Mat.

"Oh yes? What?" asked Mat.

"They are getting so expensive and it's because the Dutch fishermen are charging us far too much. They are like Mafia you know, they control the sale of mussels to us and they know that we are crazy about mussels and that people come here to Brussels to eat the mussels and so they think that they can charge us what they like," she concluded with a shrug of her shoulders.

"Sounds like they're playing it pretty tough," said Mat not wanting to get too deep into the subject, but just enough to coax along the conversation.

"Yes, but what if we fight back? What if we boycott all mussels for a week or a month? That will show them!" she said a little defiantly, her red hair shaking a little. Mat noticed a slight flush to her cheek.

"Consumer power," said Mat dryly. The receptionist was sexy, but dead earnest.

"Anyway let's not start tonight," he said.

"No *monsieur*. Perhaps I could give you a map to help you find your way to Chez Patrice?" she suggested.

"Yes, that would be very kind," he said.

The receptionist reached into a drawer, took out a tourist map, and opened it out. Then she took out a blue pen and made a neat circle around a street in the center of the map. As she did so she leant forward, so that her soft hair fell onto her face. Mat admired the clear, translucent skin of her hands and wrists.

"There you are, sir," she said, indicating the blue circle she had made on the street map. "It's no more than a twenty-minute walk from here."

She folded up the map and offered it to him.

"Thanks, that's most helpful," said Mat.

Their hands touched as he took it from her. It could have been divined by both parties as an accidental touch. But both knew it wasn't.

"I hope you have a good evening," said the receptionist.

"Thank you. I'm sure I will," replied Mat placing the room key on the counter. They smiled at one another and Mat walked out into the night.

Brussels was not quite the European capital that he had expected. Before this visit he'd only passed through the airport and never visited the city itself. Apart from the very center, most of the architecture was modern and unremarkable. All the old town houses and Art Nouveau buildings had been torn down in favor of modern glass and concrete. But then Brussels itself had changed. Its main business today is not trade but bureaucracy; the city merely reflected this new, more inscrutable character. Most Belgians have moved out to the nearby Flemish towns leaving the city itself to the Eurocrats.

At least the old quarter at the heart of Brussels had retained its character. Mat's restaurant for the evening was in one of the network of narrow streets just off the Grand Place. It had been raining earlier and the cobbles of the square glistened beneath the street lamps.

With the help of the tourist map, Mat found his way to the street where Chez Patrice was located. He paused a few yards short of the door to collect his thoughts. As he did so, his eye was caught by the window of one of the adjacent shops. It was an old-fashioned men's hairdressers and the window contained a magnificent display of men's combs, brushes, and eau de colognes as well as a marvelous collection of ocean sponges.

Mat bent forward to inspect the sponges. He had seen sponges in the deep coral waters moving idly in the stream: living things. These sponges had been brought up by divers, their outer skin torn off, beaten, dried, and then dyed in acid to create the soft yellow and white colors we think of as natural. For all this, they still retained their fascinating beauty and made him think of being underwater. Mat had read once that unique among the animal kingdom, the sponge can regenerate itself. Tear off a fragment, place it back in salt water, and the sponge will slowly grow again.

Just at that moment Mat caught the reflection of a man walking behind him. The man was wearing an overcoat and a tall broad hat, similar to a Homburg. Mat turned and saw the man disappear into Chez Patrice. Mat's heart started to pound. He walked straight into the restaurant and looked around. There was no sign of the man whose reflection Mat had just seen.

"Can I help you, *monsieur*?" asked the *maitre d'* as Mat looked about him.

"No…no…I was just looking for someone," he said. "Someone in a tall hat and gray overcoat. He just walked in."

"I'm afraid I can't help you, *monsieur*. I haven't seen anyone of that description. Perhaps at the *vestiaire*…?" the *maitre d'* suggested.

"Thank you," Mat said and went over to check his coat in. There was no one there but a middle-aged attendant.

Mat walked back into the main body of the restaurant. The interior consisted of a maze of small rooms linked by staircases. It reminded Mat of one of those Escher prints with trick perspectives and levels.

Mat looked about him. On edge, he asked the *maitre d'* whether a Mr Max Larsen had already arrived. The *maitre d'* confirmed he had and offered to show Mat to the table.

He led Mat to a room near the top of the building where Max Larsen was sitting reading a newspaper. He stood up. The first thing Mat noticed was that he was tall – over six feet – and muscular. He looked the way you'd expect a middle-aged, middle-weight boxer who kept himself in really top condition to look. He had close cropped blonde hair and blue eyes. He wore a checked jacket and soft pink shirt, blue trousers and brown loafer shoes. There was no Ralph Lauren Polo logo anywhere to be seen.

They shook hands. Definitely a fit boxer kind of a handshake, thought Mat. Definitely. His mind wandered to the missing fingertip. He wanted to take a look at Max's left hand but knew this would be obvious.

"I'm delighted you could make it to Brussels at such short notice," Max said, "Why don't you sit there, that way I can watch you..."

Mat sat down and scanned the room about him. He was apprehensive and his hand shook a little as he reached for his napkin.

Max sat down too and also picked up his napkin, holding it in both hands for a moment. The little finger on his left hand ended in a rounded knobble just above the knuckle. The Colombians hadn't done a very good job at surgery.

The two of them settled down to things and looked over the menu. Mat noticed the little memo on the front: "To cook is to create. And to create is to act with integrity." He could think of a number of chefs who had forgotten these *bon mots*.

"The *moules* are good, of course," said Max. "They cook them in white Zinfandel and dry vermouth here, with a little garlic. Quite delicious. Maybe to start with? And then we could try the *waterzooi* – it's a kind of creamy stew with chicken, fish, and scallops. I think you might enjoy it, it is quite different."

"Sounds fine to me," replied Mat.

"And some wine? I know they say you ought to drink Belgian beer with *moules*, but I prefer wine, don't you?"

Mat didn't see the need to argue.

"Sure thing," he replied. He was beginning to relax.

Max chose a dry white wine, a Piesporter Goldtröpchen Kabinett that would go well with the mussels and stand up to the cream sauce of the *waterzooi*.

They talked further, about the journey and Brussels and the state of the European Union and all the while Mat kept expecting the interview to start. Waiting for leading questions like: "So why did you leave Hardings, Mat?" But they never came. Max had other ideas.

"I'm not sure why you're after this job with us, Mat," he said eventually. "In fact I'd have to say that a Hardings consultant was just about the last person I expected on the list of candidates."

"Maybe that's why I want the job," replied Mat.

"Could be, but I suspect not," said Max, "I would guess you have some other motive. Probably personal. So let us move on to what my motives are. I am interested in you because you are obviously very capable and you are an outsider. You can look at my business with a fresh pair of eyes. That's what I need. I also need someone who is going to understand our business very rapidly."

The mussels arrived in large bowls and looked succulent in their smooth white wine and vermouth sauce. The Piesporter was cold and dry and matched the full creamy texture of the mussels beautifully. Much better than beer thought Mat.

Max tucked a napkin into his shirt collar and began to eat his mussels with athletic ease, using the shell of one mussel to scoop out the flesh of others.

"OK," he said between mouthfuls. "I am going to tell you a story, a true story about me as it happens, but it could be about anyone in my organization.

"It happened several years ago now. I was in Japan. I had been asked by the senior management within a major manufacturing company to take a look at one of their plants. I went along to the plant and met the senior executive in charge of it, whom I shall affectionately call 'Honda-san' though that wasn't his real name. Honda-san was very polite and thanked me for taking the trouble to visit, but said very firmly that there was no real point to my being there because the plant was operating at its optimum already. I was a bit confused about this since the organization had suggested that I might be able to identify some cost savings here. So I prodded a bit further, asked for the production figures, and took a walk around the plant."

Max stopped. The bowl before him was now a mass of empty shells. Mat had also finished his mussels and was glad that the boycott of the Dutch Mafia's product had been left to another day. A waiter took the bowls of empty shells away and topped up their glasses. The restaurant was full and relatively noisy; no one would be bothered to overhear their conversation.

"Anyway," continued Max. "Everything I asked for, Honda-san had ready. And everything we saw confirmed that things were pretty much perfect. They had all the world-class system elements you'd ever want and all the right numbers. I don't think there was anything missing. So at the end of this tour I had a cup of tea and a small think to myself."

Max took a sip of Piesporter and seemed to reflect again for a moment. He crossed his hands on the tablecloth. Mat studied the knobble end of his little finger, fascinated that Max probably no longer even thought of the loss. He imagined Max towering over his Japanese clients.

"Then I went back to this guy Honda-san and I said: 'OK, Honda-san. Could you please get me the current shift supervisor? I need the shift supervisor to come into the room.' He looked a bit puzzled but sure enough he calls the shift supervisor. The supervisor comes into the room and does his bow to Honda-san and his bow to me. And of course he can't speak a word of English. So I had a translator called for."

The next course arrived, *waterzooi*, with the aroma of scallops and garlic and creamy richness.

Max seemed pleased by the choice. He continued his tale: "Then I say, 'Honda-san I don't want you answering this next question.'

"And I turned to the translator and said to him to ask the supervisor if these things happen on his shift. And I had a list of ten types of classic things that happen on shifts. As soon as the translator started asking the questions, the shift supervisor starts nodding. Then the shift supervisor was smiling and nodding, not in that ordinary Japanese polite way, but as though he was really agreeing with what was said."

Max mimicked the supervisor's movements. He was surprisingly good at it. Funny and accurate.

"I asked him: 'Do you ever go to the plant's part store and ask for a part and find that the part is not there?' And the supervisor smiled and nodded."

Again Max mimicked the supervisor's actions.

"Then I asked him if his maintenance team were ever called to attend a high priority event and the call was overlooked because people thought it was some other department's responsibility. And the supervisor nodded and smiled. Then I asked: 'Have you ever sent a team out to do some maintenance and the maintenance operators didn't have the right tools and when they do get the right tools they open up that particular part of the asset and they find that the job they had been told about was in fact completely different to the actual problem?' And the shift supervisor was smiling more broadly than ever."

A big grin came across Max's face.

"But Honda-san wasn't smiling," he said. "I can tell you. Honda-san was sunk.

"Very shortly after that, Honda-san was told that his numbers might look good in abstract but the fact that all these things were happening meant that they couldn't be and he was asked to take out all these non-value-added, irritating activities and events out of the plant, which the supervisor knew were there and which Honda-san failed to acknowledge."

Max took a large and emphatic drink of wine. End of story. Point made.

"How do you like the *waterzooi*?" he asked Mat.

"Very good," replied Mat.

"Good. So is that a description of a business you want to be part of?" Max asked, not letting Mat reply straightaway.

"The choice is up to you," he continued. "Say 'no' and we'll just have dinner. If you say 'yes' and you're being honest with yourself, you'll love working with us. If you're not, you'll leave within six months like others have. I'm not taking the risk you are. Because I have to believe you're genuine. I have to believe you want to do the best. Just prove I'm right. Now, let's talk about wine. What do you know about wine, Mat?"

And with that the interview had effectively ended.

Mat took the job. Why? Because as he said subsequently: "It just felt right. I liked Max straightaway and I decided that if he was the boss then it was worth giving the company a go."

Mat was also persuaded by Max's story about Honda-san. It showed a consultant working and thinking differently. It also gave him an insight into a language of a business which he had never had before. It wasn't just that Honda-san was hiding the facts from Max in his interview – he spoke a different language to his supervisor. He used the inflated language of management, while his shift supervisor spoke the day-to-day language of problems on the plant floor. Different languages – of course, they were going to have different views of the business. Even the word "maintenance" would have different meanings for each of them.

This idea of common and distinct languages in business and within a company would return to Mat over and over in the coming weeks. It was his first new building block.

Differences emerge

The spring sun shone brightly on Mat and Marianne's apartment in Blue Key. It was early evening and the temperature was still an agreeable 76°.

Mat and Marianne had spent the day diving with the Flamingos, a diving club operating out of Fort Lauderdale, and were getting ready to go out for dinner. Marianne was in the bath and Mat was shaving. The heat from the water caused the mirror in front of him to mist, so every now and again he would take a towel and wipe himself a new patch of mirror. A new image of him. There was some kind of oil or perfume in the bath and the interior of the room was full of a heady scent, like incense in a Turkish bath.

"Hope you don't mind darling but I happened to be speaking to Anthony Elliot about some art they had rented from us and I asked him about Tactilis," Marianne said to him from the warm perfumed waters of her bath.

"Oh yes," replied Mat, "what did he say?"

"He was polite as always but said that they weren't really in the same league as Hardings. Is that right?"

"Yes, I think that's a fair comment," he said tilting his head back to shave the nick between his jaw and neck.

"So why do you want to go and work for a smaller, less prestigious outfit? I mean nobody ever quits as a partner at Hardings. You're the first…"

"Hey Marianne, you've said that a thousand times before. Remember, I left before they made me up to partner. While I still had a way out."

Marianne didn't respond to this comment. As Mat had said, they had discussed this subject a number of times before and had always found themselves at odds. He felt that Marianne just couldn't relate to his actions. Why leave the world's No. 1 consulting firm? Especially when they paid you more money than was sensible and when you were about to become one of the ruling priesthood. She just thought his actions were bizarre. I suspect if she were pushed on the subject she'd have said that she believed this was a temporary aberration on Mat's part. It was so way out of character. He'd soon come to his senses and return to that brilliant career with Hardings. In fact she wouldn't be a bit surprised if they asked him back right away.

Anthony had almost said as much to her when they had spoken on the phone. He'd said how much he admired Mat and how if he ever considered coming back, then all he needed to do was call him.

"It just doesn't make sense sacrificing your career like this. There's got to be something more behind it," continued Marianne.

Mat hesitated. He had already tried to explain to Marianne that he was searching for something new in business, something that the consultants at Hardings would never find. But he had not told her about his father's driving spirit.

"Look Mari, this is something I have to do," he said, cupping his hands and dousing his face with water from the basin in front of him. "I told you that. Besides I'm sure Tactilis are a good outfit."

Mat turned to Marianne and smiled. She took a natural sponge, dipped it in bath water, and squeezed its warm "juice" onto her left shoulder.

"How long are you going to go on this odyssey for?" she asked.

Mat reached for his bottle of Penhaligon's Blenheim Bouquet. The aftershave felt cool and fresh on Mat's face.

"I guess as long as it takes," he replied.

"And what about my timescales? What if your plans don't match mine?" she said.

Marianne stood up in the bath. Her dark hair was tied in a bunch at the back. Tiny bubbles from the soapy water caught on her skin, on her breasts and thighs.

"Look at me, Mat. I'm 32 next birthday," she said.

He looked at her. Her stomach was flat. The real flat of a young woman. Her legs were lithe, her arms slender, her breasts round and firm. She was a woman in her sexual prime. Her body was charged. She smelled ripe. He wanted her now, right now.

He stepped forward and held her wet body close to his; her breasts pressed against his chest. His hand found the inside of her thigh. She kissed him and drew back, reaching for a bathrobe.

"You're now 33. We're both getting older and we can't wait forever to think of having a family," she said. "You know I could say that your actions are downright selfish and show that you don't care very much for me after all. You're not even putting your career first – that I could understand. You're putting some crazy notion of improving business before our happiness. Throwing everything away on a whim."

She was very close to tears now, the emotional tide still rising. She was angry and she wanted him to know it.

"I can't understand you, Mat," she said, her voice raised. "You had everything. Great job, lovely home, loving girlfriend and you're risking it all. Why?"

Mat stared at her. She meant what she was saying. She was presenting him with a simple choice: me or your crazy idea.

"Look Mari," he said holding her shoulder tenderly, wanting her still. "I know it's rough on you. But keep the faith for a couple of months. That's all. Who knows I may even end up starting up my own consulting firm."

She kissed him, hard on his lips, passion flooding into her eyes.

"Don't take too long to decide that's all. I don't want to be in this position in five years' time. That's not fair to ask of me."

Back in the saddle

Houston, Texas. The Big Country, where they make more millionaires than anywhere else on earth. Here money and business walk the sidewalks together on an evening stroll, just saying to one another, "My what a wonderful world."

Some cities expand upward. They reach for the sky. Not Houston, it doesn't need to. It spreads outward like ripples on a pond over southern Texas. It's got space and plenty of it. While other cities try to impress you with their glassy towers, Houston is all about elbow room.

The consequence of this horizontal ambition is that it can take you more than an hour to drive from George Bush International into the hub of the city. But the drive is across pure American savannah: the vast flat plains of low-level enterprise. This is where photocopying franchises grow up and special offers take root, where huge Chrysler forecourts offer knock-out deals and computer stores look like supermarkets. Here's where Mary's Café takes on Sam's Diner in a battle for the best cup of coffee or the thickest rolls; where loan companies hold out hope and gas stations offer freedom; where flat-roofed shopping malls are the launch pad for new ideas; and where they put McDonald's signs on stilts as though lifting the golden arches out from the scrubland below.

You want to know what competition smells like? Come to the American savannahs. If you can make it here you can make it anywhere.

Mat drove in from the airport with a young black taxi driver whose name was Curtis. Curtis came to Houston from Connecticut ten years ago, out to make a living. He had silver wraparound glasses and a shaven head and a large silver MPV.

"Did you know that Houston is the fourth worst traffic city in the US?" he asked Mat as they drove in.

Mat said, "No."

"Yeah. The worst is Los Angeles," said Curtis with a mix of awe and satisfaction. It was the kind of fact that taxi drivers liked to know.

Mat had come to Houston to make his first "on site" with Tactilis. He was making a complete new start, not just with a new company, but with a whole fresh approach to business. He was going back to the simplest fundamentals of business. From here he would see if he could figure out his new dimension or not. It was the only way, on the ground. At the moment his idea was still vague and unformed. He was like a mathematician who senses he's on the edge of discovering some new law, in his case a new law of business. He had this obsessive feeling it was tied up in the word "human;" that was where his father was leading him. He was being challenged to rescue business from the abstract, mechanistic position it had taken up and which was so difficult to dislodge precisely because it was so successful. Business worked, it just didn't work as well as it should. That "complete picture" was the Holy Grail for Mat and he was staking everything on it. He'd already thrown up his career per se, now his girl was threatening to walk out, too.

At least Mat felt that he had started in the right place by joining Tactilis. They were the type of hands-on organization he wanted. And he'd liked Max Larsen. Max had a powerful charisma that came from being very down-to-earth and passionate at the same time. During the interview in Brussels he'd talked for almost an hour about wine to Mat. But not the usual connoisseur talk of the great vintages he'd had over the years. Or the rarity value of this bottle or that. Max was a hands-on lover of wine. He owned a stake in a vineyard and the things that he talked about were soil and climate and grape variety but, most passionately of all, about *terroir*.

"*Terroir* is the soul of a wine," Mat remembered Max had said. "It's what makes it uniquely itself. It means much more than terrain or the mix of stones and gravels in the soil or the accumulation of leaves in the topsoil. It's the whole environment. Everything about that particular spot: the way the frost acts at one time of year and not another, the layout of the vineyard and its angle of the slope to the sun, the effect that different growers have had on the land, the weather pattern, the proximity to water, or trees, how fast the temperature falls at sundown and how fast it rises at sun up. *Terroir* is every factor that creates individuality."

The words had left a distinct impression on Mat's mind. He'd never thought about all the detail behind growing wine before and that suggested there were whole other dimensions to activities he'd never thought about; dimensions that you'd only know if you'd been there.

So now Mat was in a cab driving down the freeway into Houston. He was back in the saddle. And right next to him was a brand new crocodile skin attaché case. It was a present from Marianne to wish him luck. Inside was a photograph of Mat and Marianne diving off Grand Turk. Signed on the back:

Love, Mari. Always.

A voice from the past

Mat stayed overnight at the Westin in the heart of Houston. In the morning he was up at 6.30 and did half an hour of stretching exercises. He took a shower and ordered room service breakfast: fresh fruit, coffee, and some pastries. His suit arrived back from pressing and looked good and crisp. He was going to make an impression.

Over coffee he ran through in his mind what he knew about the company he was going to visit: Southern Cropsciences. A huge plant. Third quartile performer in Hardings terms. Not a terminal patient but equally not giving the kind of return on investment that shareholders had a right to expect. The CEO was a man named Harry Dean, 55, and had spent his whole career in Southern Cropsciences. General analysts' comment would be that he was a good guy who'd got used to making do with old assets. He'd probably just given in to the conventional wisdom that says his business is driven by forces over which he has no control.

Mat took a tie from a small leather holder in his suitcase and tried it against his blue cotton shirt. It made a good match. As he was easing the tie around his collar and thinking about Southern, he had a flashback to working with Hardings.

He was talking to Brad. He was at the Wentworth head offices in Pittsburgh. And they were standing outside a meeting room and he had said to Brad:

"We give them the ideas and they put them into practice."

He could remember saying that. Quite clearly as though it was some profound insight, which no one other than a Hardings consultant would have the temerity to say.

Then Brad replied: "In a case like this, only a handful of people in the business are going to get the ideas. The rest we're going to have to reconsider. We'll take the telephone directory approach. Take out the company's telephone directory and cross out every fifth name. Given that it's a uniformly low-grade workforce, it doesn't much matter who you cut out."

At the time Mat hadn't said anything.

Now the scene was as clear to him as if he was standing there in those offices. Was he losing his nerve?

Houston Cab Company: Driver 367

A little after 7.45 Mat went down to the lobby and asked the concierge to call a cab. He wanted to make sure he was on time for his first morning.

The cab pulled up, Mat told the concierge where he wanted to go, the concierge told the taxi driver, the taxi driver seemed to nod his head, the concierge opened the rear door, Mat tipped the concierge, the rear door closed and the taxi drove off. That was all just as it should have been and Mat naturally relaxed in the back of the cab and turned his mind to the day ahead.

About five minutes later the cab driver turned round and said: "Where we going, sir?" in a very thick West African accent. That made Mat pay attention. Point one, this driver was clearly very new to the metropolitan area of Houston. Point two, he had not understood a word that the concierge had said to him. Neither point was promising.

"I want to go to the Southern Cropsciences offices at Fainthope and West."

"Yes, sir," the cab driver said.

Yet there was something in the way he said it which made Mat think: "I bet he didn't understand that either." Mat had never been to this part of Houston before, so he wasn't going to be able to navigate them out of any problem.

"You know where that is?" asked Mat.

"Yes, sir. Sorry, I am new here." The minor disconnect between these two statements occurred to Mat, but the guy seemed sure, so he sat back and hoped for the best.

They drove on, for another five minutes. By now the cab driver was beginning to take random and last-minute decisions at traffic junctions. Left, right; it was a lottery.

Then his nerve broke. Houston was just too big to bluff. The cab driver pulled in to the side of the street and said to Mat: "You can write name, sir?" They were both frankly lost. Strangers in a strange part of Houston.

Mat wrote the name out on a small sheet of paper and handed it forward. The cab driver took it, flipped open his cell phone and dialed a number. There followed a highly animated conversation in some West African dialect which went on for several minutes longer than it should have done and also called in to play the entire range of the cab driver's hand gestures. He then closed the cell phone and looked at Mat.

"All right, sir," he said with a smile.

They performed a neat U-turn in the road and drove off in the opposite direction. From time to time thereafter the cab driver would call his African accomplice as he negotiated the more tricky traffic intersections. But 20 minutes later, they arrived at Southern Cropsciences' regional offices. It was in a particularly run down district and Mat thought that probably even an experienced driver would have had difficulties. The cab driver turned and smiled at him.

"We here, sir."

"Yes, thank you. Tough ride," said Mat. He paid the fare with a reasonable tip and took himself and his crocodile attaché case to the security booth by the front gate.

The office

He checked in and asked for the Tactilis offices. Mat walked across the compound and knocked on a rather weather-beaten door. Inside there was a long, low room lit with strip lights from above. There were a series of tables linked together to form a flat surface that approximated to desks. On the desks were PCs and portable printers. Two people were seated at PC monitors and neither looked up at Mat as he came in.

In simple terms, the scene resembled a charity aid crisis hut rather than the smart office surroundings Mat had been used to. He was expecting a dip in form, but not exactly the basement.

Cabling ran criss-cross over the floor linking PCs and printers. The walls were decorated with sets of whiteboards that had graphics and data showing customer service stats, maintenance stats, distribution stats, procurement, production, and MCRS. On another wall there were posters entitled, "Project Objectives" and "Milestones."

On the window sill, Mat noticed an unlikely jumble of professional aids: a large tin of Folgers Classic Roast coffee (catering size), a glass filled with plastic cutlery, a huge carton of Advil pain relief tablets (hospital size) – offering "advanced medicine for pain relief" – a box of Band-Aid plasters, a large cannister of Raid Ant & Roach spray, a bright red can of Bee Bopper with a black top, a can of 3M SprayMount, and a plastic cup holding some petty cash.

On the desk in front of the window sill there was a coffee maker, together with a sugar pourer, two tins of Coffee-mate, offering a choice of French Vanilla and The Original flavors, a tin of Altoids – cinnamon flavor – a stack of yellow legal pads, several packs of Boise printer paper, a batch of cartridges for color printers, four whiteboard markers, a box of stationery with pens, pencils, and highlighters, a large roll of Scotch tape, a roll of brown parcel tape, and a collection of stained white coffee mugs with blue Southern Cropsciences logos.

There was also a pocket folder on the wall filled with takeaway menus from local eateries. Mat absentmindedly took one out. It was for Dino's Deli. At the bottom of the page, after a long list of delicacies, the menu announced the Dino's USP:

The Li'l Dino Difference: Quality, A Clean Restaurant Always, Friendly Courteous Service, A Smile, A Thank You.

Dive buddies

A young man entered the office from the door behind Mat. He was slight, wore glasses and a leather jacket. He looked at home but also strangely out of place. Maybe it was the leather jacket.

"Oh hi," he said to Mat, extending his hand. "Are you Mat Durer? I'm Ray Winston. Glad to meet you." They shook hands.

"Look, grab yourself a seat somewhere," he continued. "We're a little busy this morning getting ready for a Milestones meeting."

"OK, no worry," said Mat. "Just give me the strategy documents and I can get myself up to speed while I'm waiting for you guys."

A brief smile came across Ray's face. "I'm not sure what you mean, but we don't have any strategy documents."

"Oh well, what about the CEO's summary?" said Mat.

"Don't have one of those either," replied Ray.

"Fine. OK. All I need is a schedule of the executive meetings for the day and I'll take it from there. Fly it myself, if you know what I mean." said Mat hopefully.

"Sorry to disappoint you on your first day and all, Mat, but you don't have any schedule with any executives. But you do start with Frank at 9.00. He's expecting you."

"Who's Frank?" asked Mat.

"Frank," replied Ray. "He's the maintenance manager."

The first dive

Frank worked at the main production plant about 20 minutes drive from Southern's regional offices where the Tactilis team were based.

The entrance to the building was through a pair of perspex swing doors, marked "Authorized Personnel Only." Inside there was a low ceiling lit by fluorescent tubes and offices off a wide central passageway. Along both sides of the passage, leaning against walls, there were pallets, boxes, and assorted pieces of equipment. Frank's office was the first on the right.

Mat knocked on the door.

"Come on in," said a voice from inside.

Mat opened the door. Inside there was a desk with a green-booted foot on top of it. The boot was big and belonged to a dark-haired man who was leaning back in his chair, holding a telephone receiver to his ear. He had a black patch over his left eye. He beckoned Mat to come in. He finished off the telephone conversation, swung his boot down from the desk, stood up, and walked over to Mat.

"Can I help you there, mister?" he said, his one eye scanning Mat as though he were looking for faults in a product line.

"I'm looking for Frank," replied Mat.

"Well, you've come to the right place then. I'm Frank," he said. "And what can I do for you?"

"I'm new to the Tactilis team and they asked me to come over and meet with you," Mat replied.

"Oh, you're the guy Ray talked about," said Frank, taking a keen interest in Mat's crisp blue suit. "Just that you didn't look like you were part of Tactilis. I mean you're not exactly dressed like one of them."

"Yeah, I guess the suit's not ideal. I hadn't realized I'd be coming straight over to the plant this morning," said Mat.

The black patch over one eye gave Frank a threatening air. He played to it, making sure that he intimidated Mat from the first. He was the sort of guy who stood just a fraction too close

95

to you, imposing himself that little too far into your personal space for comfort.

Frank went back to his seat behind his desk; Mat pulled up a metal-rimmed chair, the red cloth around the sides was torn and dirty and the silver chrome frame poked through. Mat looked about him.

The walls to the office were littered with notices stuck onto corkboards. There were production targets and shift rosters and safety certificates all mixed up together. There were red stars, green, yellow, and blue ones on the rosters, all denoting different shift patterns. Behind Frank's desk there was a cartoon. It showed a figure sitting on a bomb just like the one in the Peter Sellers movie, *Dr Strangelove*, and the rocket was blasting off into orbit. On the side of the rocket was the name "Tactilis" written on in ballpoint pen.

"Ray said you'd be able to help out with this knowledge transfer thing he's got going," said Frank.

"Did he – fine," replied Mat, not knowing what he had been volunteered for but ready to play along for a while.

"You see I have been here near 30 years and there ain't nothing I don't know about this plant and the way it works. But the trouble is that I am the only one that really knows it. The gold is up here," Frank said, pointing to his temples.

"Ray wants me to find some way to get it down so that others can benefit. First I said to him to get lost because that was a sure way to get myself fired. I mean if I tell him everything I know then he can get rid of me tomorrow. My pension is in this gold," pointing again to his head.

"But then Ray says to me that if I ever was to retire, then this place would really suffer and he talked about how most of the farms and agricultural businesses in the Houston area and the South as a whole have come to depend on Southern Cropsciences and how it would be a shame if that didn't continue. So he kind of wheedled me round to agreeing to co-operate with him. That's his way though."

"So I guess you're here to be my secretary," he said. "What

with that neat little case you have there," he went on, laughing in a rough, hard growl.

"Well, I suppose Ray sent me over to help in any way I can," Mat replied with a brief smile. "But what about the procedures manual? Don't you have a manual that covers everything already?"

"Sure we have one of those," said Frank pointing up at a thick volume on a shelf at the far end of his office, just next to a fading silver trophy for basketball dated 1985 Houston Champs.

"But we don't use it. Don't read it. It was written by some guys in head office who'd never visited the plant and how could they know how everything worked here? Dangerous piece of literature if you ask me. Can send people in all the wrong directions," replied Frank.

Mat had shown just enough humility to get through the first phase with Frank. If he hadn't then Frank would have told him that he should go and meet Jed in one of the giant tanks. This was a way that Frank had of introducing people to the life of a major plant. The temperatures inside these tanks were terrific, a few hours spent here and you were a chastened man. Frank knew that and he wouldn't hesitate to make you experience his baptism if he felt you deserved it.

"OK we'll have a walk around and I'll try to tell you some of the things I know about this place and we can decide whether you think that's the sort of stuff that other people should know. OK?"

"OK," said Mat.

"And let me say right from the start that I'm only agreeing to do this stuff with you because Ray set me up for it and because I reckon the Tactilis team have done real well here," he said. "System availability has increased from 70% to 80% over the last six months. Preventative maintenance routines are now about 36% of overall maintenance, we've reduced inventory levels by 6% and we expect improvements in the finished product area of around 40%."

Mat heard the figures and they were all pointing upward on the curve, but he didn't know exactly what to make of them. It was strange for him to hear figures this close to the business. They were not the kind of figures he was used to dealing with; he knew about board level figures like CAPEX and ROI.

This everyday data was new to him. It reminded him of his original conversation with Max and the Honda-san story – because what Mat was listening to was another language going on inside this company. Only here it was data that Frank was talking about. Data is part of a company's language too – it's not just the words that people use. That was a big point for Mat to pick up because it was the first time he realized that if data was part of the language of a business (how it told its story) and if businesses have different languages at work inside them, then the messages can get all confused. So it's no wonder that executives can get the wrong picture of what's going on in their company. It's not that they're stupid or lazy or even distant, it's just that the data they have is measuring different things from what they believe it to be. No common language and your business fragments.

Mat and Frank set off on a walk around the plant and Frank started by giving Mat an idea of the people who worked for him – six general maintenance technicians and three instrumentation and electrical technicians. For the next three hours they visited every valve and pump around the plant, Frank giving a running commentary as they went. If Mat had been looking for business at its purest, here it was.

Come the end of the day Mat felt like he'd covered several miles with Frank. His blue suit was flecked with oil and dust. His shoes had a thick film of grime over the toes and instep. His head ached from the band of the safety helmet he had worn around the site. But there were other areas that were aching inside – changes inside his head. He was seeing things up close for the first time and not just from the perspective of a plant tour – he'd been on those with other senior executives and of course everything always worked perfectly – he was seeing through the one good eye of a maintenance manager who had been at this plant for close on 30 years. Who knew every pump and duct, who really knew how it worked. That was all a very different perspective for Mat.

Business is empirical. You learn by doing. These lessons were beginning to strike home to Mat. He was feeling a real excitement. He was on the trail of the idea, hunting it down. Putting the pattern together. And all the while he felt like he was getting closer to his father.

Dinner at Dino's

When he got back to the offices, Ray and three other members of the team were going through an outline for their next meeting.

"How'd it go? I hope that 'one-eyed pirate' act of Frank's didn't put you off none," asked Ray as Mat came in.

"No, it went OK. I think we got on fine. I helped Frank out on the plant knowledge program you wanted him to co-operate on. Actually, it gave me a pretty good insight into the way the plant came together," said Mat.

"I thought it might work out that way," said Ray. "And Frank's really a top guy. He's fine once you get him on side and he's come to show us some respect in recent weeks."

Ray seemed even younger than he had on first meeting. He was probably still in his late twenties, so Mat was surprised he'd been able to deal with such a tough customer. He asked Ray about it.

"Yeah, Frank was one of the biggest skeptics around," said Ray. "Just thought we were making more work for him. But it's often the way, the ones you think are going to be a big problem, when you win them over, tend to be the biggest allies."

"It seemed like he felt he owed you one," said Mat. "How d'you win him round?"

"Just with small practical changes. Small wins we call them. Give them something that makes their lives easier, probably something that they've wanted to change for years: like the way a shift operated or helping them to establish a daily meeting to plan their work, small changes like that. And once life starts to get better for them, they'll start to trust you more and it builds from there. It's the small changes added together that really turn a place around."

Mat thought about this and about seeing a company differently. The knack was to see a company as a myriad of tiny events that you have to get right. Calling this attention to detail is correct, but it also entirely misses the point. Attention to detail is abstract. Thinking about a company as a mosaic of small wins puts the focus on the practical human dimension. You have to deal with emotions to help people work better.

Anyone can set a target of 5% cost reductions in a company, but you only achieve that target through lots of small wins. A few months ago at Hardings, Mat would have said of course he knew that, but in reality he would have had no idea what it meant in terms of actions. To Hardings setting the target was enough in itself.

Mat turned back to Ray. He was listening more intently than ever.

"And you want to know what's best about all this?" said Ray. "When I got to the bottom of why Frank didn't want to work with us on that knowledge capture program – you know what, it wasn't because he was afraid he would be laid off. Not at all. It was just that he can't write very well. He's nearly illiterate and he was worried we'd ask him to put everything down on paper himself. It was pride that was getting in the way. Just shows it's the emotional baggage you have to deal with first if you want to change things."

After they'd finished up, Ray, Charlie, and Marcia – the other Tactilis consultants on the team who were around that evening – asked Mat if he wanted to join them and get something to eat. He felt starving and also felt it was sensible to see how the team worked together after hours, so he agreed. They thought about a Chinese but they ended up deciding to go to Dino's Deli for a bite to eat.

Dino's was about half a mile from the office and Ray said he'd drive them. He had this big rental Ford and the four of them fitted in quite comfortably. Ray put on the radio and tuned it to some country station Mat had never heard of. They got to Dino's, which was on a small parking lot with a dry cleaning business and an office supplies company. Inside the place was bright and cheerful; all the staff smiled (that "Li'l Dino Difference").

It was here that Mat had his first Southern Steak Sandwich with shredded slices of beef and chilli sauce. The other members of the team treated him to it.

Charlie was middle-aged, by the look of him didn't take enough exercise, and probably hadn't eaten a fresh vegetable for several decades. He wore large glasses and puffed a little as he walked from the car. He was also one of those people you just couldn't help but like. He had this smile on his face most of the time like he just wouldn't mean any harm to anyone and you got the feeling that he was that rare person who never said anything unkind about you behind your back. He was just a good guy.

Marcia was smarter and more difficult to read. She was living with "a nice nine-to-five professional" as she put it. She was dark-haired and very earnest and lived in New York. She flew home at weekends to her partner who seemed to be doing everything to organize their imminent move to a new apartment. The two of them were also just about to get married and both Ray and Charlie were invited to the wedding.

Ray was the youngest and brightest. He was very fresh-faced with short brown hair and blue jeans. He wore his leather jacket as a totem more than a threat. He was from the cell phone generation.

Each of them asked Mat a few polite questions about his life and his role at Tactilis, presumably to satisfy themselves as to what level of operator they were really dealing with. They then seemed satisfied to treat him like the equal he was – or more accurately they chose to indulge his innocence in their ways and were genuinely keen to instruct him into the way that they worked.

While they were seated at the neat little formica tables in Dino's, Ray suggested that Mat should do a Day In the Life Of study some time soon.

"DILOs are quite simple really," said Ray. "We just follow a guy around all day and note down his every movement so that we can build up an exact picture of what the guy does and what the frustrations are in his day. It's not about judging the guy or trying to do some time and motion study on him. What we're looking to do is to experience what it feels like to do that work, we put ourselves inside someone else's shoes and understand the sorts of practical issues they face."

"And how do the employees react, being followed round like that?" asked Mat, taking a large bite of Southern shredded steak and chilli sandwich.

"Well it can be a bit nerve-racking for them," said Charlie, taking a large drink of Coke out of his plastic cup. "So the first thing I usually tell them is that I'm not going to use their name on the study, it's just a generic title of the role I'll use. I tell them all I want to do is understand the sorts of problems they have to put up with, the things that actually prevent them from getting on with the job. After that they usually see we've got the right interests.

"I guess we just think that people are fundamentally positive," he went on. "And that most people derive satisfaction out of doing a job well. They don't get out of their beds in the morning thinking, 'How am I going to screw up today?' They want to do their best. But what happens is that 'stuff' gets in their way. Colleagues don't tell them things, communications break down, old practices and habits close in on them. So while you're doing one of these Day In The Life Of studies you'll usually pick up literally dozens of little things that would improve their lives. And surprise, surprise, people actually want to know about these and learn from them and make their jobs better."

Detailed analyses like this were nothing new to Mat – in theory. He had read about them naturally. But he'd never actually come up close to the practice himself. It was something that you might cover on a course but, let's face it, it wasn't going to change the destiny of the company. Was it?

Mat was beginning to see work differently.

"And do you pick up a lot of bad behavior, too?" he asked.

"Sure," said Charlie. "While you're doing a study you'll see things like people bunking off or taking a half-hour break when they should be taking a fifteen-minute break, but that's not really what we're interested in. That's up to the supervisors and they pretty much know what's going on anyway."

"The people tell you all the stuff in minute detail that prevents them getting on with their job," Ray added. "You build a detailed snapshot of how a business really works. It's great because you actually build a complete narrative in five-minute increments throughout the day."

A narrative in five-minute snapshots. The idea crackled in Mat's brain. The connections were beginning to come together for him. Small wins create change…the company is a narrative in five-minute snapshots…these ideas were all in the same territory. That was important. They weren't clichéd observations about business, they were fragments of another way of seeing and understanding – put the fragments together and you would have a coherent picture, which was original, fresh, true.

The five-minute narrative especially struck a chord with Mat. It seemed like a new way to describe a business that was both practical and highly analytical. It focused on people doing work. No matter whether the subject was an engineer, or an accountant, or a software developer it would reveal the truths about the way they worked. It would reveal the petty difficulties that were getting in their way: the missing invoice, the missing part, or the missed telephone call.

Mat wanted to get into a DILO, find out how it felt to be in the five-minute stream. He wanted to experience that language for himself.

"Anyone for desserts?" asked Marcia. They ordered three chocolate sundaes for themselves and a cheesecake pie for Charlie. Afterward, they headed off back to their hotels. Marcia, Charlie, and Ray were all staying together at a small hotel near the site, but Ray kindly offered to drop Mat back to his hotel.

Back in his room, Mat rang Marianne. She had just got back from a private viewing at a gallery in town and was tired from having to be "nice to all the same faces all the time."

"So how did your first day go?" she asked.

"Oh fine, really. Bit tough at times," he said.

"Poor you, did you manage to get some dinner. Bet you've been to my favorite McCormick & Schmick's, just to make up for a hard day."

"Not exactly," said Mat. "I went with the rest of the team to Dino's Deli. Had a shredded steak and chilli sandwich. My first."

There was no edge to the conversation, no bitter words. Marianne had been very sweet and concerned. It was just that to Mat it seemed like they were talking about very different data.

Deep diving

Mat arrived at the main plant gates at 7.00, got his security pass and went to Frank's office to pick up his contact. Frank was pacing around his room and barely lifted his one eye to acknowledge Mat. He was busy and sent Mat over the passage to find Rick who would take him to meet the maintenance supervisor – called CJ – who he would be following.

Mat took out his Shaeffer pen from his inside jacket pocket – he'd left his attaché case back at the hotel for safe-keeping – and got ready to make entries on the DILO sheets Ray had given him from the car the previous evening.

He made his first entries:

7-15 The supervisor is drinking coffee and chatting about last night's football game with a fellow supervisor.

7-25 Supervisor walks to his office picks up a two-way radio and the work schedule for his department for the day. The supervisor also has a two-week plan but doesn't need that today. He is responsible for MIC, MCB Syn Gas, and Chlorine and Caustic. Syn Gas is due to be sold to another chemicals company in three months.

7-35 Supervisor walks to MIC control room.

7-37 Supervisor enters MIC control room. There are six operators in the control room engaged in non-work related conversation. The supervisor goes to the LOTO (lock out tag out) area. A LOTO card details the safety procedures, which need to be carried out before work on a maintenance job can start. The card includes details of equipment identification, jobs to be done, and danger level, shut down and start up procedures. The supervisor pulls out the necessary cards, which are needed to go with the jobs on the daily schedule.

The pen felt electric in his hands. He was describing work and business in a whole new way.

Now, you could say this picture of a company was just banal and insignificant if you like. Or you could see it as Mat was beginning to – as a description of how business really is. "No strategy, no big ideas, no incentive schemes," thought Mat. "If you want to direct or change or drive a business this is where you start. With the reality of work."

From this moment the DILO was like a deep dive. Strange new forms and shapes appeared at every foot. For instance:

> 7-55 The supervisor goes to the MIC production area. The supervisor explains that he came from a plant in the next town and finds life here very disorganized. "There is no maintenance organization to speak of. I have my areas for which I am responsible but there is no coherent preventative maintenance. I do so much running around, reacting to problems and putting out fires. I should have joined the fire brigade."
> I have discussed this with my boss and he says, 'We are all too busy to look at the problems properly, our job is to keep the plant running'."

Or how about:

> 9-12 Supervisor walks to building 507 where the Syn Gas plant is located. He explains that the two-way radios look good, but they are quite useless, so hardly anybody carries them. He feels that this is just an excuse because in the plants the radios work fine, it's just when someone from the main production office calls, reception is bad because the distance is quite significant, as was the case with the call from Capital Projects.

Note the comment about two-way radios. The importance of communication. Or put it the other way round, the interdependence of people at work. Most businesses simply don't make enough of this. Interdependence, interaction, whatever you call it – it's like joining two wires; you get a spark. Or not. Business breaks down when people cease to understand how they need one another.

10-30 Supervisor walks past MCB scrap metal yard.
There are four fitters working on building a ramp.
The supervisor explains that before he came, the
forklifts were always having accidents on the
entrance to the yard because of the kerbing, and
by building a ramp which was his idea, they would
save at least three hours a day of forklift time.
Supervisor also explains that another huge problem
is the number of contractors who aren't very skilled
but that they have to use because "we are not
organized enough to do it ourselves." The cost of
contractors is estimated at 35% of the total
maintenance budget.

Thirty-five percent of maintenance work is outsourced! How much is that costing the company? And building one small ramp could save the company hundreds, even thousands of man-hours. One small item, one small win.

Don't think these examples of inefficiency just belong to life in some blue-collar factory. If Mat had been doing a DILO on some smart software outfit, it would still have been about chatting around the water cooler, talking about vacation plans, sharing baby pictures.

10-44 Supervisor walks back to his office in building
507. En route he gets a call on his two-way radio
asking for authorization to withdraw 2 caustic
valves from stores, the supervisor approves. He says,
"You see, Bill, who called me, always uses his radio
and that just saved me a 20-minute round trip."

How many other "20-minute trips" could be saved if they got the right interdependence-ware going? How much money could be saved?

11-00 until 12-00 Lunch.

Mat went into the canteen. Like most works canteens it had its own particular smell. Something had been fried a little too long. None of the other workers in the canteen would notice this smell; they had become used to it.

Mat picked up a plastic tray, some cutlery and a thick Duralex glass. He helped himself to the salad bar. He was the only one at the salad bar. The others were going for hot food.

He sat down and started to read through his notes. The five-minute history. A living network of interdependencies. That's what he was dealing with. He was watching an organization happen.

He got ready for the next immersion.

12-15 Supervisor returns from lunch explains that the number 3 unit overheating problem has caused a major shutdown in MIC which will cost a fortune in lost output he says. "I bet contractors did the last maintenance work on that - it's always the way."

12-25 Supervisor goes to conference room for the daily meeting.

12-30 One fitter is present. When asked where the other 11 people are he shrugs his shoulders. The supervisor reviews the work of the one fitter and lets him go.

12-37 Three more fitters arrive and they talk about the overheating problem on unit 3 that has shut down MIC. They all agree that if it had been looked at quickly it wouldn't have needed a shutdown.

Mat was with them every minute – there was no way that he could avoid empathy and becoming engaged. He was experiencing their problems not just recording them.

1-19 Supervisor works on daily schedule for tomorrow - he looks at the plant downtime report, the preventative maintenance schedules on SAP and writes out jobs, and loosely allocates them. "I can't be hard and fast as to who'll do what as I don't know who'll turn up."

Reminds one of that phrase: strategy unravels at the first contact with the enemy.

Back to work:

1-34 Supervisor phones home. Engages in non-work related chat with his wife.

1-43 Checks email, has received one message, which necessitates a change to the schedule for tomorrow.

1-47 Surfs the Internet looks at football website and various other non-work related websites.

1-58 Supervisor makes 20 photocopies of the schedule.

2-05 Supervisor goes to MIC and pins a copy of the schedule on the board.

2-45 Supervisor returns to office. When asked how he thinks he spends his time, the supervisor said 60% active supervision, 15% administration, 10% working as a fitter, 15% passive supervision. When asked how he would ideally spend his time, he said: 60% active, 20% passive, 20% administration.

3-00 Study ends.

At 3.00 Mat put his pen and paper down. He was exhausted.

Going this deep into work forces you to think in different ways. More, it makes you start to feel in different ways.

As Mat later said, "It isn't an intellectual exercise, it's experiential. That's fundamental to understanding why it's so valuable. Don't expect to surface with treasures from the deep, they'll never make the change in pressure. What's different is inside you, you have changed for the experience. And that enables you to interpret data differently in the future. That's the boon you bring back."

But back then Mat's immediate problem was thinking through the consequences of measuring a business in five-minute intervals. How could you operate at that sort of intensity? And yet it was here that things got done. CJ had showed him that. It was here you understood why things worked or didn't work. Take the two-way radios for example. One simple fix would have improved the productivity and costs of the whole place.

For Mat the truth had opened up. In the past he'd thought that overviews of business were what mattered. The view from 35,000 feet so to speak. Now he was seeing things through a different prism. He was learning that the truth about a company's performance lies in these five-minute sequences. That's where results get made.

At the same time Mat also recognized that the five-minute narrative might be useful at the ground floor, but how could it help the CEO or the executives make the big decisions? How could a directive in head office ever really influence what CJ did in the five minutes between 8.00 and 8.05? Equally how could a problem at CJ's level have any influence at board level. There was a complete disconnect.

So the big question for Mat now was: how could you connect the CEO to CJ? How could you give a CEO a tool that would shape the company every five minutes? It was clearly impossible.

Big Yellow Cabs:
Driver 4568 Owens

It had been a long week and Mat was glad to be flying home. He was looking forward to seeing Marianne and having some time together over the weekend. Maybe they'd go for a dive together on Sunday. He didn't know how he was going to describe to Marianne what he'd been doing all week. Partly because in one sense he didn't know. He'd had a variety of experiences which had changed the way he thought but as yet he didn't have a neat way of describing the difference. And if you can't describe something succinctly and completely people always think it can't have been that important.

He felt himself changing and that she inhabited another world. A world where the surface was all that mattered.

The difficulty for Mat was that he was going back to basics and as a result he was rewiring his system. Going back to basics: sounds so simple doesn't it? Like we could all do it. But the real difficulty is that in doing so, Mat and any voyager like him, has to question their basic assumptions. That's the challenge. Everything comes under scrutiny. Not just the way you think but the way you feel. You have to unlearn your prejudices. What's more, once you have done so there's no going back.

For Mat there was no going back to the old world of Hardings and big company strategies. He couldn't do that any more. It was also causing him to question other parts of his life – even his relationship with Marianne. For the first time since their relationship had begun, he was questioning whether she was the right one. He wouldn't know the answer to that question until he'd reached somewhere further on.

But in the meantime, life was going to get more complicated. He hadn't reached the safety of a new destination. He was searching for his new view of business but he had not reached land yet. In fact he was far from certain he would reach land at all. Unless he could reconcile the gulf between the CEO and CJ, he would have nothing at all. Just a series of more or less useful insights into the practical nature of business life. Not much to sacrifice a career for is it?

So Mat could be forgiven for being in a mixed mood as he prepared to leave. Exhilarated at what he'd experienced, but exasperated that it seemed to leave him in such a blind alley.

He said goodbye to Ray and Charlie and Marcia and said he hoped their paths would cross again. Then he ordered a cab to take him to the airport. The taxi arrived. It was driven by a middle-aged woman with thick blonde plaited hair and spectacles that looked like two magnifying glasses. She picked up his case and put it into the trunk. You might describe her as "chunky."

"Where we headed, mister?" she asked.

"The airport please," said Mat and got into the back.

In the past, Mat had tended to be distant and silent in the back of cabs. All the more surprising then that on this journey he actually wanted to talk. He was intrigued by this tough woman in her big yellow cab.

So when she started to talk about the weather and the traffic, he went with the flow and pretty soon she was opening up her life to him.

Her name was Susan. On the dashboard of her taxi was a photograph of a small white poodle.

"I'm a white lady doing a difficult job," said Susan. "And I'm in this business for the money not the men. Though most other drivers are men."

"So how did you get started cab driving?" asked Mat, just to see where her story would go.

"Well let's see now. I started out driving school buses up in the Pittsburgh area," Susan replied. "And I remember I used to pray for it to snow so that I didn't have to go to work. And when I became a taxi driver, I just hated the snow 'cos it stopped me from earning and that's one of the big reasons why I moved down here to Houston to get the better weather. I had a friend or two down here as well so that helped."

"So why give up on the buses?" Mat asked.

"I gave up my job working on the school buses because I didn't like the responsibility of driving all those children. It used to worry me. And I guess I had some pretty good times with them. You know I only ever once refused to drive and returned the children to school and that was with a kindergarten class. Boy, were they mean.

"After I left off the school bus driving, I started to work as a barmaid in the Pittsburgh Strip District. Actually, the bar was a striptease club. I just loved that job. Hanging out with guys all day and them giving me money. And the money was just great. I used to clear $400 in four days. I really never had it so good. I reckon I'd still be there if it wasn't for this guy I was dating at that time. We was getting pretty close. He wanted to marry me and I met his mother and she was one of these deep religious types. She was very strict and she didn't like the thought of her son's future wife working in a strip club. So she starts to put pressure on him and then he puts pressure on me and I give the job up. I left the job in March. And you know what? By September we'd split up.

"It was a shame really, because I had a lot of good times at that club," said Susan staring out at the road in front of her. "One time this guy said to me, 'I really want to kiss you' and I said, 'See this finger. No ring... No ring. No kissing. Now if you want to do something to change that...'" and with that Susan burst out laughing and Mat laughed, too.

"Yes, sir, I made a lot of good friends in those days at the bar. Like with the pizza restaurant guys next door. They were Arabs. Lot of people don't like Arabs these days, but I made friends with them and met their families and I thought they were good people. I even spent three months in Oman during one summer and really enjoyed it although they need to improve their attitude to women some. And also they were a bit strange – sitting in a bar with a white cloth on their heads – drinking Heineken. It was just a bit ridiculous."

"Then after the club I worked for a limousine business out

of the airport. That folded after 9/11 and I turned to working in a cab. Then I moved down here to be sure of the weather."

"And do you think you'll go back to Pittsburgh. I mean, eventually?" asked Mat.

"Oh sure," said Susan. "I couldn't be away for too long. It's in the blood."

Back to Boston

Mat didn't go diving with Marianne as they had planned that weekend. In fact they hardly spent any time together at all. On Saturday morning, Mat got a call that his sister Anneka had been admitted to hospital in Boston.

Mat was very worried by the news. His sister was never ill, never even took a day off work. What's more, he remembered how tired and drawn she'd looked at their last meeting at the Mirage. If she'd been admitted to hospital, it had to be something serious and he'd decided to fly up to see her on the Saturday afternoon. Marianne was naturally disappointed that their weekend together was going to be cut short. They'd hardly had time to talk about Mat's week before he was off on another plane.

Anneka had been taken into Massachusetts General Hospital on Fruit Street in the center of Boston. Mat flew to Logan and caught a cab to the hospital arriving there around 6.00 p.m. Anneka was in a private room and was sitting up in bed when he arrived.

"Na was denn Professor, immer noch im Bett?" said Mat as he walked in.

"Ja, warum nicht?" she said, smiling to greet him. *"Ich habe alles was ich brauche hier. Komfort, erstklassige Bedienung und 'Friends' im Fernsehen. Toll, nicht?"*

The shadows below Anneka's eyes were even darker than when Mat had seen her previously and she seemed, if anything, a little thinner. He did not like to see her in bed like this, vulnerable. She was the tough one, the one who always looked after him. He remembered being a small boy, perhaps seven or eight years old. One day he had met some older boys who were smoking cigarettes. They had offered a cigarette to Mat and he had taken a few puffs. When he gave the cigarette back to them, the boys had said: "Now you're going to die. You're going to die at midnight tonight because you have smoked this cigarette. The Bad Man will come for you at midnight."

Mat had been terrified by their threats and had told Anneka all about it when he got home. She had told him there was nothing to worry about and that she would protect him. That night Anneka stayed up with him. She told him that there was no "Bad Man" to fear. But nevertheless, both sat squeezing one another's hands as midnight came.

Now, he leaned forward and gave her a big warm hug.

"How are you feeling, really?" he asked.

"Fine thanks. Just a little tired that's all. Guess I've been overdoing things, working on my next paper."

She sat up in bed a little, pulling the crisp white sheets around her. She wore a pink cardigan and there were yellow flowers in a small vase beside her. She did not look like a Professor very much right now. Perhaps that's why Mat felt so uncomfortable about seeing her this way. It wasn't "her."

Mat moved a little closer to Anneka and tried once again to get under the radar of her irony.

"So, what's wrong with you Professor?" asked Mat directly.

"Not sure to be honest. I passed out yesterday morning before a class and they brought me in here for tests. Plugged me into various machines, didn't tell me what's going on, it's just *my* body after all – you know the sort of thing."

The ironic tone had come to her voice. It was so difficult to get a straight answer from her. Mat decided he'd have to go along with her jokey explanations.

"Yes I know, you're only the patient so they only tell you what they think you need to know, which is very little," said Mat, taking a seat at the side of her bed. "And trust you to come to MGH with all these nice young Harvard Med types around, Professor. They'll be in there conferring about you no doubt. Learning all about you."

"Yes, one thing you learn from a life in academia is that you don't ever want to be part of someone else's learning curve, but that's another issue," she said and gave him a look he knew well. It meant change the subject, immediately.

"Now what about you, *Junge*. Are you recovered now?"

The word "recovered" resonated between the two of them. It conjured all the concern she had had for him after the hijacking.

"Yes, yes," he said quickly.

"So how is life after Hardings?" She took his hand and held it lightly on the bed covers.

"Oh I'm fine," he said. "I have a new job and I'm starting to get into it. Things are very different. In fact, the complete opposite to Hardings. No intellectual baggage at all."

"And have you sorted out in your head that stuff with Dad?" she asked.

"No, not exactly," said Mat. "In fact, I have seen him again."

"What?" said Anneka in a concerned voice.

"Yes, twice in fact. I'm more convinced than ever he's trying to communicate with me. He's telling me to sort out things he left undone."

"What things?" asked Anneka.

"About work really. I think he wants me to prove he was right all along about his theories. At least that's how it seems."

"Mat, you can't let yourself get all eaten up like this."

"I know. But it's what I have to do. Right or wrong I have to get it out of my system."

"OK *Junge*, but for heaven's sake. Talk to me about it will you?"

"Yes I promise," said Mat.

"What about Marianne, how's she taking things? All this change of lifestyle must have been quite a shock for her, too." asked Anneka.

"She's been very supportive," said Mat. "We had a great time on the Turks diving. It was just excellent and it was so important to have some real time together. But I can't say she's so OK about what I'm doing right now. She can't understand why I would leave Hardings and go to work for another firm."

"Have you told her about your experiences?" asked Anneka.

"No," said Mat.

"Don't you think you should? It might help her understand why this matters so much to you."

"Maybe. But I can't right now. I have to get into this thing on my own terms. I can't have the extra burden of worrying what people think about me. At least, not what she thinks about me. I get the feeling sometimes that she just wants me to be part of a smart world. And smart people don't believe in ghosts."

"Well as it happens she may have a point," Anneka said.

"Sure," said Mat in frustration. "It's easy to dismiss what I have seen. How could any smart person do otherwise? But what I'm saying, is that 'smart' is not the only game in town."

"All right little brother. I don't doubt you…"

The conversation would have gone on, but at that moment a young medic came into the room. He introduced himself as part of the team who would be consulting with Anneka. He was tall, straight-backed, considerate but nonetheless distant. He was dressed in a white coat with a shirt and tie, every inch the expert. In other words, he was a junior Harvard Medical School student who was there to check in on her. He was polite to Mat, gave him a card, but also made it clear it was time for him to leave.

Mat was angry. He didn't want to go. He wanted to stay and look after Anneka. He wanted to pick her up in his arms and take care of her. But he was being given no choice. So, reluctantly, Mat kissed his sister goodbye and said he would call again tomorrow to find out how she was.

As he walked out of the door, he looked back to see her sitting in bed, in her pink cardigan, in a room with yellow flowers. He did not like the feeling, it was new and uncomfortable to leave her this way.

Mat made his way back to his hotel above Copley Plaza and put a call in to Marianne. She was pleased to hear from him.

"So how was Anneka?" she asked.

"Fine, I think," replied Mat. "But you know her, she never lets on very much."

"Have they said why she's there?" asked Marianne.

"No. She just said that she was undergoing some tests and intimated that they didn't know what was wrong with her."

"Oh, so she's not in a serious condition or anything?"

"No I don't think so. It was just upsetting to see her in hospital that's all."

"And will you be coming back here tomorrow?" asked Marianne.

"Probably not," replied Mat. "I've got this trip to Norway, so it makes more sense really to fly out from Logan to London, rather than hike down to Miami and then go on from there. Besides even if I did fly back, I'd only be around for a couple of hours."

"No. I know," said Marianne, a bitterness seeping into her voice. Then she recovered her composure. "It's OK really. I'm just disappointed at not seeing you over the weekend. But there's next weekend and we can plan lots of nice things then. Maybe we could go out with the Flamingos for a dive Saturday morning?"

"Sure. But really, Mari, if you'd like me to fly back tomorrow I will. Honestly."

"No, no, sweetheart. It would be senseless and just put more pressure on you. You get a good dinner and a good night's sleep and we'll talk tomorrow before you go."

A chance meeting at the club

To lighten his mood after the phone call, Mat decided to treat himself at an old favorite, the Capital Grille. The Capital is one of the old-style steak houses on Newbury Street and it serves just about the best steak you'll find anywhere.

Mat enjoyed his dinner and left the Capital with a reasonably warm glow. He decided to walk over to the Burlington Club for old time's sake.

The Burlington was a very upscale private members' club in the heart of Boston. Its membership was strictly limited and required several personal referees. Mat had been put up three years ago. Hardings' employees supported one another's election. The place was a bit old-fashioned but had a great charm. When you stayed there for a night you didn't pay on departure. They sent you a bill at the end of the month.

Mat walked through the reception to the club and went into the lounge area. He looked around for a moment and was about to leave when a voice from behind him called out:

"Goodness me, Mat! What a pleasant surprise to see you here!"

It was Anthony Elliott. He walked toward Mat and shook his hand. He was as immaculately dressed as ever in a dark pin stripe suit, probably from London. He smiled with genuine warmth at Mat, who although a bit taken aback at the coincidence of meeting Anthony, was nonetheless pleased to see him.

"What brings you back to Boston?" Anthony asked.

"I'm here seeing my sister," Mat replied. "She's in MGH."

"Oh dear. Nothing serious I hope," replied Anthony.

"No she'll be fine I'm sure. Just a few tests," said Mat.

"Will you join me for a drink?" asked Anthony. "Sagradio has gone to bed and I have decided to have one last single malt before turning in. We've been to the opera this evening, Handel's *Xerxes*. Quite fascinating. Are you sure I can't tempt you?"

"No thanks Anthony," Mat replied. "It's very kind but I'm staying over by Copley Plaza and I just passed by to see how the old place was."

"Well, it's much the poorer for not having you around Mat. Such a delight to see you. I understand you spent some time on the Turks after Christmas. One of my favorite places."

"Yes we had a magical few months there," Mat replied. "My diving improved a little and we very nearly bought a boat and stayed."

"Can't think of a better place to be or better company to keep. How is my lovely Marianne?"

"Oh she's very well thank you, Anthony."

"Delighted to hear it Mat," Anthony replied. "In fact, it's a rather fortunate coincidence we have met like this Mat because I have been thinking of calling you up for some time, or at least calling Marianne. The partners are looking to do some refurbishment and her name came to mind as someone who might be able to help us with some advice on art. I'd like to feel I was being of some support in difficult times. I could give her a call at the office, but I thought it might be fun if I invited the two of you to join Sagradio and me on the boat one weekend. We never did get the chance to say goodbye properly. I could ask Marianne about art and I know that Sagradio would love the chance to talk to her for the weekend. Just a thought, but maybe we could talk about it together sometime."

"Well I'm sure that Marianne would love to, Anthony," he said.

"What's your cell phone number these days?" asked Anthony, withdrawing the slimmest leather note pad from his inside jacket pocket and taking out its tiny silver propelling pencil as Mat recited the number.

"Good. I will talk to Sagradio this very evening and we'll settle on a date some time soon."

"Thank you that would be fine," said Mat.

"By the way, I'm sorry that my introduction to those bankers didn't work out for Marianne. As I said to her, anything I can do to help, anything at all...."

Mat didn't know exactly what Anthony was referring to, except that he remembered Marianne meeting with some bankers Anthony had put her in contact with while they were still on the Turks. Mat remembered how he had resented the meeting at the time and now it opened old wounds. It was like Marianne was still in the old world, the Hardings' world and wouldn't move on from it. She felt safe there, while he had left its protection. He felt this as disloyalty, that she wasn't with him all the way.

What is intelligence?

Mat got up later than usual, and ordered breakfast in his room. He was still troubled by the events of the previous day. His visit to his sister had disturbed him. First, she was obviously not well and the doctors weren't immediately able to diagnose the cause. Second, it seemed that even his sister was doubting him now. It was not that he expected her to believe that he had seen their father's ghost, merely that he didn't want her to disbelieve. That made him feel even more isolated. Then there was the phone call with Marianne. She obviously doubted him, too. And finally, to top it all, the chance meeting with Anthony had only served to remind him of how much he had given up. Was he really right in pursuing this crusade of his?

The doubts mounted.

He took a shower and was about to do some stretching to take some of the stress out of himself when the door bell rang and the room service waiter brought in his breakfast tray.

"Where would you like your breakfast sir?"

"Put it on the table by the window, thanks," said Mat.

"Would you like me to remove the plastics?" asked the waiter.

Mat was unsure for a moment: what were "the plastics?" He decided to say "yes" on the basis that plastics were probably not a good thing in any case.

The waiter nodded and stripped off the Gladwrap stretched over the glass of orange juice and the milk jug. There, the plastics were dealt with!

He handed Mat the room service bill for signature and left.

Mat sat at the table eating some of the fresh fruit and sipping the orange juice and connected his laptop to the hotel's ethernet so that he could log on to the Web.

The only way to quell the doubts going on in his mind was to get down to some work.

He had been thinking lately about smart people and how most companies he'd worked with had either wanted – or bemoaned the lack of – smart people, or as they usually referred to them: "talented people." Reassuringly, talented people almost always had a good academic background. "Cram your company with talent and you'll be all right" was the mantra. But after his experiences in Houston, this was making less and less sense to Mat. Talent or intelligence weren't going to fuse the gap between the CEO and his workforce. Intelligence alone wasn't going to get to the heart of the five-minute narrative.

Following on from these thoughts Mat had been doing some research into intelligence and had come across references to recent work at Columbia University. He'd linked into the University website and searched out the various references to the work of a psychologist named Dweck.

The main thrust of the articles on intelligence seemed to be that this psychologist had undertaken tests which suggested that people have one of two strong beliefs about intelligence: either that it's a fixed trait or that it's malleable and can develop over time.

Those who believe that it is a fixed trait tend to care so much about looking smart that they will even act dumb – for instance they'll pass up the opportunity to attend a class which could help them improve because if they attended it might show they were lacking in some way. Whereas the person who believes that intelligence is malleable will go to the class to learn more.

In another experiment, the psychologist divided a class of students into two groups. One group was praised for its effort, the other for its intelligence. Those praised for their intelligence were then less keen on tackling difficult tasks (unlike those praised for effort), presumably in case they were exposed.

Equally those praised for intelligence were likely to conceal their real scores in tests from other pupils – in a world that defined them by their innate talent, they found it difficult to admit that they were ever wrong. In contrast, those praised for effort were more open.

But the really interesting area that this and other articles on the site made him think about was the true benefit of intelligence to businesses. Were businesses so obsessed with employing the brightest and the best that they created environments where people avoided taking on difficult tasks and did not admit they were wrong? That wasn't too far from his experience at Hardings.

Then Mat started to think about the whole talent thing in business and how this obsession with talent creates divisions within a company: a fault line if you like. People think of a company as being the sum of its star performer or performers. Hence the cult of the celebrity CEO: "We'll be all right because we've got this brilliant boss at the top." What an abdication of responsibility that is. How was some stellar intelligence going to affect the performance of CJ or Frank?

In fact, it was clear that Frank's and CJ's intelligence mattered to their business, mattered as much to that business as what the boss was thinking. Yet they were in an environment that did not recognize their kind of intelligence and so that made them reluctant to put it to work. What a ridiculous position.

It was dawning on Mat that the talent myth he'd lived out for much of his life didn't work for him any longer. He was moving away from its source of power: the talent machines, like universities and business schools. And the further away he got, the less influenced he was.

I have to sympathize with Mat on this. We're surrounded by organizations that put way too much emphasis on the few "natural athletes." We're all looking for the guru. But what if we looked at performance rather than intelligence as the key test of business, the key test of who we hire. (An absurd notion I suppose, but one we should play with for a moment.) If we took performance as the key to business and promotion, we would not select the gifted but the performer. We would measure people by what they actually do, not just their potential. We would do performance evaluations that were based only on – performance.

And if we got away from intelligence being the best test for a company's stars, maybe we'd start assessing the smartness of an organization as being the sum of all its parts: like distributed computing.

Makes you think doesn't it? Maybe the key is to link the systems; get the system itself to deliver its intelligence.

In-flight entertainment

The next stop on Mat's tour of Tactilis projects was SOL Oil in Norway. Max had specifically asked him to go to the SOL installation.

"You've got to get yourself into a bigger site where there's a lot of middle management involvement and capture what they bring," Max had said. "That's why it's so useful that you're going to the SOL Oil terminal up in Norway. It's a massive place and it's a long way from head office, so it's a middle manager's territory. What's more, it's a bit off the executive radar. No new technology or exciting finds to be had here, so the executive focus has moved on."

Mat flew from Logan International to London, where he got a connecting flight to Norway. The flight was busy and Mat sat next to a middle-aged man in a purple striped, open-necked shirt who played logic puzzles throughout the entire duration. He had a magazine full of these brain teasers. It was crammed with math puzzles, word math, and logic quizzes: 72 co-ord arithmetics, 15 figure logics, 4 math mazes, 30 cross sums, and 9 number places. For some reason, Mat found this guy and his logic puzzles intensely distracting. Each time Mat looked over, he had started another one.

Now you may not have experienced this particular frustration but it is extremely difficult to read a book, any book – slight novel or heavyweight fiction – if a man sitting next to you is doing puzzles. You get the wrong brain waves or whatever being emitted into the ether. It happened to me once on a flight to Chicago. I was reading *Farewell My Lovely* and the man next to me was doing anagram puzzles. He was using his logic mind; I was using my imagination. I was seeing the guy with the gun walk into the imaginary room and save the imaginary heroine and he was there doing anagrams: "militarism" to "I limit arms;" "conversation" to "voices rant on;" "Presbyterians" to "best in prayers;" "President Clinton of the USA" to "to copulate he finds interns" and most telling of all, "Marlon'" to "normal."

I reckoned the guy had to be called Marlon and I found Marlon's obsession with logic disturbing. I spent the whole flight peeking over his shoulder to see whether he'd cracked the anagram to "Eric Clapton" yet . (It turned out to be "narcoleptic.")

Perhaps that was what was going through Mat's mind. This man with his logic puzzles captured how sterile and impractical such thinking was becoming for Mat. Everything was fine and under control in a puzzle book, but when would you use a math maze in real life?

Dangerous driving

Mat had several hours to wait before his connecting flight to Norway, so he decided to check in briefly to one of the airport hotels, get a shower and some extra rest.

He took a cab to the hotel and checked into a room that was more like a Japanese overnight box than a European hotel. He lay down on his bed and dozed a little.

His cell phone started to ring.

He rolled over on the bed, picked it up, and answered the call. "Hello, Mat Durer."

"Mat, how the devil are you?" It was Brad Johnson, Mat's erstwhile colleague at Hardings.

"I'm fine thanks, Brad. Chilling out at Heathrow Airport actually," said Mat, staring up from the bed at the ceiling that was not that far above him.

"Yes, I heard you were back on the road with another consulting firm. Jolly good news for them," said Brad. There was the sound of traffic and a car horn hooting in the background.

"I'm also in Europe as it happens, in the Netherlands. Driving up to meet with a major energy client in The Hague. That's why I had to call you. This amazing coincidence you see," said Brad.

"What coincidence?" asked Mat.

"Well, when I went to get my hire car from Avis they had reserved me this great big, handsome blue BMW. It looked exactly the same as that BMW you had trouble with in Pittsburgh. I'm driving the damn thing right now. Spooky huh?"

"Yeah spooky," said Mat without a trace of sarcasm.

"And since they never recovered that vehicle," continued Brad, "well, I just wondered whether it was the same one. Maybe those crazy bums drove it all the way to Europe," said Brad laughing.

"Yeah, very funny, Brad. Glad to hear you're still that sensitive son-of-a-bitch I knew and loved," said Mat.

"Miss me?" asked Brad.

"Every day," replied Mat.

"Knew you would," said Brad, then changing his tone "But seriously, you should keep in touch with us at the old firm. We like to know what happens to our former stars and you never know when there might be an opportunity for mutual advantage."

"I'll bear that in mind..." said Mat and was about to carry on when he was interrupted.

" Jesus..." shouted Brad.

There was the sound of screeching brakes followed by a heavy impact and the sound of breaking glass.

Mat got up sharply from his bed and put the cell phone closer to his ear.

"Brad...Brad...Can you hear me? Are you OK?" said Mat raising his voice.

There was no reply.

"Brad, can you hear me? Brad?"

Still no reply. "Christ he might be dead," Mat thought.

"Brad!" Mat shouted.

A longer silence.

"Yeah," said Brad. "I'm here. I'm OK I think."

"What's happened?" asked Mat.

"I've crashed into some kind of post on the side of the road," said Brad, breathing hard. "I hit my head on the windscreen and I feel a bit dazed. My knee hurts too. Think I hit it against the dashboard..."

"How did it happen?" asked Mat. "Was it me being on the phone to you?"

"No, it was this guy," said Brad. "This guy in a big old overcoat and hat. He just appeared from nowhere and walked out in front of the car. I had to swerve to avoid him. Now of course the bastard's nowhere to be seen…."

Northern Lights or fogbound?

Four hours later Mat was on a connecting flight to Bergen in Norway. He'd made sure that Brad was OK and that help was coming. But after all, there wasn't much Mat could do for him at this distance. Nevertheless, the incident had scared the hell out of both of them, but for slightly different reasons. For Brad it was just the shock of an accident. For Mat it was the shock of knowing he had been right.

During the flight he kept turning over in his head those long conversations with his father and wondering how all this would end. He was on a mission now, and he knew there was no turning back from it.

From Bergen, Mat flew up the Norwegian coastline by helicopter to Trudheim, a remote location about 100 kilometers north. He was visiting a SOL oil terminal where the Tactilis team had been based for some months. The helicopter flight north should have been spectacular, with great views of the fjords and dramatic coastline. In fact, much of the journey was shrouded in fog.

So when Mat arrived at Trudheim, it seemed a little like he was landing at the edge of the world. He was entering into a mysterious landscape of fog and half-light. Trudheim was so far north that even at midday it was only barely daylight. It was a place where the strangest things might happen and yet appear commonplace.

The site itself was a vast installation of pipes and towers, separation units and storage tanks set on the edge of a romantic, open bay, which provided the deepwater harbor for the oil tankers. It was set within a range of soft hills, which stretched around it in a green embrace. The conventional attitude of course would be that this sort of installation was a blight on the landscape – industry tearing up nature. But you had to be there to appreciate the magnificence, the audacity of the place. To create this huge, complex industrial environment within such wild surroundings, well it was a work of art.

What's more you had to feel a sense of awe at the engineering achievement of it all. Thousands of kilometers of pipes formed into a system that took raw hydrocarbons and prepared them for their long journey into usable energy and products. Like one vast storage unit that held the energy which lit homes and fired factories, which made hospitals, schools, shops, and stations all possible. How dangerous it is to praise such glamor. It's almost taboo.

Yet, the whole adventure of the oil industry and, in particular, the North Sea oil industry is full of glamor. It glows with the light of the pioneering spirit. You can't get away from it. The crazy audacity of building communities on stilts and calling them platforms, then towing them out to sea and turning them upright to stand or float in hundreds of feet of ocean – and produce oil and gas. That's some feat, to bring that off. It makes you believe that anything is possible.

So although Mat felt a little unnerved by the dim half-light and the fog and damp air, he also felt good being in this world; it was his level. He might not know much about oil terminal management, but in terms of economic significance it was definitely in his league.

The Tactilis team leader at Trudheim was Jennie Macpherson. She was short, jolly with blonde hair and a lot of sensible clothing to keep out the wet, chill wind.

Mat shook her hand.

"Welcome to Trudheim. Good flight?" she asked.

"Reasonable, it would have been a lot better if I could have seen something out of the windows," he replied, motioning up to the fog above.

"Oh yes, it's a bit foggy isn't it? Can get a lot worse though. Quite often we're marooned here for days at a time. Very unpredictable, some days it clears in seconds, others it hardly gets light. One of the helicopter pilots told me once that this was the only place in world where you get 50 mph fog. And he meant it."

Mat took another look around him, at the wet gray sky and wet green hills; he saw no reason to doubt the pilot's word.

Jennie helped Mat get his bags stowed in the project office and then suggested that they get started on the day. She had a long schedule of meetings to attend and Mat was welcome to join her. He agreed, saying he'd like to sit in as an observer and get a feel for the operations.

They passed a few minutes inside and then went out in to the wet air to await the bus that would take them to their first meeting on the other side of the site.

"The driver of this bus is quite a character," said Jennie. "The story goes is that he's a convicted getaway driver from the south of Norway. Came up here looking for work and this job was all he could find. Think of it. He gets this driving job and he's as pleased as punch to be in the driving seat again and then he finds that it's actually his private hell on wheels, because the maximum speed you're allowed to do around site is 20 mph."

Mat imagined a wild-eyed driver, hunched at the wheel emerging from the fog. When the bus did arrive, the driver was short, chubby, and gray-haired. He did not look like a hoodlum, rather more like an amiable grandfather. He smiled and opened the door for them. In fact, to Mat he seemed utterly at peace with his lot. Perhaps he'd been cured. He even drove away carefully and stuck well within the 20 mph limit.

For the next 40 minutes Jennie and Mat looked out of misty windows as Jennie pointed out various buildings. The site was huge covering over 700 acres and handling around 800,000 barrels of oil per day. In effect, it was a giant buffer zone between the Norwegian offshore oil fields to the west and the oil tankers that came here to collect crude oil that would then be delivered to refineries around the world. The site had 14 crude storage tanks, so that even if bad weather prevented tankers from coming into the harbor, there was sufficient storage to ensure that the offshore oil field could continue production safely. Six of these tanks held enough oil reserves to supply Norway's total energy for one day.

The bus took them past the oil and gas processing plant, the storage tanks, the liquefied petroleum gas storage tanks, and then around to the four huge jetties where the oil tankers berthed. These stuck out like steel arms into the sea and the tankers waited there patiently gaining their load. They drove around the stabilization unit for the crude oil and then the compression and fractionation units which handled the natural gas. There was also a power station generating electricity for the plant, a flare, a fire station, and various admin buildings.

The lights on the separation units and storage tanks were orange and flickered like stage door lights in the gray mist. This was industrial theatre on the grand scale; no one could question the ingenuity or talent required to create this plant. At that moment, Jennie said something which cut across the splendor of what Mat was seeing.

"We've got the job of taking a big slice of the operating costs out of this terminal over the next year or they'll have to reconsider its future," said Jennie.

How could that be? How could a site of this importance, with all this money and investment and excellence and skill behind it, run into difficulties? It's got everything, from the backing of SOL's world-class management team, to leading-edge technologies and yet this was a site in trouble. That was a non sequitur for Mat. If it had all the components that were likely to ensure its efficiency, why was it performing so badly?

Now I suppose that you could ask why the fate of a huge oil terminal should have any relevance to ordinary businesses. It's my experience that major companies, like outstanding individuals, exhibit the same weaknesses as the rest of mankind – only more so. That's what makes them so interesting. And it's why Mat was determined to analyze the situation as best he could.

Dinner and stories

"We thought of going out tonight – given that it's a Thursday evening and wondered whether you might want to join us?" Jennie had asked. "There's an old hotel with a restaurant about 10 kilometers from the site. The setting is fantastic and the food is quite OK."

"Sure that sounds a great idea," Mat had replied and they had agreed to meet in the reception area of the admin buildings at 8.00 p.m. Gunter, another consultant on the team, had a car and would drive them round to the Hotel Hulsta. Mat had met Gunter earlier and had found him rather untypical of the Tactilis consultants he had encountered so far. A small thing but he seemed to dress smarter – or maybe not smarter, but more aware of how he looked.

The road to the hotel took them along a stretch of breath-taking coast road with views down to rocky coves and deserted bays. The wind had picked up since the afternoon and as they drove along, Mat could see waves crashing against rocks and the surf rising in white towers. At one point the road went closer to the sea's edge and spray billowed into the air above and around the car, as though they had been enveloped in droplets of ocean.

The Hotel Hulsta was situated in its own bay about 100 meters up from the sea and nestled under the lee of the hill for protection from the wind. The hotel was a large, old stone building with massive walls and windows set irregularly within them. It had once been the home of a local clan chieftain and had been converted into a hotel about 20 years before, primarily for salmon fishing trips and tourists who came north to see these wild fjords. Inside, the walls were four or five feet thick, so you just knew what kind of winters they had up here.

"You know they say that this place is haunted, " said Gunter, as they took their seats in the long, low dining room decorated with simple tapestries and fishing memorabilia.

"No, I didn't," said Mat looking at the surroundings, and pretending to be uninterested in Gunter's comment.

"Maybe Mat doesn't want to hear your scary stories, Gunter," said Jennie sensing that Mat was turning away from the subject.

"No, no. It's all right really," said Mat. "Up here anything is believable."

"OK, well, I will tell you this sad story," continued Gunter. "The house belonged at one time to the Ulin clan and to a famous chieftain Ragnar Ulin. Ragnar had six sons and six daughters and they all lived here in this house."

"His wife Agnes had a sister, Ailsa, who was married to another local chief named Tore. Tore and Ailsa died from the smallpox and their only daughter Beata was taken in by Ragnar and Agnes and brought up as one of their own. Beata was a bright, good-looking girl who soon became a favorite with everyone."

Gunter was obviously enjoying telling the tale and was becoming slightly theatrical, raising and lowering his voice for effect.

"As I said, Ragnar and Agnes had six sons," he continued. "Two of these died in infancy. Of the surviving sons Erik was the eldest and on the occasion of his eighteenth birthday he and his three brothers, the family's tutor, and one of the family's servants decided to cross the fjord to visit their uncle Ulf on the far side. The boys often took Beata on these trips, but not on this day. Roads, as such, were unknown at that time and the boys had crossed this fjord a hundred times and were well accustomed to it in all weathers. On that day the weather was calm and as bright as anyone could remember. There was hardly a ripple on the waters. The boys, their tutor, and the servant set off before lunch. They were due to return after dinner. The evening was still and warm, but the boat never returned. The following day Ragnar and Agnes searched the fjord and found the boat, floating the right way up with the tutor's hat and staff inside, but none of its occupants. For two days they and the rest of the clan and servants searched the banks of the fjord and on the third day a body was found. It was Erik. His was the only body recovered.

"When they dragged his body to the shore, Beata threw herself down and clasped the body of young Erik. Unseen by anyone she took a note from his breast pocket, a note she herself had seen him place there."

Gunter took a deep breath and went on.

"Six months after the tragedy a boy was born in the attic of the house. He was born to Beata and his father was Erik. The note had been their promise of betrothal. The boy was named Bram and grew to be a strong, fine young man who would inherit the whole estate on the death of old Ragnar. Terrified of the waters of the fjord, Beata forbade him to ever go out on the fjord. This he obeyed throughout his childhood. But on his eighteenth birthday and sensitive to the fate of his young father, Bram was determined to take the boat out on the fjord.

"No one saw him leave but they found the boat gone," he went on. "Beata stood on the bank below the house and called and called his name, her voice echoing around the fjord. It was another calm, bright day; still and warm. But the boy never returned nor was his body ever found. Just the boat alone was recovered, again three days after the incident. Once again floating the right way up.

"The death of her son unhinged poor Beata and she never left the house again. She had the windows of her room boarded up so that she could not see the waters. She died one year to the day after her son had disappeared. Her spirit still wanders the house, looking for her son and husband. They say she will sometimes stroke the cheeks of male guests who sleep here, as though in remembrance of her loved ones.

"And you know what?" said Gunter, concluding his story. "A couple of months ago one of the senior executives from SOL decided to stay here because accommodation on site was full. He's a great big guy, a keen rower; your typical tough oil man. Anyway, he swears he woke in the night and looked up and there was a young woman stroking his face. He left the place there and then. Drove straight back to the plant and spent the rest on the night in his office."

Mat was looking distinctly uneasy at the end of the tale.

"Like I said, up here anything is believable," he said. "What's more, they always say you never believe in ghosts, until you've seen one."

"Well, enough of the spooky stories," said Jennie. "Shall we order?"

The menu was short and simple, but it did offer fresh reindeer steaks and snowberries. Mat decided when in Trudheim, it was only right to try the local fauna.

"So do you enjoy working for Tactilis?" Mat asked Gunter.

Gunter and Jennie looked at one another. There was an obvious exchange between them and Jennie nodded as if to say: "Yes go on if you like…"

"Well, not entirely," he replied. "In fact I am thinking of leaving at the end of this month."

"What don't you like?" asked Mat. "Is it the location?"

"No, although that can be difficult," said Gunter. "No, it is more the work. I joined the Tactilis team because I thought that I would be giving advice, telling people what to do. Instead I find I am asked to help people do work which is many levels below me."

"But surely you get some satisfaction in seeing them do things better?" asked Mat.

"Yes, but I think I should be involved more in the management decisions, in making bigger, bolder changes that would really lift the production here. I wanted to have an input at a strategic level, not at the everyday work-face. After all, I am dealing with a lot of not very clever people and that is not good for my career."

"Where do you want to take your career then?" asked Mat.

"If I'm dreaming – I want to work for a top consulting firm at a senior management level. That's where you can make a real difference to companies. All this level stuff, it's saving peanuts. I want a career that allows me to use my imagination, be creative about the directions that business might take."

"You mean you want to work the big ideas," said Mat.

"Yes, that's right. Ideas are what make a difference in business and that's where I think I have something to offer," replied Gunter.

"Well, you may be right I suppose," replied Mat, not feeling it was his place to argue with Gunter's youthful enthusiasm.

Mat and Jennie exchanged glances. It was clear to all that Gunter would be moving on, although Mat had some sympathy for the way he thought. A few months previously perhaps, he would have been saying the same things.

As they left at the end of the meal Mat paused. He looked out at the bay below the hotel and the waters of the fjord. Tonight they were thrashed by wind and he could just make out the white tips of waves caught in the half-light. How much safer it was now than on a calm, still, warm evening.

Meeting the managers

Over the next four days Mat went from meeting to meeting trying to listen and understand what had happened to the terminal.

His first meeting was with the site operations manager, Anders Fulstrom. He had a small office in the main administration building at the end of a long corridor lined with other small offices. Jennie had agreed to accompany Mat and introduce him to Anders – and then leave the two of them to talk. Inside Anders' office there were the usual charts of the North Sea oil fields on the wall as well as photography of the local area and wild life. It gave a sense of the twin preoccupations of any such facility: get the oil, but please don't screw up the countryside.

Jennie and Mat waited for Anders inside as she explained to Mat that Anders had been having problems with some of the safety groups on the site. Anders was late. Jennie said this was not unusual.

"I'm sure he'll be on time one day," said Jennie, "then I'll really know I've turned the corner with this guy. When he realizes that being late for meetings isn't macho or a sign of how busy he is, it's a sign that he can't manage his own time. And if he can't manage his own time, then how's he supposed to do it for others?"

Anders came into the room, in an apparent rush and put a large pile of papers and files on the table. He was tall, slim with very light ginger hair, thinning on top.

"Sorry I am late," he said. "My team meeting overran and then I bumped into one of the union leaders in the corridor and had to talk to him. You know what people like that are like?"

"No problems," said Jennie, "but if you think this meeting is unimportant then we'll cancel it right now."

"No, no," said Anders quickly. "Of course I think it's important. I ran over in my meetings, that's all. Let's get started shall we?"

Jennie introduced him to Mat and then left as the two of them discussed the major issues facing the plant right now. Anders was very helpful and talked about the history of the site and how many people had been there for 13 years and some even for 25 years (although he himself had only been there two years). That of course meant that a certain culture had built up over time and it was very difficult to break down. People had become very entrenched in their positions and it made change very hard to drive through. To some extent they had had it too good for too long, in the 1980s and 1990s the throughput at the terminal had been three times what it was today.

"You know in the old days," he said. "We even used to hire a helicopter to fly in the Sunday newspapers for us. Can you imagine! That's the kind of culture that got embedded here and that's what we've got to disentangle."

Anders also explained that there was a lot to do in terms of right-sizing the equipment.

"We've got a key job to do in right-sizing our kit. The kit is pretty much the same today as it was in our heyday. So in simple terms, we have got three separation trains running. We had planned to come down to two naturally over time, just doing things normally, but now we're planning to come down to one. We think we can operate on one and that would mean big savings," he said with a certain glint in his eye. "The same for power generation. Right now we're running with three gas turbines and we're doing a piece of work to see if we can get to one."

Anders was very helpful and talked about the terminal and the changes he'd seen already. He was also keen to let Mat know that he was only here for one more year and then was hoping to be involved in an LPG plant that SOL were setting up in Indonesia.

"I hope that this place can change enough, we'll do our best. But it's a big ask," Anders finished.

After Anders, Mat had talked to dozens of other middle managers at Trudheim. He crossed and re-crossed the site many times and in many slow bus journeys. The bus driver would approach in the mist and rain, pause at the stop, open the door and take Mat on board. A simple, easy complicity arose between them – there was no need to hurry to where they were going.

Mat talked to one manager who took him through a recent presentation they'd done on benchmarking against other terminals worldwide, looking at how they should be managing assets of this size and significance. The benchmarking had strangely not been an impetus to improve but a justification for their current difficulties. Of course they were behind other sites, but then none of the other sites had the particular set of problems – geographical or inherited – which they had to deal with.

Another manager had talked about the need to define the critical issues that they faced and that without clear definition they would never get buy-in from the senior management team for some of the more difficult decisions they would have to make. "We need a strategic framework to work within," he'd said.

Another member of the management team talked to him about the complacency in some groups and troublemakers in others. He recounted a story about the loading masters as a way of showing how different groups played the safety card to protect their empires.

"We currently have five loading masters, one on each shift," he'd said. "And because of the throughput through the site, we have fewer ships coming in now, so rather than have one on each shift, we're only going to retain some of them on days and transfer some of their existing accountabilities to other members of the shift team. Their point of view is that for the 20 odd years we've had them as highly professional, highly qualified individuals and as a result of that we have a very good reputation in terms of our marine performance, incident, spills, and so on. And they're exactly right, we do have a world-class reputation. So their argument is that if we take that role away we will have incidents, we will lose that reputation. And my argument is that we are not taking those skills away we are retaining half of it in a different part of the organization and we are transferring the remainder of their skill into another group of people, so there is no reason to believe that we will jeopardize our performance. But we're still in discussion."

One manager told Mat that the worst thing to deal with was the "silo mentality" when different groups wouldn't co-operate because they felt it was not part of their departments' responsibility and how they had to get more co-operation between departments. Another said that it was the remote location of the site which made things difficult: the Trudheim factor he called it.

"We don't feel part of the world here, so how do you expect people to feel the same urgencies and pressures that you would in a normal economic environment?"

He got stories on the lack of accountability and the problems of running a site of this size and complexity. Some managers said they felt the organization was too hierarchical and that it took too long for information to cascade across the 600 people employed here.

Every which way, Mat got a plausible explanation about the poor performance of the terminal in recent years. It was a big project to change a site of this size and it would take time to achieve. But the management were heavily invested in the program and Mat didn't doubt for one moment that they were sincere in what they were saying or what they were trying to achieve. He had to admit that change on this scale was very complex.

That's what he was coming to think as he waited for the bus one last time on the Thursday afternoon. The fog had lifted a little during the week and they had even had some relatively pleasant afternoons, with sunshine which had made Mat wonder what it would be like to dive in the deep gray waters of Trudheim Bay. But that afternoon the fog had come down once again and it was thick enough to obscure the tops of the hills around the site.

The bus eventually arrived and the driver pulled up and opened the doors to let Mat in. They had nodded to one another over the past days, but had kept a mutually convenient silence. On this trip however there was no one else on the bus and the driver seemed keen to chat with Mat.

"Closing in again," he said, almost pleased that the fog was once again regaining the territory for its own.

"They say the weather is going to get a lot worse over night. It might make the helicopter flights out tomorrow a bit tricky. Could be they'll have to cancel them."

"I hope not," said Mat. "I'm due to catch a flight out and back home tomorrow."

"Oh you're just here for the *week* are you?" asked the driver with a slight tome of disapproval in his voice, as though Mat wasn't tough enough to take any more.

"Yes, that's right."

"One of those consultants are you?"

"That's right. I'm with the Tactilis team."

"Yes they've been here for about six months now. Just get used to one team and then another crowd arrive. I must have seen six or seven different consulting firms here during my time. They say you're better than the others – but we'll see," he said.

Then he turned his body slightly toward Mat.

"Of course they never ask me what I think," he said.

"I'm not surprised, you're a bus driver with a criminal record," thought Mat but didn't say so.

"I could tell them a thing or two," continued the driver. "I hear everything that goes on in this plant. They all talk in the back of my bus you know."

"Like what?" asked Mat.

"Like the fact that one of the managers was saying the other day: 'We now know how many contractors we have on the site, the thing is that we don't know why they're here.' I mean how can you say a thing like that?" snorted the driver.

"Well, he was probably joking," said Mat.

"I don't think so," said the driver. "How about this then. Last week they were talking about the power station. And they were saying that there are two ways to fuel the station, either with diesel or with gas from the site. Well it turns out that we've been flaring gas for the past two months and yet we've also been buying diesel for the power station all that time. And no one knew. Two months burning fuel at $150 a ton. And they said it was all because there was no proper reporting system, like they got the figures and facts but they never got the story behind them, so someone knew we were flaring gas, but not why."

Mat didn't think the driver was telling tales any more. It was exactly the kind of story he would have heard if he'd been touring the plant with a supervisor like Frank. But on this occasion he hadn't picked it up at all. He had listened to the middle managers like he would have done at Hardings; like a consultant. Both sides had been obeying that unwritten treaty which demands that professionals talk to one another in proper, professional language: with terms like "right-sizing" and "culture" and "change management complexity." It wasn't that the managers hadn't been straight with him. In their terms, they had. They had told him what they thought consultants should know, and they had spoken to him in the language and terms that they expected him to need. It wasn't their mistake; it was his.

The bus arrived at the main building. Mat got up from his seat.

"Look, thanks very much for what you've told me. You're right, maybe the others should have talked to you. But at least you put me right now."

A broad grin came over the driver's face. He was genuinely delighted that he'd said something useful to Mat.

"Well it's a great pleasure," he said. "Any time you want to know what's going on, I'm your man."

Mat turned to get off the bus and as he did so the driver said, "You know last week I got the old girl up to 130 kilometers an hour – down by the jetties. But don't tell anyone...."

Working out and language lessons

Mat got back to his room still cursing himself. He'd wasted a whole week, thinking he was getting insights when all he had been doing was lapsing back into a Hardings approach. He felt cross and frustrated. He couldn't concentrate and paced the room. The only thing to do in such circumstances, he'd found was to take some exercise. Burning up some energy would at least clear his sense of frustration.

He'd brought some jogging gear with him, but it looked dark and miserable outside. He'd go to the site gym instead. He'd taken a look a few days before and as you'd expect of an oil installation it was set out with all the latest gym equipment.

Mat changed and walked over to the gym.

He peered through the glass swing doors. Inside on one of a long bank of running machines was Anders Fulstrum. He was running at a medium pace; a reasonable work out.

Mat walked in and Anders nodded in welcome.

"Good evening. Mind if I join you?" he asked.

"No not at all. Just don't put me to shame by setting your machine too fast," said Anders.

Mat got on the machine and started to pound rubber. Both men looked forward, staring into that inner space of running: "Just the next corner, just to the next ridge." That was how you conned yourself to keep going when the muscles started to burn, even when there was no next corner or next ridge.

"Tell me the real story, Anders. Tell me what you really feel about this place," said Mat.

"Not sure what you mean. We spoke at length earlier in the week. There is no real story, nothing's being hidden," said Anders with some surprise.

"No, you haven't meant to hide anything from me. I just haven't asked you the right questions. Like what was the worst thing you had to do today?"

Anders looked across at Mat. Both of them running into that distance just out of reach. They were also running side-by-side and though perhaps he wouldn't say that he was knowingly competing with Anders, Mat was nonetheless aware that he was forcing the pace that little bit more. He certainly wouldn't have wanted to be outdone.

"The worst thing…" Anders said. "The worst thing was being shouted at by a bunch of angry firemen."

"That's it," thought Mat. "He's being real now."

"Go on," said Mat.

"I had this meeting with the terminal firemen. The meeting was meant to be just with the leader of the firemen. But as it turned out there were 15 firemen in the room when I arrived. And all these firemen are really big guys, if you know what I mean," said Anders gesturing with his hands to indicate big, broad shoulders.

"There were all these guys and me. It's not easy you know."

"Sure I can understand that. Why were they there?" said Mat.

"Not certain I got to the bottom of that. It was very difficult because these fifteen men were very angry. They just wanted to shout at me. That's not easy to cope with and you tend to react in the same way and then nothing gets done.

"I felt they just wanted to make me out to be the bad guy. I don't want to be seen as the bad guy in all this. I have to live with these people in my own community. If they lose their jobs here, where else do they go? Nowhere. And I will have to see them every day, in the shops, in the cafés.

"Later, I had a coaching session with Jennie and she was pretty helpful because she explained that these firemen are big, tough men and they're very proud of what they do. But they don't have the education we do. So their answer to problems is not to offer logical argument but to use aggression, to let their emotions do the talking for them. They can't express what they want to express."

"That's what I have been experiencing," said Mat. "You have to get behind what people say and find out the emotional story. For four days, I have had nothing but rational cool-headed explanations from the managers I have spoken to them about the terminal and its loss of efficiency and I just get the feeling I have got to the heart of it."

"That's because none of us, on our own, know precisely what's wrong," replied Anders. "If we did, the first thing that we would do is to try and fix it. That's what we're here to do. People go on about layers of management and so on but all we want to do is to get a good job done."

"And so what's preventing you?" asked Mat.

"Lots of things. Lots of things get in the way. People and characters and emotions. Like those firemen I was talking about. They wouldn't understand the logical argument for making changes to their working pattern if I explained all day long to them. They have a set of beliefs and that is what they're going to stick to. So part of it is that we're dealing with a very messy, imperfect world of relationships and attitudes and feelings and there isn't a perfect solution to any of these.

"The frustrating thing is that because we have consulted people and listened to people, but not necessarily done what they've said, they get the wrong impression. They say: 'I told them that we should do this, they haven't done it, so they haven't listened to me' – so how can you win?"

Anders took a swig out of the plastic water bottle he'd placed on the top of the running machine read-outs.

"But then there are other things," he continued, "which show we can do better, but haven't found the way. So many of the problems come from one group assuming that another is doing something or is in control of something when in fact they're not. For instance, there was an effluent discharge over and above the standard and I asked the manager of that area about it and he assumed that someone else was taking care of it. He knew about the problem but wasn't going to fix it. Multiply that across the site and you start to understand."

"Yes, I'm beginning to," said Mat.

"And then there's the whole issue of measurement. We measure lots of things, but often in isolation and with no overall plan. We don't have a common language for measurement. We have some of the facts, but none of the story that will put them together. So we end up collecting the wrong information and we pass it on and then the people down in Bergen make a decision based on that wrong information and then we are asked to do something which is patently wrong and we complain and it takes weeks of our time to sort it out. All because a couple of facts were wrong in the first place. It's the sort of thing that drives you mad. We talk about keeping within budget and we bust a gut to do so, but in fact we don't know what the right budget should be."

Consciously or unconsciously Anders stepped up the pace on his running machine. Mat responded.

"Then we make all of this messy, complicated, irrational world of people and business even more difficult by constantly looking for new initiatives," he said. "As managers, we're forever either sending out or responding to new directives. It's like an addiction we can't kick. I suppose it's because we're sitting on this asset worth hundreds of millions of dollars and it encourages us to think big, to come up with the next initiative. And the same goes for our bosses in Bergen. Constant streams of new initiatives, because that's how they measure themselves: by the ideas they have introduced, the differences they have made.

"But what we all overlook is that the last lot of initiatives haven't been finished off yet, in fact nor have the previous set. And it's this absurdity that adds to our problems – too much change around the edges – not enough focus on the center. So what ends up happening? Paralysis. We're all reporting on a new initiative and why it isn't in place yet, when of course it has no chance of being implemented properly.

"Somehow we've got to learn to back off innovation for its own sake," he said.

Anders slowed down and got off the running machine, reaching for his towel. He was breathing in short, easy shallow breaths, relaxing himself.

"Why is all this so important?" he asked. "Because no one ever says we're going to focus on these three simple things and we're going to stay focused on them until we get them right. Whose career is that going to help? No one's! It's almost as though no one is prepared to say that the basics aren't working – because if we did admit that they aren't working we wouldn't be believed or worse we'd be sacked. How can the basics not be working in a multi-million dollar site? How would any of us explain that one away?"

Mat stepped off the running machine. He noticed he was breathing much harder than Anders. But it had been worth it. He'd been running on the spot, but he'd made some significant strides forward. He'd come face to face with the awkward, emotional, fuzzy side of managing a business but he felt that Anders was stopping short of a real breakthrough. Anders was stuck in the difficulty of it all. What he needed was some approach or style that would make sense of this randomness, that would bring order to it. Anders was getting some of the information he needed, the business was constantly being monitored and measured, but the measurements were not making sense or were being given to the wrong people.

Mat picked up his towel and wiped his face. He was still breathing heavily whereas Anders was quite normal.

"So Anders if you know all this, why don't you get it through to your senior management? Why don't they understand? What are they doing?"

Anders looked at him straight.

"I don't know," he said. "But you can ask her yourself. Just so happens that Ilsa Peters, the senior VP in charge of this place, is passing by tomorrow. Maybe you'll get a chance to speak to her."

Talking to the top brass

When Mat awoke, the storm from the previous night had gone and there was an extra layer of silence in the air. He looked out of the window. The fog had come down once again and was as thick as at any stage over the past week.

Mat showered, changed and checked his palmtop for flight times to London and back to Miami. He had been planning to take the first helicopter flight out the following morning to Bergen, and then to fly on via London back home. That would put him back in Miami in the evening on Friday and give him the whole weekend with Marianne. But he'd decided since speaking to Anders that if there was a chance of meeting with Ilsa Peters he could take a slightly later flight out and still make it back on Friday night. The connections were tight but it would work.

He then called Jennie on her cell phone to see whether there would be any chance of seeing Ilsa the following day. Jennie had said it was unlikely but she would try. Jennie was meeting Ilsa at 8.00 a.m. and she could see whether there was a slot somewhere in her diary.

Mat got breakfast in the canteen. He then went over to the travel office and checked on the availability of seats on flights out of the site later that day. It seemed he would be able to get on a morning flight without too much problem. He made a provisional booking on the 10.15 a.m. flight and then made his way to the project team office. Jennie was in her meeting with Ilsa Peters and Mat waited, reading through his week's notes and feeling ever more frustrated that he'd allowed himself to miss the story.

About 30 minutes later, Jennie returned to the office.

"Jennie, how did you get on?" asked Mat as she walked in.

"Do you want the good news first, or bad news?" replied Jennie.

"Good news," said Mat.

"Good news is that she does have half an hour in her schedule when she could see you. Bad news is that it's not until two o'clock. Do you still want to take it?"

Two o'clock. That meant earliest a three o'clock flight out of here. He would be cutting it very fine to get a connecting flight out of Bergen for London and if he missed it, he wouldn't get back in time for his promised weekend in Miami. Should he risk it? "Hell," he thought, "when am I ever going to come back here and interview the VP of global production? Besides, if I'm lucky with the connection I should make it."

"OK," he said. "I'll go for it. I'll book myself on the four o'clock flight out and I should make my connections."

At two o'clock, Mat was sitting in the executive suite waiting area. The secretary had warned him that Ilsa was running a few minutes late.

When the door did open to the executive suite, Mat was greeted by a tall, well-groomed woman with brown hair flicked at the bottom to create a curve that sat neatly on her neck and shoulders. She had a broad smile and walked forward to meet Mat.

"Good morning. Ilsa Peters," she said stretching out her hand.

"Mat Durer," he replied. "Thank you very much for finding the time to see me at such short notice."

"No problem. Please have a seat," said Ilsa. "Jennie said

you've just joined from Hardings. Interesting move. I know Anthony Elliott very well. He's a charming man."

"Yes, he's very well respected," replied Mat.

"And now you are on a fact-finding mission for Tactilis? Sounds intriguing."

"Well, I'm not sure it's a fact-finding mission, more of a fact-feeling mission really. I've recently joined the firm and the task they've set me is to find out what makes the consulting firm tick, what are the real levers that makes us successful."

"Good for you. So how can I help?"

"I wanted to experiment with you," he said.

Ilsa raised an eyebrow and smiled.

"Do tell me how? I reserve the right to object of course," she said, as though she might enjoy a game.

Mat was in familiar territory with a senior executive. As a Hardings man he knew how far he could push and his new role at Tactilis gave him the licence to be unorthodox. He could be off-beat but respectful.

"Of course," he said knowingly. "What if I asked you five questions about your life as an executive and we see what they uncover?"

"OK," she said, "we'll see how we go."

"Good. First question is what's your worst fear as an executive?"

"I suppose that would be the getting in a situation or position which I can't handle," she said. "Getting beyond my capabilities. It's like you have a successful career and you go from achievement to achievement and then suddenly you hit the limit of your capabilities. That would be frightening, because by the time you'd found out it would be too late. You'd be in that situation and your executive colleagues would know. And let me tell you that life as an executive or senior officer of a corporation isn't quite as clubby as it may seem. You have colleagues who want your job or your budget or your resources – there's a constant struggle for resources. Some are jealous of your relationship with the CEO, others see you as a threat, others simply long for you to fail so that they can add your department to the empire they're building. So, if you fail, the vultures will encircle."

Everything was polished. Every sentence finished. As though she had installed the ultimate "Word" package.

"What aspect of your life would you say is least understood by people in your organization or people generally?" Mat asked.

Ilsa raised herself to the game. She was enjoying it, too; enjoying the fun of being open and talking openly about aspects of executive life.

"I think people underestimate the huge emotional pressures at the top of a business," she replied. "They think it's all about hard-edged, commercial decision making and that the decisions are reached in a logical environment. That is true, of course, but it doesn't describe the emotional pressures adequately. Let me oversimplify it for you: the CEO makes a commitment to his group of analysts to take the business to a certain set of figures. He then comes back to you, his team, and makes it clear that you are part of that delivery process. From then on you are tied to those commitments and they are constantly on your mind. Can I deliver? That's emotional pressure not intellectual pressure. Within all of this, each executive and each department has its own agenda. And making sense of conflicting agendas is what keeps you up at night."

"What's the biggest frustration you face?" asked Mat.

"I'm not sure it's frustration but it's certainly the biggest question: how do I get people to go in the direction I want them to? How do I get people to implement at a local level what we decide at a corporate level?"

"Following on from that, what is the role of the executive management team?" Mat continued.

Ah, the big question! The one where you can really let yourself go, really test yourself against the wisdom of every other exec and every other guru or commentator.

Ilsa looked down for a moment and then spoke clearly. What she was describing was a deeply held conviction; more than that, she was describing her duty.

"Our purpose is to set the goal for the company," she said. "We set the company's direction, given all the different factors and criteria we face and given all the duties we owe to our stakeholders – duties to make a sound return on their investment, to operate ethically, to respect people's rights, and so on. Once we have agreed this direction, our job is to communicate it down through the company and create the framework through which it can be delivered.

"And finally, why do you think that process doesn't work?" asked Mat. He was pressing it, but he wanted to see how far he could go.

"I think it does work," she said surprised by the change in direction of his question. "It may be imperfect because implementing a strategy over a large organization is a complex task. But it's about getting the right organization in place and the right team of people in line so that the company achieves its goals. How else can we respond to our stakeholders unless we operate as an entity with fixed objectives?"

Mat was at the end of his interview. He carried on talking to Ilsa and asking supplementary questions for the next ten minutes or more, but he had found what he was looking for. Ilsa was a very committed, articulate, and responsible officer. Exactly the kind of executive most companies would be proud of. Textbook.

It was her job to set direction. Performance, strategy, organization, investment were all subordinate to the goal. You had to have a goal in business just as you do in life. And the goal when described would sound rational and eminently desirable. You could read it and not argue with a word of it. Oh yeah, it's that simple.

After the meeting with Ilsa, Mat went to the project office.

Jennie was there waiting for him.

"Bad news, I'm afraid," she said. "They've had to cancel the four o'clock because of bad weather in Bergen. Looks like we're going to miss our connection to London. Bang goes my weekend in the garden."

The call

"Look, I'm really sorry, Mari," said Mat. "Truly I am. This opportunity to meet the VP of global production just came up and I thought I could still make it back. If it hadn't been for the lousy weather I would have done."

"Mat, I know – it's part of the job. I know. Don't worry, darling. We'll just have to put off our dive with the Flamingos until next weekend that's all. I'm disappointed, but I'll cope."

Mat had not been looking forward to breaking the news to Marianne that he wouldn't be back for the whole weekend. This was the second time in a row that things had come in the way of them spending time together. And although that wasn't entirely unusual, he had had urgent projects in the past for Hardings which had eaten into weekends, it was slightly different now. Since leaving Hardings they'd spent more time together, gotten used to one another's company, and as part of that familiarity they had assumed that they would carry on spending more time together. Now it wasn't proving that way.

So Mat was relieved that Marianne had been understanding on the telephone and he promised to make it up to her next weekend with a long diving trip off the coast. They hadn't been diving together for some weeks now and they both missed it. It was when their relationship worked best.

Mat did get to Bergen on a later helicopter and was able to make it to London on the last flight in. There were no flights to the US until the following morning. Since Mat hated staying at the soulless hotels around airports, he decided to go into central London and stay somewhere with a little character. On previous trips with Hardings, he had often stayed at Brown's Hotel and they fortunately had a room available.

On the flight over to London, Mat had picked at the food and had taken a small bottle of champagne. He went over his notes from the meeting with Ilsa.

Mat was still contemplating her last comments about executives setting goals. And he was still unsure as to what they meant for business. These were external goals, generated not from the heart of the business but from the top, with all the clarity of a lookout seeking land. But often without charts. That was it. You couldn't impose a direction without knowing the reality of the business beneath you. But too frequently management saw its job as finding a goal, and then forcing the reality of their business to match it. Indeed management had become obsessed with identifying "the goal."

The trouble with the goal philosophy was that you rewarded anyone who contributed to the goal – in middle management especially – and admonished those who didn't. Performance, the insights of the five-minute snapshots, the potential of local knowledge, all of these were secondary to the goal. The goal was to be No. 1, rather than doing all the basics so brilliantly that you became No. 1 as a natural consequence.

If a business is defined by an external goal, how can it understand its internal voices, the five-minute intervals where work gets done? The two were just incompatible.

I remember sitting in an airport one time when I was young waiting for a plane and I got talking to a guy who was on the same flight. He asked me what I was going to do with my life. I said I didn't know, but I had to find a way to make money. He told me never to make money the goal. "Make performance your obsession," he'd said. "If the performance is perfect, the rest comes naturally as day follows night." He was an older guy and he knew what he was talking about. Yet it took me a long time to see the value of his words.

Now Mat was getting there, too. He was beginning to see why ideas brought Wentworth down.

Mat arrived in London a little after nine o'clock and got the Heathrow Express into the center of the city.

He liked London. He hadn't been here for over a year now and it was fun to take a black cab from the station to the hotel. It was fun being in a cab where the driver talked, whether you were listening or not.

"I dunno, this station just gets worse and worse," the taxi driver began. "Ever since they brought that Heathrow Express in. The police and traffic authorities never asked for our advice, did they? Went ahead and designed it on their own!"

He paused, waiting for a laugh.

"And it doesn't work…"

Another pause for laughter.

"Which serves them right, really. Only thing is that it's the passengers and us that suffer."

The driver turned his head slightly as though expecting a comment from Mat.

"That's right," said Mat.

"I mean, you'd think they'd ask us wouldn't you? After all, we use the streets of London more than anyone else. So we should know what works. It's not like they're designing a nuclear power plant or nothing. They're designing a taxi rank in central London. And who don't they ask for advice? The taxi driver!"

"They always think we'll have some agenda," he continued with an obvious sense of grievance.

They arrived at the hotel after various further short conversations about President Bush, "that Tony Blair," and the cab driver's last visit to Disney World with his children.

Mat got out, paid the fare with a reasonable tip for the education value of the trip and walked through the wooden doors of Brown's Hotel on Albemarle Street. He had a large single room at the front of the hotel.

It was now just before ten o'clock and Mat was in London. What should he do? He could have dinner in the hotel or take a walk down St James's Street or just turn in. But he didn't feel like any of those options. He was in London, on a Saturday night.

He decided to call an old friend from Harvard, Sophie Ranger. She'd come back to London and was now working for an executive training outfit.

He got out his palmtop and called her number. There was no answer and it clicked over to her voicemail.

"Hi Sophie, this is Mat. Mat Durer. I am in London unexpectedly and just thought I'd call to say hello. Sorry to have missed you, but let's catch up again one of these days. Bye."

He put the phone back down on his bed and was about to choose between the hotel restaurant and a walk when his cell phone rang.

"Hi Mat, it's Sophie. Screening my calls I'm afraid. Didn't want the world to know I was sitting at home on my own on a Saturday night. Not good for a girl's image and image is everything wouldn't you say?"

"I certainly would Sophie. How are you?"

"Fine. Still single, but fine. How about you?"

"Yes and no," said Mat.

"That's a technical yes," said Sophie. "And anyway 'yes' makes me feel better. What are you doing in London?"

"I missed a connecting flight back to the US and so I'm just here for the night. Fancy meeting up? Be good for your image."

"Oh Mat, you're so shallow – such an endearing trait in a man. Far better than all that brooding meaningfulness. Sure let's meet up. Or do you want to come over here? I live just off the park."

Twenty minutes later Mat was walking into Sophie's flat in Notting Hill Gate. It was smart and bright and the sitting room had yellow curtains and two big pink sofas.

Mat took a seat on one of the sofas. And Sophie got him a glass of wine. She was in her early thirties, blonde, slightly round, and full of life.

"I suppose you still don't smoke," she said, taking a cigarette from her packet of Marlboro Lights. "When are you ever going to get any proper vices, Mat?"

"Like?"

"Like evil, envy, lust, for starters. That's what you need, some proper vices. Relax you a bit."

Sophie was sitting on the other big pink sofa with her legs tucked up under her. She sipped the wine and looked at him.

"I think I'm laid back enough as it is," he said. "Gave up my job at Hardings."

"My God, did you? Why? Did you get a conscience about earning all that money? You could always have given some to me you know?"

"No, it just kind of happened one night. I realized that I wasn't believing the hype any more and that I had to find something else to do."

"So what are you up to now?"

"Still in consulting but with another smaller firm. More fun. I think I'm beginning to enjoy work again."

"Do be careful," said Sophie taking a drag on her cigarette, "enjoyment can be habit forming."

"How about you? Still in training?"

"Sort of, yes," she replied. "Media training more now. And we also handle big name tours of business people – celebrity speakers. We had Jack Welch over last week and there's this amazing management guru, Justin Walters, who's packing them in at the moment. Does a great 'guru' show, if you know what I mean?"

"Yes, I think I've come across the breed."

"Another glass of wine?" asked Sophie.

"Sure, please," said Mat. Sophie got up and walked to the kitchen. She was wearing jeans and silk top. No shoes.

She came back with a bottle of wine and topped up Mat's glass. Then went over to the stereo and put on some music. Stan Getz and Jobim.

"You introduced me to this," she said as it started to play *The Girl from Ipanema*.

"Remember?"

"I do remember. I used to play it all the time in my reckless youth."

Sophie sat beside him on the sofa, curling up cat-like on its soft pink cushions.

"Life turning out the way you wanted it?" asked Sophie.

"More or less," said Mat. "You?"

"Less," she said, close to him.

"It's no fun being single. Well it's fun, but not ultimately satisfying.

Like a cigarette," she said exhaling. "Don't know why you bothered with a hotel. You could have stayed here. I've got plenty of room."

"I didn't know you'd be in, remember?"

"Poor excuse from one so gifted."

"I naturally assumed that you would be out with another rich and famous boyfriend."

"Better," she said. "Are you sure you can't feel any vices coming on?"

"What the evil, envy, lust ones you mean – or did you have others in mind?"

"No, those will do."

"How would they feel, those vices, if I could feel them?"

"Like this," she said kissing his mouth.

He kissed her back.

For a moment, one of those ridiculous moments, he could have made a choice. He didn't and the girl from Ipanema went on walking by.

The morning after and thoughts on architecture

Mat got up early the next morning. He wanted to take a walk through London in the half-light. He walked down St James's Street, across St James's Park into Parliament Square and stood on Westminster Bridge as the milky half-light rose from the water.

London was Mat's father's favorite city. His father had worked here as a young man and the way of life had made him think differently about cities. For that reason, for Mat, visiting London was always done partially through his father's eyes.

London was a great city but it never ceased to amaze him how much it turned its back on the Thames. As though the Thames was no longer important to its prosperity.

Mat knew the truth was more prosaic. He'd learnt at school how the Victorians, in their ardor for cleanliness, had installed

London's main sewer system in pipes that ran along the Thames now buried underneath the Embankment. With one engineering masterpiece the new sewers had done more to improve health and living standards in London than any medical breakthrough. But at what cost? London had lost its link with the Thames forever, cut off by a wide strip of busy road.

But perhaps London had lost its links with the Thames even earlier, spiritually. All along the Thames were great buildings, Whitehall, Somerset House, but it was only when you got to the Tower that the buildings showed any feeling for the water nearby. Otherwise they rose up disdainfully. Like buildings with a different, imposed purpose. He thought of a phrase he'd read about the architect Moshe Safdie:

"He believes in contemplating what a building wants to be…While another architect might experience the design process as a search for inspiration, Safdie experiences it as a search for constraint."

Mat thought about that some more. And he thought about what Ilsa Peters had said and how it seemed that managers seeking a goal are like those who seek inspiration, they force the form on the building, they won't listen to what it wants to be. But mostly he thought about Sophie.

Mat walked back to his hotel and picked up his bags. He was just checking out when his cell phone rang. Should he answer it? Would it be easier if he did not answer it? He did not want to explain anything to Sophie. The phone kept ringing.

At last, Mat answered.

"Hello," he said in a soft voice.

"Hello, Mat. It's Max. I hope I haven't got you out of bed, but I needed to get hold of you fast. I want you to come to Atlanta on Monday. I want you to be part of a pitch team I'm putting together for a big piece of new business. The pitch is against Hardings."

A bar on the edge

Mat sat at the bar in the hotel lobby. It was one of those cool hotels in the new affluent suburbs of Atlanta and the bar was long and dimly lit. The sort of place where you'd meet Mrs Robinson.

Behind the bar was an enormous tropical fish tank. It took up almost the whole wall behind and emanated a strange electric blue light, like it was some kind of screen that opened on to another world. Inside there were fish of every kind, size, and color. Brilliant yellows and iridescent greens moved across the screen in slow motion. It reminded Mat of his dives off Grand Turk – lying there on the bottom of the seabed as the shadow of an eagle ray passed over him.

Mat turned to the barman and ordered a bourbon on the rocks. A little while later he ordered another. He didn't drink normally, but this was not a normal time. He was at a turning point. The trouble was he didn't know whether he was headed up or down. Too many things were going on that were causing the perspectives to shift.

First, he'd got a brief message on his cell phone from Anneka saying that she was still in hospital and undergoing tests. She expected to be out any day, though, and would call him once she got home. The message had truly worried Mat. This wasn't just a routine few days in hospital for a couple of tests. It was something serious. So serious he was trying to hide from it by pretending, in the way Anneka was pretending, that she would be out any day now. But deep down that's not how he saw things.

Then he thought about Sophie. Nothing had happened between them and in retrospect he was relieved. He wanted to stay friends with Sophie and not complicate the friendship. But it had been very close; he had almost let the situation develop. That made him worried about his life with Marianne.

When he had phoned Marianne last she had been in a good mood. She had been contacted again by Sagradio Elliott. Sagradio was following up on Mat's conversation with Anthony at the Burlington Club in Boston. She had invited Mat and Marianne for a weekend with Anthony's yachting team. Sagradio had said that Anthony wanted some help in choosing some works of art for Hardings' newly refurbished offices and that he'd like to talk to her about it over that weekend.

At the time, Mat had said they should accept; it would do them good to be away for a weekend together. But that was before he knew about the pitch and the fact that the opposition was none other than Hardings.

If he tried to get out of the weekend now, he knew Marianne would be upset. There was little choice but to say nothing about the pitch to Marianne and trust to Anthony's innate good manners not to mention it.

Finally, the real tipping point, was the pitch itself. It had an uneasy feeling of being a set-up to Mat. He joins Tactilis and within a few weeks he's being asked to take on Hardings in their own back yard – all too much of a coincidence.

It was clear to Mat that there was a hand at work here. He was beginning to believe the impossible – that his father's ghost or some other supernatural power was having an influence on, even determining, events. For the rational, cool-headed Mat Durer to admit this to himself was itself a turning point. The whole ghost experience, the fleeting glimpses, the sense he had of sometimes being watched, the coincidences, Brad's crash in an identical BMW – all of these things were coming together to not only raise doubts in his mind, but to actually make him think differently. He was having to accept as possible, suggestions he would in the past have ridiculed.

Mat felt the pitch was being given to him. He was being invited to put his new ideas into action. How? It wasn't clear to him. But Mat felt certain this pitch was being put forward as the perfect, no the ultimate, opportunity to test one belief against another. The chance for Mat to expose the flaws in Hardings faultless ideas, by presenting his own more radical humanist alternatives. That was the way it was going to be – and it was getting to Mat.

He'd read recently that one of the signs of extreme stress is that you start to see yourself as an actor in your own life's drama. A sign of losing control. Was that what was happening to him? Was he losing it? Mat wavered endlessly between doubt and certainty. His rational mind was telling him one thing; his instincts another.

As he ordered his third bourbon, Mat hit the moment. The first time in his life he had made a real decision.

He decided that this pitch would be all or nothing for him. With this decision he felt an enormous calm, as though he had in an instant been released from the months of doubt and concern. He was going to consign himself to fate; what a feeling of freedom that brought.

If he was being presented with a turning point, then he would take it. He would go through with this pitch, he would follow his internal voices and if necessary he would also allow himself to be played out by them. He would do what he thought his father wanted. That was fine. He would let the pitch decide.

If he found some way to articulate his emerging ideas – his father's philosophy – and the pitch was successful, then he would know that was the right direction, whatever the consequences on his relationship. If not, he would give up this whole wild enterprise, stop looking for a new business philosophy, settle down with Marianne and maybe even go back to Hardings.

Mat raised his glass in the direction of the huge tropical fish tank.

"Here's to diving and the Wall," he said and downed the remaining bourbon in his glass.

That was it. No more equivocation. He would let the pitch decide.

The pitch briefing

There's an art to winning pitches, but I don't know what it is. Something inside me doesn't want to know. I prefer the unpredictable nature of it all, because a pitch is here and now. Pure win or lose, no middle ground; no comfort zone, no blaming it on others.

The five members of the Tactilis team gathered in the meeting room in Atlanta were all experienced in the art of pitching.

Max, the man who had escaped FARC guerrillas in the jungles of Colombia, was the obvious leader. This was a man you could trust when the odds were stacked against you, when you were staring down the muzzle of the competition's guns.

Eric Stadler was an obsessive. Fifty-five years old, he had had a whole career with Daimler-Benz and then switched to consulting because "it is my adventure." He worked every hour that God provides, day and night, on every angle and twist. A pitch to him wasn't a matter of life and death; it was more important.

Elias "Katz" Katzonopolis was a thinker (as opposed to an intellectual). He was the analyst, the mathematician, and a Scrabble genius.

Nancy Dearden was the quiet one; she had glasses and a strange way of smiling only with the very front of her mouth. She was Ms Organized, never late, nothing forgotten, she'd whip any team into shape. In her late forties she'd also worked out of consulting for much of her career. But she was born to it, drawn to it. Why? Because she was about getting things done. She had no time for small talk or clever reasoning – just get on and do it.

Finally there was Mat. The new boy, the fresh-faced recruit to the Tactilis squad, still finding his feet with the new surroundings. In fact, his selection was typical Max, who always liked to bring in the unexpected. Shake up the comfortable squad. You never win the next pitch by relying on what got you the last one. However, in this case, Max also had a very good reason for bringing Mat in: the pitch was against Hardings.

Max was sitting at the head of an oval table. Eric was cool concentration. Katz had taken to doodling on the complimentary pad. There was something about complimentary pads that just had to be doodled on – and not on the first page either, randomly on different sheets. Nancy Dearden was sitting to attention, aware of the time. And Mat Durer? Mat wasn't sure what to make of it at all.

Max made the opening remarks.

"First I'd like to introduce Mat Durer. He's very new to the organization and comes fresh from none other than Hardings & Co. – our competitors in this pitch."

There was a mild look of surprise around the old stagers: no one in their right minds would expect a new guy to be part of a pitch team for such a big piece of business as this. And certainly no one would expect him to go head-to-head against his old firm.

"I know I'm taking a risk asking Mat to be part of this team as he knows very little about us at this moment. But that's my responsibility and I want you to help him get Tactilis into his blood very quickly. Because Mat's new, I hope he'll bring some fresh ideas. Because he knows Hardings, I expect him to tell us how they'll be thinking and how they'll approach this piece of business. That inside knowledge could be invaluable. We've lost every time we've taken on Hardings in the past. That's not surprising. They are the best in the business. But it doesn't prevent us from giving them a run for their money now."

"Excuse me, Max," said Eric, staring intently at the highly polished table in front of him, "But we have tried something similar before, a few years back. We involved an ex-MPC guy in a pitch and what happened? We found out later that he'd been giving the inside track to his old colleagues – on us. We lost out on a $2 million slice of business because he was leaking information."

"We don't know that's what happened, Eric," said Max. "My guess is that we weren't going to win that business anyway. And what's more I have every faith in Mat. Every faith."

"Yeah, but they always say once a Hardings man, always a Hardings man," said Eric, casting a distrustful glance at Mat. "It's like *Hotel California*: 'You can check out any time you like, but you can never leave.'"

Katz laughed; Nancy smiled with the front of her mouth.

Mat said nothing.

"OK I'm not trying to be hard on Mat," continued Eric "I'm just telling you how I feel Max, right from the beginning."

Mat looked across at Max and then toward Eric.

"I appreciate the honesty," he said. "But I can assure you I am not a Hardings spy!"

Sensing there was more to the argument than a few short remarks, Max took over the conversation once more.

"OK, can we move on?" he said. "We have a lot to do in a very short space of time. The client we're dealing with here is Oxytec."

There were brief glances of recognition and approval between Eric, Katz, and Nancy. This would be a big account to win.

"Oxytec have asked us to put initial recommendations to them within four weeks," continued Max.

"That must mean they are hemorrhaging money real fast," said Katz. "Unbelievably fast. What's their stock price doing?"

"Low but stable. No big falls in recent days. Analysts haven't had the chance to pick up on the news yet. Looks to me like Oxytec have a situation with their investment bankers."

"Who are the bankers?" asked Nancy.

"Bond & Co.," replied Max.

"It's not their style to take a pre-emptive strike, so it could be that the numbers are hidden in some way, or that Bond have been unnerved by something internal," she said.

"Could be you're right, and I'll bet Katz will find out the full story soon enough," replied Max. "Right now, the scope of the project as we have been given it, is that the healthcare and life sciences division of Oxytec have an unacceptable level of profitability, which is holding the whole group back.

"The official line is that the clients are under enormous pressure from the investment community to increase shareholder value. In addition to efforts to improve margins, there's also a major cost reduction program worldwide. The institutions want both delivered, and delivered faster than the current status. That means we're going to have to take a look at cost reductions based on improved productivity, efficiency, and organizational effectiveness and on taking out any non-value-added activities – and then find ways to improve price margins."

Max paused.

"In their words, they want a quick transfusion followed by sustainable recovery. We've been brought in by Gunther Claus, the manufacturing VP which makes me think that he feels his empire is on the line here and he needs some way out of it, where he maintains control. He knows we've done good work in other projects and he sees us as an outfit he can trust."

"And we suspect that Hardings have been brought in by the CEO?" asked Nancy.

"Yes, that would be my guess," said Max.

"Or a mix of the CEO and pressure from Bond & Co.," said Mat. "Don't forget that the bankers will be pulling a lot of the strings here. Do we have a link into Bond?"

There was a brief silence.

"Well, no matter, if you've got contacts within the manufacturing situation that's just as good," said Mat.

Of course this was not strictly true. He knew that the investment bankers would be very likely to have a big say in any critical activity and would almost certainly be canvassed by the CEO as a way of taking the investment community with him. Manufacturing on the other hand, would be unlikely to carry much influence, even though Oxytec was ultimately a manufacturing company. That's often the way of it in companies these days.

"So, we have very little time to pull together a very big pitch," said Max. "We'll work as a team, but split into two pairs for the first couple of days. Katz and Nancy, I want you to get into a meeting with Gunther Claus fast and set up a pre-analysis project with Oxytec at a couple of the key sites in Europe and the US. Mat and Eric, I want you to go to Alanstown."

"Excuse me, Max," interrupted Eric. "But Oxytec don't have an operation in Alanstown. That's a Northern Utilities site."

"Exactly," replied Max.

"I want you to take Mat to Northern Utilities and pull together some really compelling examples of the way that we've worked there – especially the way we've helped out on behaviors. That'll be invaluable material for the pitch, and it will also give Mat a chance to take a deep dive into our business."

Mat looked up.

"Just one question. Northern Utilities, isn't that the business that Jim Bates turned around?" he asked.

Eric was on him in an instant.

"No it was the place that we turned around but he took the credit for," he said with some force. "Just like all those celebrity CEOs do. Anyway he's no longer at Northern. He's moved on."

Eric made another rather hostile glance at Mat, and then turned to Max.

"So you're telling me that you want me to take two days out of an unbelievably short four-week pitch schedule to gather a few client examples with Mat here? No offence to either of you, but wouldn't it be better on this occasion to get someone more experienced – there'll be plenty of other opportunities for Mat to get involved in pitches. Besides we've already got a whole host of examples from other clients."

"Yes, I know, Eric, but Northern Utilities are bang up-to-date and, more importantly, Peter Smith, the CEO of Oxytec is also a non-exec of Northern Utilities. So they'll be examples that really have some relevance to him. He knows the success story of that place; we just have to drive it home to him. As to involving Mat, well I am going to take the risk. If things go wrong, then I am to blame. Is that OK?" said Max.

Eric hesitated for a brief moment, just long enough to register his disapproval.

"OK whatever's best," he said.

"The reason I want Mat in on this is, as I've said, that he might bring some fresh ideas. We all know that we'd do a far better job for Oxytec than Hardings, but we have got to convince Peter Smith and his board and the bankers of that. We need them to engage with us, in exactly the same way as they'd engage with a proposal from Hardings."

Max then turned to Mat. "What would you say our chances are?" he said.

"Hardings have a head start in terms of reputation, that's for sure. No CEO is going to get fired because he hired Hardings. In fact, it will be the reverse. Hiring Hardings works like an expensive insurance policy. If you get the best in the business to help and things still don't work out then no one is going to blame you personally – it was obviously a terminal case."

"On top of that," Mat continued, "Hardings will flood this pitch with some of their heaviest hitters. They'll bring them from any corner of the world they have to. They'll line up all their client references and then they'll go into that final meeting with a classically simple set of messages. One: we're Hardings, the world's leading consulting firm. Two: this is how much money we've saved clients just like you. Three: here's the model of how we're going to do it. No detail, just smart, elegant thinking around the client's problems. Those three are as near to a sure-fire pitch winner as you're likely to get."

"Looks like Mat is already having doubts about being able to turn over his old employers," said Eric.

"Not at all. As Max said, the one thing I can contribute is an intimate knowledge of the way that Hardings works and thinks. Oxytec has sales of over $10 billion – it's one of *Fortune*'s most admired companies, so it's a big prize for Hardings, too. They won't want to lose out, and especially not to a smaller consulting firm.

"They'll come out with all the strengths they can muster; their industry expertise. They'll have all the comparative financial and sector data you can imagine to support their proposed model. They'll have all the language of long-term vision and understanding trends. They'll be ruthlessly scientific. It will all be so carefully worked out and presented that it'll feel to the board of Oxytec that they're watching a scientific experiment with only one outcome, only one possible reaction."

"But we all know that science and formulas and neat little models don't always work in the real world," said Nancy.

"Exactly," replied Mat. "And that's where we'll attack them."

His use of the word "attack" surprised him. He was charged up.

Max had tuned in to the change in mood.

"I think we'll have a lot of fun on this pitch," said Max, smiling across the table. "I know all of you are winners and that you're going to do Tactilis proud on this. Just stay true to our philosophy and we can do it."

"Like they say in Scrabble tournaments: stay focused, have ice for blood," said Katz and they all got up to leave.

Eric, Katz, and Nancy, old friends on the pitch trail, walked out together already planning their next moves. Mat and Max were left briefly behind, pulling together their papers.

"So when did you get to know about this pitch and Hardings' involvement?" asked Mat.

"Oh, they first called me up about three weeks ago, for a very informal, initial discussion," replied Max, as though unaware of the significance of the question.

"So, was that before you hired me or after?"

"Before, of course," said Max. And they followed the others out.

The guru in the lobby

Mat had got his overnight bag and briefcase together and was waiting downstairs in the lobby of the hotel. He and Eric had agreed to take the 11.15 a.m. flight out of Atlanta and hoped to arrive in Alanstown mid-afternoon. They'd spend the next two days there and then meet up with Katz and Nancy.

Mat sat in one of the big white lobby chairs. A meeting had just broken up in one of the conference rooms and the delegates were walking out and talking animatedly as they did so. Mat noticed the name on the conference room notice board: Justin Walters, Business Pathfinder. He was the management guru that Sophie had told him about in London. She'd handled his European tour. Now here he was in Atlanta. Mat was intrigued and walked over to the board to see what Guru Walters was talking on:

Justin Walters'

NETWORKING INTELLIGENCE

How to connect with the magical dynamism of your company's potential

The delegates who were still filing out from the conference room certainly looked as though they had got in touch with their "magical dynamism."

These days business gurus jet around like a pop stars, doing a gig here and there. They're the great communicators of our time, outside of the TV preachers of course. Come to think of it the two of them have a lot in common, they both emanate a sort of evangelical glow; they have found the "truth."

And the way the guru works his audience! Pacing the stage, embracing those provocative ideas, which are all very well for him, he never has to put them into practice. It's magical performance art, like a big one-man comedy show.

I remember going to this one event and the Master saying to his disciples: "What I'd like you to do is to pick a partner. I don't want you to talk with the guy you came with. I want you to pick someone on the other side of the auditorium and I'd like you to spend 20 minutes and I'd like you to answer two questions: what are your biggest regrets and what are your greatest achievements? And I want you to really discuss this."

Then right away some grumbling started up, probably by some Germans or Belgians and they were saying, "No, no, we want to listen to you. I don't want to listen to the guy over there. I can listen to him any time. You only come to Europe three times a year."

Then another section in the audience started saying, "No we need to go with this. I'm sure there's a good point to this." And the Master watches and thinks very carefully and then says in a low voice, "Anybody like to describe how they see this situation?" And a huge Belgian gets up and spouts incomprehensibly for a few moments and sits back down and the Master says, "That's a pretty good characterization of the situation. But you know what's really going on here?" and he lowers his voice even further. "It happens all the time…" and the audience knows at this point they are about to be let into one of life's most mystical insights.

"This is the best possible introduction that you're ever going to get to...polarization."

What a performer! He had the audience eating out of the palms of his hands. You have to give it to him, he understands that communication is nine-tenths of the idea.

You have to admire such rhetoric and showmanship. Gurus entirely justify the cost of the ticket because they give a great performance, while conning you that they're getting you to think "differently" ("out of the box," "out of the envelope," etc.) for a while. Of course they do get you to think differently. They allow you to flirt with big ideas, which sound nice but lead nowhere. Therein lies the danger. Because what these guru-shows don't do is lead to action. They're all about theory of management. No one actually goes and does anything as a result of having been to one of these shows. In fact, and this is important, they are actually a substitute for action. Just go to the talk on quality and somehow you'll have acquired quality. It's all built around thinking not doing.

Which is probably why these gurus always end a discussion with a feel-good moment. They stand on the stage, with one arm folded across their stomach holding the elbow of the other arm and a thoughtful and very caring finger to their chin, looking out into the audience and humbly saying, "Did I answer your question?"

Mat was about to take a look inside and get a peek at the great communicator when his cell phone rang.

He took the phone from his jacket pocket and answered in a low voice:

"Hello, Mat Durer."

"Mat, old boy. It's Brad again. Don't worry, this time I'm not driving."

"That's a relief," said Mat. "How are you feeling?"

"Oh, I'm fine," said Brad. "All recovered. I was just a little shocked at the time and had a bit of a bump on my head – that's all. But that's not the reason for my call. I thought I would just see if there was any help I could offer you?"

"Thanks Brad, but I'm not sure what you're getting at," said Mat.

"With the Oxytec pitch, of course. My sources tell me your firm is pitching against us for the Oxytec business and I just had to believe that you'd be in on the deal."

"As a matter of fact I am, Brad."

"Good, well we'll look forward to catching up with you. And if there's anything at all I can do for you, please don't hesitate to call," said Brad with mock concern.

"Well, that's extremely kind of you, Brad. I think I'm OK at the moment but you never know when I might need a bag carrier again."

That made it evens.

"Nice one Mat, your sense of humor hasn't deserted you. Mind you, leaving Hardings for another firm, that sure shows you've got a highly developed sense of the ridiculous. Oh, I nearly forgot. I caught up with the guys from Bond & Co. this morning for a breakfast meeting. We put on a great show and they were most appreciative. What's more I think Anthony has a meeting with Peter Smith at Oxytec lined up for sometime next week. I might go along if I have time. Would you like me to ask him anything?"

"I'll have to get back to you on that one."

"Sure thing, I'd be glad to help in any way I can. Bye bye, now."

"Bye, Brad. See you around the forum some time." Mat closed off the phone call and scowled; he hadn't found Brad's attempt at humor at all amusing.

At that moment, Eric appeared at his shoulder.

"Not bad news I hope," said Eric.

"No, no, not at all. Just a friend calling up for old time's sake," said Mat, wondering what Eric would make of the fact that he'd just had a call from one of the Hardings team.

"Well, let's go then. Before we get taken," Eric said, nodding toward the notice board announcing Justin Walters. "One thing I can't stand is management gospel."

Discovering "The flow"

Eric and Mat talked little on the flight to Michigan. Eric was clearly the kind of person who liked to work on flights. That suited Mat as he wanted to read through the provisional summary of the scope of the Oxytec project and get a handle for what they needed to cover. They did speak briefly when the stewardess brought round the tea and coffee.

However, Mat had wanted to find some way to ease his relations with Eric; they'd be working pretty closely over the next four weeks. He decided to break the silence.

"Do you know a Tactilis consultant called Danny O'Connor?" asked Mat, thinking this would be an innocuous place to start.

"Yes, we all know Danny, though few have met him," replied Eric. "Why?"

"It's just that when I was down in Houston one of the consultants suggested that I talk to him as he'd have some interesting insights on the way Tactilis worked. I left a message on his voicemail but he hasn't come back to me."

"Doesn't surprise me. Danny is a lone gun. He's never in our offices and rarely makes meetings."

"Why did the others think I should speak to him do you think?"

"Probably because he's very successful," said Eric with a quick smile. "If you want, I can call him and see if I can get him to contact you. Maybe that would help."

"Yes, that would be great."

"OK, I'll do it once we get to Alanstown."

Eric was about to turn back to his papers. Mat wanted to keep the conversation going.

"So what made you become a consultant?" he asked. "Why leave the comfort of a settled job with a major manufacturer and come to a world as difficult and unpredictable as this?"

"As I have said to other people: I wanted an adventure," said Eric. " I had reached the age when my children had left home and, frankly, my wife did not need me around any more. Our way of life was very comfortable. So I decided to do something for myself. Other people reach this stage earlier in life; for me, I did not. Perhaps I did not have that luxury before."

"It must have been very difficult giving everything up," Mat went on.

"Yes, and many people did not understand. But for me it was a release. I had felt for a long time that I wanted to find out something. I wanted to see whether I could help people to change, to think differently, and I wanted to do this all the time. It must have been the same for you, Mat – to leave Hardings?"

"There are some similarities," said Mat, avoiding a straight answer. "And how did your wife take it?"

"We are both happy with our lives," said Eric. The conversation closed at that point, both of them going back to their papers.

Once through the airport, Eric and Mat hired a car and set off for the Northern Utilities plant at Alanstown. It was about a 30-minute drive, and Eric spent much of the time on his cell phone talking to the Tactilis team on the ground and sorting out meetings with people at Northern Utilities. He also left a message for Danny O'Connor to call Mat.

"Don't suppose you've ever been to a water treatment facility before, have you?" Eric said as they arrived.

"No I haven't," replied Mat.

"Well, it's no different to a software company really, or a financial institution – it's still about getting people to work together to produce results. Of course, some consultants would rather work in a software house or a bank, but that's because they don't like getting their suits dirty. And they cover this up by saying this is "just blue collar." As though the same smart-world rules don't apply. Well, if you think that, you haven't reached first base – and never will."

Eric had stated the ground rules; Mat was suitably warned to get his attitude straight.

The treatment plant was on the edge of the metropolitan area. It consisted of a collection of low, red-brick buildings spread across a wide site surrounded by rusting barbed wire. Although the site was old, the company itself was a relatively new water and utilities business. It had been formed from seven smaller units serving the Michigan area. It was a classic example of a business morphing from the public to the private sector, with all the problems that brings.

Eric had been part of the original analysis team at Northern and knew his way round the site pretty well. After checking in at security, they made their way over to the Tactilis project office. When they arrived it was empty but had the same feel as the offices in Houston and Norway. Formica tables arranged in rows with PCs and printers and a couple of silver Toshiba laptops. Walls covered with posters headed: Items, Activities, Deliverables, Milestones, each broken down into simple short sentences and graphics. Photographs of team members and people around the plant – the latter looked like they were snapped while working and enjoyed the idea of someone taking an ordinary shot of them, the way you'd take a photo of one of your family around the home.

On a trestle table near the window were the obligatory tins of coffee and Coffee-mate together with cartons of Westminster tea bags and a bunch of sachets of Sweet 'N Low sweetener. Next to them were some Niceday Post-its, a half drunk bottle of water, 3M SprayMount, and – stacked at the end of the table – a very large roll of brown paper.

Eric and Mat found a place at the tables and put down their bags.

"Nobody around then," said Mat.

"They're all at customer meetings," replied Eric in a way that suggested he would have been surprised to see anyone back in the office this early in the day: it was just after three on a bright, late spring afternoon.

"I thought that the team were finishing up here," said Mat. "Isn't implementation all through?"

"Depends on what you mean by implementation. If you mean handing over the blueprint to the client then, yes, that's over. If you mean implementation as we do – staying until the last change is cemented in – then I'd guess that the guys are still at work making sure that everything's in place." Eric was points scoring again.

"OK, but all the costs have been taken out and the place is running smoothly, right, otherwise why would we be here?"

Eric carried on unpacking his briefcase.

"Any idiot can take out costs from a business, but you've got to be smart to make sure it still works afterward and even smarter to build it in a sustainable way. That's where we were at with Northern Utilities."

The comment felt like another taunt, as though Hardings would only understand the first cost-cutting phase of a project and that because of his past with Hardings, Mat would think that way to.

"Look, Eric, what's your problem?" asked Mat.

"I don't trust Hardings consultants," said Eric, still looking through the papers in his briefcase.

"That much is clear," said Mat. "But why not?" He stepped closer to Eric as though he was physically confronting him, the way that Frank had done to Mat in that office in Houston. It was time to take this thing head on. He was being treated by this balding old guy like some junior without any brains, or worse, some junior who thought he knew all the answers and had to be taken down a peg or two. "What is it they do so wrong?"

Eric turned to Mat; he also recognized the need to clear the air.

"It isn't just Hardings consultants I don't trust, it's anyone who comes along with a formula or a theory and tries to impose it on a business. That never works. There are a whole lot of technology solutions that go wrong because they come in with a pre-defined solution which ignores what's unique about the customer's business. It's the same with management solutions. You can't impose a formula because a formula has no internal systems.

"Whenever things have gone wrong," he continued, "it's been because we've assumed we knew the answer before we arrived. It's so easy to look at a business and say, 'Oh, it's in the manufacturing sector so it must be suffering from manufacturing problems.' Never make assumptions. Always base your solutions on known facts – facts that you've gathered yourself. Don't take the client's word for things. The client might tell you that the problem is staffing levels or poor productivity or poorly trained staff. They might be right, they might be wrong. What they say could be based on poor data – or simply on hunches or prejudices. Always check the facts yourself."

Eric was getting a little red in the face, like he was getting onto a stream of thought that went very deep inside him.

"Take a look around you," he said. "Does this look like an operation where we impose on clients? The hell, no."

He paused.

"It's all about people," he said, gesturing at the photos. "And their simple, banal, everyday acts."

"I get that, so why do you think it's beyond me to understand what you do?" said Mat.

"Because it's about humbling yourself," said Eric, straight into Mat's face. "And I'm not sure you can do that."

Mat felt that river ice shift from under him. Maybe he couldn't. He hesitated.

"I have come a long way, Eric. I have given up a lot and been through a lot. So don't say I can't do something I want to do. I am here so that you can show me the way, remember?"

Eric turned away a little; it was the first moment of acceptance he'd shown Mat. Like a fighter who, having stood toe to toe, turns away to think of his next move.

"OK, I'll show you. Let's get back to this room, this empty room," said Eric.

"Like I said," he continued, "the guys are out there working with clients – maintenance supervisors, production assistants – and they're coaching them. Helping them to understand situations, making the job of work more easy. They're not telling them how to do things; they're letting them have the first say. They're subsumed into the workflow here. And once they're in the workflow, they can start helping."

He paused for emphasis.

"Outside the flow, you just don't understand."

"How do I get in the flow?" said Mat. He had nailed one small part of Eric and the coach in Eric was now responding to the pupil.

"You have to connect with the people. You have to get them to talk to you about what they do on an equal basis. That means dispelling any notion that you're the expert. Often, I'll say to them: 'I'm not going to tell you anything about your business. You are the expert at your business, not me. In fact, the last thing you need is more experts. There are plenty of people in your organization with over ten years' experience. All I can do is focus your knowledge and understanding in a slightly new way, so you'll find solutions for yourself.'

"After that, you have to understand that the flow you're trying to get into is all about people's behaviors. It's a journey by road as opposed to rail – and it's not straight down the track, either. It's down the byways and lanes. The ways most experts ignore. There's a lot of social work to it; dealing with people's emotions – often negative emotions, taking people with you. The rate of change of an organization is really governed by the slowest person not the fastest."

"That makes it sound touchy-feely and random. Like I'm some form of counselor," said Mat.

"That's because you're still stuck in the world of management fads, and you think that dealing with people's real problems is beneath you."

Eric had got resentful again and was pacing round a table.

"OK, give me some feel for how to get in," said Mat. "I really want to find out what's going on here."

"To get people to open up, give them a quick win. Something small where they can feel the difference, like a meeting. Find some way to get people talking together, and talking about their common ground, and pretty soon they'll be suggesting ways to one another about how to improve things. Sounds so trivial, doesn't it? And you say to yourself, 'X company is a world-class business with operations in 20 countries, so of course their production and maintenance team will be talking to one another.' You want to bet?"

Eric now sat on the corner of a table and picked up a green felt marker pen. He used it almost like a conductor uses a baton, emphasizing thoughts and moods.

"I know all this because I was once in a client company. And we were working with a Tactilis team. And they got people in my organization to change. I saw for myself that people could change, and that organizations could get better and that there was a method to it, a real method not some management fad. These guys weren't talking to top management, they were changing things in the flow of business. I wanted to be part of that, too, so I looked for a new job."

Mat looked down at his feet, a little embarrassed at Eric's revelation. Eric took this as a sign that Mat wasn't listening and stood even taller.

"Remember that guru we saw this morning?" he said. "He'd convince you. Maybe, that's what I should do, too."

With that, Eric stood up on one of the formica tables and arched his body a little as though on stage. Mat was used to most moves but this was great, there was no holding the man back. Eric began to perform:

"We all have a set of values and beliefs, you, me, the supervisor, everyone," he said pointing around his imaginary audience. "These core values govern the way we act and the way we act determines consequences. Essentially there is a set of relationships I like to call the 'ABC set of relationships' – Antecedents govern Behavior govern Consequences – but it's the same thing."

With his green marker pen, Eric drew an imaginary A, B and C in the air and pointed to them whenever he needed emphasis.

"Now, the thing about this set of relationships," he said, jabbing upwards with the pen, "is that because we humans don't like messing around with our core values or antecedents – they're wired in deep after all – we have set up a system that protects them from the C word, consequences. And the result is that behaviors never get changed. We protect our antecedents by using soft data – rather than hard facts – to shape our judgments about the consequences of our actions. So, for example, we don't listen to a tape recording of a meeting, we rely on our memory of it – colored as that is by assumptions and inferences and emotional baggage such as the fact that we didn't like the moderator or that the meeting room was too hot. In most cases, this soft data will support our motives for a certain action – the moderator, we tell ourselves, was stupid – and we will carry on behaving in a certain way. In those troublesome cases where the soft data doesn't suit our motivation, we go into defensive mode or denial and simply cover things up. Maybe we heard the moderator incorrectly or maybe the moderator had got us wrong: 'if only he knew how smart I was, he wouldn't keep dismissing my opinions!'"

Eric was reaching his summit; his life's work was being settled into a few sentences. He looked down at Mat and his voice was steady but strong and full, like this was all he had to give.

"Now if the ABC relationship is true, what needs changing is the antecedents or values, and to do that we have to present ourselves with hard facts. Businesses have to be based around systems that deliver hard facts or what I call valid information, data that's been verified. We have to present that openly and to the people who matter most, those who have generated the data. The difference between Tactilis and every other consulting firm is that we show the data to the people who create it. Every other consulting firm shows the data to the board, which then has to react to it with a set of remedies that in effect do nothing to change behaviors."

He paused for emphasis.

"The key to changing behaviors is measurement."

Jab went the pen at Mat. Jab. Jab. Jab.

"Measure performance and then tell people the results. Sooner or later these hard facts can't be denied and the antecedents start to change. People stop thinking that maintenance are a load of time-wasters and realize that they don't have the information they need to do the job better – when that happens the whole organization can cut 20 percent off its costs."

Eric now got down from the table.

"OK, that's the official version," he said. "Now let's go and walk the walk."

Mat was surprised at Eric's outburst and by his attempt at theatricality. While it wasn't quite up to the guru's performance, it struck Mat that Eric had felt an instinctive need to find some more powerful form of expression. Like the expression had to release the idea. One idea implemented is worth more than all the great ideas that remain unfulfilled – that was a Tactilis theme. But ideas only gain credence in expression.

Feeling the flow for real

Getting into the "flow" of work – the phrase kept kicking in Mat's brain. It was right in the same territory as the five-minute snapshot. It was about getting to the same level of intimacy and experience. Mat was excited by that; the five-minute snapshot wasn't an isolated discovery, it was tied into a whole way of seeing a business – a way that people like Eric knew because they had experienced it. And the experience made them passionate about it, like it was something you could only really get to if you'd been there. Mat wanted to find where that place was and with it some way to capture the associated ideas.

Over the next 48 hours, Mat and Eric, sometimes together and sometimes separately, talked to people of all levels and skills across the NU plant. They met technicians, supervisors, call handlers, secretaries, managers, and customer service reps. They immersed themselves in these people's stories, going into their flow.

Among the first of the NU staff Mat met on his own was a water treatment plant supervisor called Sally. She was black and probably in her late forties, though she looked younger. She wore her hair in narrow braids with brightly colored beads on the end. Eric told Mat that Sally was a quarter American Indian and very proud of her heritage. She certainly had striking looks and a charisma that most would die for. She was independent and not afraid to speak her mind.

"I was thinking, 'here we go again, someone else trying to tell you how to do your job,'" she said to Mat about her first impressions of Tactilis. "And I really felt it was going to be a waste of time and money. I did not see how they would be able to capture what it is that we do and understand what it is that we do. So my first impression was that it was just something else to go through to get control back of my plant."

But Sally was also clever and articulate and she kept making telling observations like: "I learned that if you want something, the first thing that you've got to have is an action that you've got to get done."

Sounds simple enough, but if you think about it, this is a pretty key insight: planning means nothing if it isn't tied to a specific list of actions.

Mat kept talking and gently probing, not asking her to give some easy testimonial but to tell him about the reality of her work. And then he hit a story.

Sally was responsible for this treatment plant and she knew it like the back of her hand – she'd been working there for the best part of 20 years. She had worked her way up from an operator and was now responsible for the whole plant.

Then one day her worst nightmare hit: there was a brown water incident and then another and another. People were calling non-stop and they were all complaining of brown water.

"Yeah, I can really remember it vividly," she said. "Last year at the beginning of January we started trying to do a chlorine reduction program. It was really a cost-saving measure but the plants were not equipped to drastically reduce the chlorine, and we had some brown water instances inside our plant.

"Well, next thing we knew the phone lines were lighting up. The citizens were constantly complaining. It was on the news, 'Brown water everywhere.' While we were in a meeting one day we got a message that the soda factory had to shut down production because the water was so brown it was causing problems. There were also problems at the hospital… And they were mostly coming from our plant."

Coming from her plant meant that it was her responsibility and Mat didn't get the impression from talking to her that she'd take that lightly. Which of course she didn't. Sally set about finding the cause and it led her straight back to the cost saving. Lowering the chlorine levels meant that they were not oxidizing any iron and manganese in the water.

"And if you don't oxidize them in the sedimentation basis and the pre-treatment process," she said, "it's too late. It all goes out in the distribution system. That's why we had brown water calls all over the place."

Sally knew in her bones she'd found the source of the problem – and that's when the work started.

"I thought I had identified the cause, but nobody wanted to listen: they were focusing on the cost savings and did not really identify the problem in the plant. They were all trying to tell me that it was phosphate or something else. I kept saying it was the chlorine, and they kept saying, 'It can't be that, it can't be. It's got to be the phosphate doing this with the element.' I was trying to say that both plants have the same type of phosphate, that I'd been here for 18 years and knew we'd had this phosphate for over ten – that it could not be a phosphate problem."

Trouble was that Sally was not being listened to. The company had brought in an expert to look at the problem and he was a qualified scientist. How was an uneducated black woman going to know better?

"I didn't have a college education or a science degree like him. So people assumed he was right. He had more influence and he was trying to say it was about distribution, but I was trying to tell him that it was chlorine."

They were going nowhere and the brown water problems were on the increase. And then something unexpected happened.

"We were in this round-robin meeting," said Sally. "I had been made to feel that my presence wasn't really required but that I could attend if I wanted. Anyway, we got in there and everyone was giving their opinion as to what the cause of the problem was, and then the meeting moderator said: 'No, we are going to do this based on the facts, on real data... Let's do away with opinion, let's just deal with the facts and let's work out where we need to get those facts from and what we need to do.' Suddenly, the whole thing changed. The meeting wasn't about opinions any more, it was down to data. And when we looked at the data, they had to agree: everything pointed to the chlorine level."

A few days later, they put the chlorine levels back up and the brown water calls all but disappeared.

"I think that day," said Sally, "it hit really hit home what using data was all about."

Sally wasn't angry or even resentful about this incident. She had taken something positive out of it; she had even come to understand other people's motivations better.

"Sometimes," she said, "you come up with an idea and you want to see it work; you don't want to say that it didn't work. Instead of honing in on the right problem you look at other possibilities. I think the two or three people who wanted to keep me quiet knew what the problem really was, but could only admit it after we focused on the facts.

"It wasn't done intentionally, it was done really to optimize chemical dosage, but I think that we all learned from this that you don't use your plants to experiment with."

Sally had given Mat a theme to work with: how data set

people free. It set people free of status or qualifications, assumptions, and inferences. Mat remembered how, back in Houston, CJ had been worried about being part of some measurement program. CJ should have seen the guys up here at NU. They were being given the data to measure themselves by, rather than have others use data to measure them. That was the big difference; that was what was so liberating, so empowering.

Like with Cassie. She also worked in water treatment – at a smaller plant on the other side of town to Sally's. She knew that getting information into people's hands could make a difference to their outlook. What she hadn't realized was that no one had bothered to check what facts were being given to which people.

"Once I started having my daily meetings," she said, "and I started utilizing the tools like key performance indicators, or KPIs, things began to change. I realized that we had KPIs in the plant that I hadn't recognized as KPIs until then. Before it was like this, it was just information we had in the plant. But then I started noticing through the data how you can start focusing your time and your days and your meetings."

Mat wondered how many of the CEOs he'd met would associate with Cassie's remarks about KPIs. To her what mattered is that people listened to the facts.

"Suddenly everybody got more focused in their daily meetings about what they actually had to do," she said to Mat. "They would be held accountable for things, too, because the next day we would review the actions and we could start seeing the things that had happened and things we could take off the list and then we started developing a new list. So every week we were seeing what we've achieved. The meetings also gave us all a chance to network together and other people put their ideas out and it bonded us closer together as a team it seemed."

Hold that thought… Facts and data aren't just setting people free they're also changing the way meetings are held. Like with Sally's story, Cassie noted that introducing facts into a meeting meant that people got things done, easier and quicker. Now it wasn't all about opinions, it was simpler and more straightforward. Behaviors had begun to change. Particularly when the information was spread to everyone.

"Everyone saw the data," said Cassie. "We posted all the data daily. Now we have a board and we update the KPIs, the parameters, all the time, just to let the operators know how we are doing for the state, for the city. I now know where the real problems are."

The result of the redistribution was that no one was left feeling threatened by data – which is the usual liberal, romantic view of things. They were actually being extended by it.

Such a simple story – feedback on what you're doing improves performance. That was the way to engineer the five minutes and unleash people into the flow of work: create the continuous feedback of hard facts. Simple, yet how few companies, or organizations, or even *individuals* actually do feedback based on facts.

Two cheese melts and fries

"So how did you get on with Janice Richie?" asked Eric.

He and Mat were sitting in Draco's, a small deli a few hundred yards from the entrance to the Alanstown plant. They had ordered toasted cheese and ham sandwiches with french fries. They had been busy for two days, talking to people, going through milestone charts, re-piecing the project at NU. Mat and Eric were still a little distant; but working together for the past couple of days had given Eric the opportunity to witness that Mat was capable and bright and most of all wanted to understand the mechanisms that had turned the NU Alanstown plant into a success.

"OK," said Mat. "She's an interesting woman. Real upfront about the demands that being part of a project like this places on you as a manager. She was talking about the physical exhaustion of just talking to people all the time. Sixteen hours a day talking to staff and union officials and colleagues. It was obvious that she found it really emotional work."

"Yeah, Janice is a really good lady," said Eric. "Very conscientious, and pretty brave, too. She worked on the project team that installed a single common IT platform across the business. When they first asked her to run part of it she refused – unless the senior management recognized it was a change program not just a technology one."

"TWO CHEESE MELTS AND FRIES!" the young guy with a peaked cap shouted from behind the counter.

Mat went over to pick them up and brought them back to the table. Eric carefully squeezed a little tomato ketchup on to the side of his plate.

"She told her bosses: 'You can't take 140 stand-alone systems and transfer them into one without having a huge impact on people's power bases.'"

"Yes, she told me that story, too," said Mat. "She understood the political side of the project. Setting the data free transformed work for people like Sally and Cassie, and that was great. But Janice also recognized the flip side: the reality of why people protected data within their departments. Data was power."

"Too right, in a business like Northern Utilities where each of the VPs was used to running their own patch and therefore their own data, a single integrated system spelled nightmares. Suddenly, everyone got to see all the inappropriate things that were going on in finance, or supply chain, or procurement. All those areas of business that are often to one side, which nobody really pays that much attention to because they don't think they know anything about it."

"That's the impression I got," said Mat. "She told me that it truly shook the organization up. Especially in a department like finance who weren't at all used to other people getting a look at what was going on."

Eric took a bite from his cheese melt and wiped his mouth carefully with a paper napkin.

"OK, well I'm glad you had a chance to meet with Janice.

This afternoon we'll talk to some people who were part of the IT project."

The limits of perfection

Riordan Hanif was waiting for Mat and Eric in his office. It was at the corner of the building and was light and bright.

"Come in there, Eric. Take a seat please," he said as they walked in.

He greeted Eric and then introduced himself to Mat. They sat and discussed the various merits of cheese melts at Draco's Deli and then got down to business.

Riordan was an experienced manager with a long history in the business; in fact, Riordan had worked his way up from a field engineer all the way into senior management. He was a square-bodied guy with a heavy scar across his forehead and a refreshingly simple outlook on life: he just wanted to get it done and then move on to the next job. So as one could predict, he'd proved a very capable project manager. His focus was on action not perfection. For, as Riordan had discovered, perfectionism can undermine your business sometimes.

Riordan was responsible for actually installing the single integrated system that would act as a common base to drive and calibrate work. It all came to a head over one weekend: the Go Live weekend.

"Everybody was in over that weekend," said Riordan. "I am no techie and I couldn't help the IT engineers, but I felt it was important that I was there to make decisions if they came up. And you know those kinds of events... We had over 100 people in the building, transferring files and a lot of them were in for 48 hours straight. It was classic intense stuff. High excitement. No time to go out to get food – living off take-out pizzas and that kind of thing.

"In essence what we had is all these systems, 140 standalones, and we had to just shut them down and then start up the single new platform on Monday morning. So that weekend was a very critical weekend and if you've got people who weren't on board and were not going to get their tasks done it would start to cascade on everyone else.

"Well we hit this problem on Saturday evening," said Riordan. "One of the guys Geoff, a top IT engineer, just lost it. I had to order him out of the building."

"Why?" asked Mat. "What happened?"

Riordan got up and walked the room, like the story needed a little animation to do it justice.

"Well, the truth was that he was getting everybody else spooked. IT engineers are their own worst enemies sometimes. Engineers will not throw the switch until they think everything's 100 percent; damn the timeline, damn how much money is being spent. To them it's got to be perfect. Well, I'm sorry, boys, but not on my project. We had that 80/20 rule going and we were going to make it stick. By golly we were going make it stick."

The 80/20 rule was one of Tactilis's basic beliefs: do first, don't wait for perfection. If something is 80 percent right then put it into action and you'll build in the remaining 20 percent on the way. At the heart of this simple belief is the recognition that you will *only* reach perfection through putting something into action. Those systems that are built to be perfect from day one, they will always fail. They lack that magic ingredient: action. We've come to believe perfectionism is something that can be installed off the shelf. It can't. Riordan was discovering that and also discovering what a useful excuse perfectionism can be.

"This guy Geoff kept saying to me 'the data inside the system wasn't right,'" said Riordan. "And I kept saying back, 'Well, I know it's not right, it's never been right.' You know, you've got 140 stand-alone electricity systems and lots of people out in the field feeding in different data. So of course it wasn't a perfect match up. But the thing was, he couldn't make up his mind which one to pick.

"So I said, 'Well, pick one, Geoff.' Like 'I don't care which one it is because, you know what, you have to start somewhere.'

"In hindsight, he now realizes he wasn't being too smart at the time."

"Or he was being *too* smart – period," thought Mat.

"So we got him out of the building and we went on with the installation. And, you know what, everything turned out just fine." Riordan continued, "I met with him on the Monday and I went through what had happened, and we both recognized that he'd frozen because he was tired and stressed. The stress led him to become so fixated on making everything perfect that he could never really nail down the decision."

Eric, who'd been quiet up to this point, got to his feet too and he and Riordan had this weird moment together, when they sort of moved around one another, like they were two kids shadow boxing or a pair of adults getting to dance.

"The key is to get people acting," said Eric. "There are always a thousand excuses not to act. But you have to get people acting and moving and then start measuring. Move, then measure. Don't wait for the perfect storm."

The scene was being stitched into Mat's mind. These two middle-aged guys getting all excited about doing things, about making things happen.

Mat understood. Action is the magic ingredient. Action is what opens things up.

I have to agree. I remember meeting a very senior London moneybroker once. He ran an organization that was trading in millions every few seconds. He was a soccer fanatic too as I recall and was on the board of a major soccer club. I remember how he said that some mornings he'd go into the office and he'd have no idea which way the money markets were going to go. So what was his answer? He'd say it didn't matter, just start trading, on the pound or the dollar. Either way, but just start trading. Because the only way you're going to know which way the markets are moving is when you're part of the action.

It's fashionable in some quarters to talk about the "knowing–doing gap." The truth is, you can't know outside doing.

Chicago taxi driver No. 454767

Two days later, Mat was sitting in the lobby of a Westin hotel in Chicago. He and Eric had completed their research at NU and were now supposed to join Katz and Nancy at an Oxytec plant in Germany – more precisely, at a town called Erfurt, in what used to be East Germany. But Mat had to come via Chicago. Max had called him and asked him to meet him there.

The reason for the meeting had not been made clear on the phone. And when it took place, Max was in a hurry and only had time to give a rough sketch of what he wanted.

Max said he'd spoken briefly to Peter Smith at Oxytec and Peter had suggested that it would be a good thing to meet his assistant Shakira Price. Max believed this was a genuine steer and that it was ideal ground for Mat. "She's bound to be one of those ultra females you're used to handling, Mat. I think you'll understand her language better than the others on the team. So I want you to make the call to her and set the thing up."

That was about it. Just call Shakira and find out what Oxytec wanted. No problem for a man of Mat's caliber! It concerned Mat that if the others found out about it they might feel left out or jumped over. Perhaps that's why Max had called him to a meeting on his own.

More importantly, Mat worried at the apparent ad hoc nature of the arrangements. He thought about the way Hardings would be going about the pitch. He knew for a fact that they would have set up meetings not only with Peter Smith but also with the team from Bond & Co. And for Mat, the investment bankers were probably going to hold the key to who won the pitch. They wouldn't influence things openly, of course, they would simply make the casual suggestion, the loaded remark, which would leave no one in doubt as to whom they favored. And it would be conclusive.

What's more, Brad would have a whole team working constantly gathering data, comparative data which would show, conclusively, that the only way forward for Oxytec was the one that Hardings would be proposing. Above all, Hardings believed in security in numbers.

How could Tactilis ever hope to win in these circumstances?

Mat didn't have an answer – not yet, anyway. But he did feel that his time at Northern Utilities had opened other new doors of perception for him. Spending time with people up and down the company, experiencing their work and insights, had made Mat aware of the flow in a business. The real flow inside a business which got the work done and which often ran like an underground stream. He'd felt genuinely excited by this experience. Furthermore, discovering the idea of flow had given him a sense of having learned a new skill. It wasn't just an intellectual skill, it was a physical thing; like learning to play a musical instrument.

Mat was fascinated by this physical sensation. He thought about diving under the tutelage of Jean-Claude Daran and how that had made him feel.

He also thought about something a friend from school days had once said to him. The friend, Richard, was English and had joined the Army as an officer cadet. The training involved ten weeks intensive training at Sandhurst. But the interesting thing which Richard had pointed out to him was that at the end of this time, the cadets truly became officers. In other words, they were real leaders of men. Yet the same people might spend four or five years at trainee level in business and emerge with little or no leadership qualities at all.

The difference, Richard had said to him, was that the Sandhurst experience was physical as well as mental. That caused the change.

Mat recalled that insight now. It was like the skills he had learned at NU were part of the same phenomenon. They had a physical dimension, even though they led to an alternative intellectual understanding of how to improve performance.

Together with the five-minute narrative, the idea of flow had given Mat a new way to see a business. Right now he had to believe that these new skills would add up to more than Brad or his team could come up with. It wasn't much to hope for, but he had said to himself, "let the pitch decide," and that was how he was going to play it.

So Mat made the call to Oxytec and set up a meeting with Shakira for the beginning of the following week, since Shakira was also traveling until then. That seemed fine and it would give Mat time to work in whatever he gathered from the meeting into the pitch presentation. For some reason he got the feeling that he would be leading the ultimate pitch to Oxytec.

After a while, Mat went out on to the hotel driveway to wait for a taxi to the airport. He told the porter he was waiting and placed his overnight bag and attaché case on the ground. It was a warm sunny afternoon in Chicago. The breeze fluttered through the flags above the entrance. Mat felt good about being on his way to join the pitch team. He was going to prove something.

The taxi driver helped put his luggage in the trunk. He was a big guy, wearing blue jeans, a blue jeans jacket, and a blue peaked denim cap. The slogan on his T-shirt read: "I've seen them crash before, but never actually burn."

"Where are we going sir?" asked the driver.

"The airport please."

"OK, sure thing," replied the driver and he pulled off the hotel apron and out onto the busy routes around Chicago.

Mat looked at the driver. He had long gray hair and big sideburns. Mat also noticed that the driver's blue peaked denim cap was decorated with a multitude of Harley Davidson pins. That was an interesting start. He was the sort of person you just had to talk to.

It turned out that the driver was the head of the local Hell's Angel chapter. He'd driven his bike "all over the United States, many times." Once, he'd driven to San Francisco in 72 hours – only stopping for gas.

"Of course, we had a little chemical assistance on the way, if you get my meaning," he said.

"Why did you make the trip so fast?" asked Mat. "I mean

it sounds like the sort of journey you could spend a few weeks enjoying."

"We were called to the meeting, sir," replied the driver. "It was a *mandatory* meeting."

The way that the driver pronounced "mandatory" was enough to convince Mat that in the Hell's Angels mandatory definitely meant "be there."

Mat had never been this chatty with a real live Hell's Angel before; it was an opportunity to ask the question he'd often wondered. What's more there was a thin metal grille between him and the driver.

"Maybe a stupid question," Mat said. "But what's the attraction of being a Hell's Angel?"

The driver turned his head to look in incredulity at Mat. They were driving close to 60 on the freeway and his gaze was fixed on his passenger.

He said one word: "Brotherhood."

Daring to relax

Marianne had been looking forward to spending the weekend with Anthony and Sagradio Elliott. To her, the invitation was a sign of belonging – or rather of being asked back in to the fold. It would also be great for her business. What's more it would be exciting being part of such a glamorous boat race in Miami.

The Elliotts owned an ocean racing yacht, *Masquerade*, and had entered her in the Maxi Yacht Regatta at Miami Beach. They were taking their other sailing yacht, *Espresso*, down to Miami to watch the racing and had asked Mat and Marianne to join them.

Despite Marianne's excitement, Mat was less comfortable about the weekend. In fact, he was tense about it. In part this was because he felt it was going back to the old world, the world he had left behind. He was also filled with a foreboding that this was not the right place to be. His rational mind put it down to feeling guilty at spending time off while his colleagues were working on the pitch. In fact, he had brought some of his research from the Alanstown meetings with him in his attaché case to work on if he had time. Finally, he felt uneasy that he was seeing Anthony socially at the weekend and then planning how to beat Hardings in a pitch during the week. Of course, Anthony was far too much of a gentleman to ever mention work over a weekend like this.

But another part of Mat, the sixth sense he had become more attuned to in recent months, felt a real sense of apprehension. He felt an atmosphere around him as they drove to the weekend, as though something was about to happen: the way birds stop singing just before an eclipse.

As a consequence of his sense of responsibility to the pitch team and his overall misgivings, Mat told Marianne that he would not be able to spend the whole weekend with her, but would need to fly back to Europe on the Sunday. It was a compromise and, although not altogether happy at the result, Marianne felt it was the best she was going to achieve. At least she would get to be a guest on board Anthony and Sagradio's yacht.

Mat and Marianne arrived at the marina at about 7.30 p.m. They passed the crowds milling around the Sailing World Racing Village looking at the boats, parked and walked over to where Anthony's yacht was moored. For them, it felt a little like old times in the Turks: big boats, big sky above, and before them an azure sea.

Anthony and Sagradio were on their yacht *Espresso* and welcomed Mat and Marianne aboard. Everybody seemed to get on well. Anthony shook Mat's hand and was genuinely pleased to see him. Sagradio had given each of them a big hug and then she and Marianne got into a huddle to talk about Harrison and other things. The two had been friends for a long time, in fact it was Sagradio who originally introduced Marianne's gallery business to Hardings.

Mat had stayed with Anthony in the lounge area of the yacht. Although the yacht wasn't enormous, it was comfortable and impeccably furnished. There were soft blue carpets through the living areas, sensible chairs and wooden furnishings, a mix of art and photographs on the wall and a bronze bust of Sagradio at the far end of the room. It was a yacht to enjoy, rather than a statement of one's power or status (though arguably all yachts are status symbols). It was definitely a weekend craft.

It's interesting the divide we create between work and leisure. I sometimes think we try to create as much distance between them as possible. It's a very modern notion. The ancients never considered leisure time as something distinct from the rest of your existence. It was all one. In the past the distinction was that in work time you did things you had to do to survive. In leisure time, you did things for yourself, things that had meaning for yourself, say like the pursuit of beauty or writing poetry. And even more interestingly it was the quality of the uses to which you put your leisure time that marked out your status, not the job you worked at. Everyone could do enough to survive, but philosophy, politics, art, poetry, music; these were matters for real admiration, the pursuit of beauty.

Anthony and Mat made themselves a couple of Martinis and Anthony started explaining his fascination with ocean racing.

"It's such a change from the office, a very different set of people and problems," said Anthony. "Physical problems such as how to cope with weather conditions. There's always something unforeseen happening which requires instant ingenuity. There's also the fun of being in a closeknit team who are all pulled together in a big, dramatic race. But above all, of course, there's the ocean itself. Dealing with the unknown – that's the great challenge."

"Yes, I know what you mean," said Mat. "I found the same on Grand Turk, diving everyday, literally going deeper into a strange and different world. It changes you..."

At that point, Sagradio and Marianne came back into the room, laughing, arm in arm with one another. The conversation moved to Marianne's business, how well it was doing and how pleased that Anthony was to be able to have the chance to talk to her about some art for Hardings' newly refurbished offices.

"Nothing too grand, you know, Marianne. Intriguing, I suppose is what we are after," Anthony had said and they talked about different styles and what the latest Hardings offices looked like.

After that, they all went to their cabins to change for the evening ahead. Once inside, Marianne grabbed hold of Mat's arm and pulled him close to her. She whispered to him:

"She's pregnant... Sagradio's pregnant again," she said in a hushed voice, as though this was the most important and controversial news she could give him.

"You're joking," said Mat, feeling compelled to copy her hushed tones.

"No, I'm not. I wouldn't joke about something like that. She's over the moon about it."

They got dressed in silence. The news had changed their mood. They were no longer simply thinking about the evening in front of them; it was their whole future they had been reminded of.

However, neither Mat nor Marianne would let their emotions show in public. They were guests of the Elliotts and needed to respect that courtesy. You and I might call it putting on a brave face.

They spent the evening with a group of about 20 other boat owners, sponsors, and VIP guests who had been invited to a small party on board the *Espresso*. It was an enjoyable time. No one asked the awkward question, "So what do you do?" since it was assumed that everyone was past the career stage when such things were necessary to enquire after. You obviously did something important otherwise you wouldn't be there. Marianne was dressed in white Armani trousers and a silk Hermès blouse; Sagradio in a soft patterned dress that left her shoulders bare. The two of them quite stole the show and that night Marianne looked just like Jackie O.

Anthony was the charming host and took great delight in preparing his specialty – crêpes suzette. He held the pan in his left hand, gently tilting its face so that the pancake mixture was warmed by the yellow and purple flames. The scent of orange curaçao and brandy filled the evening air.

World Maxi Racing Regatta
Miami Beach, Florida
Weather Report

Severe Weather Warning

Hurricane Christina, currently expected to hit Cuba and Western Haiti at between 3.00 p.m. and 5.00 p.m., appears to be changing direction. Race organizers are therefore issuing this severe weather warning to all competitors as a caution only. Although Christina is not forecast to travel over the Miami Beach areas, race organizers will keep you informed.

Early morning call

Mat had spent most of the night awake. The swell had picked up and even within the calm confines of the Miami Beach Marina, the *Espresso* was listing from side to side. Nothing violent, yet a noticeable change from the calm waters of the evening before.

Mat looked up at the ceiling of the cabin. The light was just beginning to seep in through the blinds. Marianne lay asleep beside him, her face turned toward him, the curve of her breast against the white sheets, her breaths regular and peaceful. He thought of the previous night and how she had rolled away from him when he had tried to hold her. She had felt cold and distant. He understood that the news about Sagradio's pregnancy had upset her, but how could he do anything about it? It was fine for Anthony and Sagradio, but right now Mat wasn't able to commit to Marianne. He was too unsettled in so many other areas of his life.

Suddenly his cell phone started ringing and he grabbed it rapidly to prevent it from waking Marianne. His heart raced a little. For a moment, he didn't want to answer; the sense of apprehension he had felt on the way to the weekend was still with him. It was just a phone call wasn't it?

"Hello, Mat Durer," he said.

"Hi *schatz*, it's me," said Anneka.

She sounded frightened and tense. She was obviously in pain.

"They've had the results of my tests back and the indications weren't clear. So the team here want to carry out an exploratory operation. I suspect they think that it's the pancreas that's causing the problems."

"What do you think?" asked Mat.

"I just don't know any more… Anyhow, they're going to keep me in for a further week's observation. Could be that in that time things settle down. They've put me on a new course of medication, which should help. All I can do is wait, I guess."

"Seems like it, professor. Is there anything I can do to help in the meantime?"

"No, no. I'm fine really. I shouldn't have bothered you. I was just feeling a bit sorry for myself. That's all."

"No, you're not bothering me. And I need to know about these things. I'll call again in a day or so and in the meantime promise you'll call me if you get any more news?"

"Sure, *schatz*, I promise."

Mat was shaken. Anneka had been in and out of hospital for several weeks and now they were talking about surgery.

He put the phone back down on the shelf beside him. Marianne moved over a little.

"Who was that?" she asked, her eyes still closed.

"It was Anneka," he said. "The medical team at MGH say they want to carry out an exploratory operation."

"So why was she calling you at 7.30 in the morning?" said Marianne.

"I think she was just scared and feeling a bit lonely," said Mat.

Contacts and races

"Looks like we're in for a bit of rough weather," Anthony had said as Mat and Marianne joined him and Sagradio at the breakfast table. "Hurricane Christina has turned north a little and we may catch the very tail end of her as she moves up the coast. Shouldn't interfere with the regatta, but it might make for more interesting racing."

"How exciting," said Sagradio, pleased that something unplanned was about to heighten the tempo of the weekend.

She was looking stunning, even more radiant than usual. Mat wondered whether he thought this because of what he knew or whether she really was blossoming.

"It could be," replied Anthony.

"Not too exciting I hope," said Marianne.

"No, I'm sure not. Just a little rough weather. That doesn't worry you, does it Marianne?" Anthony replied, almost teasingly.

"No, I was just thinking about Mat, that's all. He's had a phone call from his sister and he needs to make sure she can get hold of him on his cell phone if she needs to."

Mat looked across at Marianne, slightly embarrassed that she had mentioned his sister to Anthony. Her comments were true, though. He'd said to Marianne earlier that he was worried about reception on the boat. What he was really saying was that he was worried about being on a boat and only contactable via cell phone at this time. It was all part of his general unease about the weekend.

"Oh dear," said Anthony. "Nothing serious I hope, Mat."

"I'm afraid it is," said Mat. "Do you remember when we bumped into each other in the Burlington Club I said I had been to see my sister at MGH? Well she's just been re-admitted and is obviously in quite a lot of pain. They're even talking about surgery."

"Yes, I can see that is quite serious. Who's looking after her at MGH?"

"I'm not sure. I just met one of the medical team briefly."

"Well, as I said in Boston, if you want me to get on to someone at MGH for you, then I'd be very happy to. I know the senior surgeon there very well and I'm sure he could help out."

"Thanks," said Mat, "the more I think about it the more I think I should talk to someone about her condition."

"Fine," said Anthony. "I can give him a call when I get back into the office and see what I can set up for you."

"And the weather," said Mat. "Do you think the hurricane is going to hit us here?"

"Oh no. I'm sure not. It's just the weathermen taking sensible precautions. What they really mean is that we're likely to get rather more interesting conditions than we'd bargained for."

"But you can't be sure," said Mat.

"No. That's why it's far better to be warned in advance. So that we can make allowances."

Anthony was doing his best to make light of the weather, but Mat was still unconvinced. The weather warning was right in line with his premonition. He didn't like this sense of having premonitions, much less of them beginning to be proved right.

After breakfast the four of them went over to Sailing World Racing Village to take a look at Anthony's racing yacht, *Masquerade of Marblehead*. She was named after the start point of the oldest ocean race in America, the Marblehead to Halifax ocean race.

Masquerade was taking part in the Maxi Yacht Racing Regatta which had attracted entrants from as far away as Italy and Sweden. She was a majestic boat, designed by Frank Stapleton of Boston Marine and skippered by Ron Colins, a hugely experienced mariner who had been part of the *Stars and Stripes* America's Cup program. (Anthony Elliott was only ever going to recruit the best.)

Ron was supported by a huge cast of experts: from the grinders who worked the primary winches to the headsail trimmers who ran the headsails and spinnakers for maximum speed, to the mastman, pitman, bowman, helmsman, rules advisor, and performance manager. Not to mention, of course, all the shoreside support that this type of boat needs. It was like a Formula One Racing team, all geared up and ready to charge. And they needed to be: over the weekend they would be facing some of the strongest competition anywhere in ocean racing.

The clouds darkened, the temperature became a little fresher and the wind picked up. By 9.00 a.m. the crowds had already started to arrive. This was the first big day of the weekend, when the boats competed for the first time out on the water. So, along with the ocean racing aficionados, there were families, couples, and casual onlookers all milling around the beach front and the boats. It was quite a carnival atmosphere with balloons and music and roller skate artistes.

There was also a huge sense of excitement and anticipation everywhere, as though the mere sight of these majestic ships had imbued everyone with a new sense of what was possible on this earth. The ships with their super-smooth hulls, gigantic sails, and rigging appeared masters of all they surveyed. They cut through the water as if not bound by the rules of ordinary craft, but driven forward by other supernatural forces. With winds gusting well over 12 knots, they looked as though they had been released on turbo charge.

The Regatta started at 11 o'clock sharp, with a cannon blast. Anthony, Sagradio, Mat, and Marianne watched from on board a luxurious Riva motor launch. In a few moments, the sea around them became alive with boats and sails. Bright blue and red and yellow and white hulls crashing through the mounting swell. The flash of silvers from the rigging and wires. The frantic activity on board as the crews jockeyed for the all-important positions going into the first of the big race turns.

Mat put his arm around Marianne's waist; he felt her move away a little. Not enough so that anyone else would see, but enough for him to know.

After a little over two hours of high drama action involving everyone from the helmsman to the grinders, the *Masquerade* took second place behind Pierre Luigi Camara's *Duc de Savoie*. It had been a much better outcome than expected, given the strength of the overseas competition, and there was much hugging and congratulating among the shoreside support team as the *Masquerade* made her way back to them. They were in a great position to press for the lead in tomorrow's round of racing.

A dream and disaster

Mat and Marianne attended a race party at the Bermuda Triangle Bar in South Beach with Anthony and Sagradio that evening and then the four of them returned for dinner on board the *Espresso*. It was a pleasant evening, although much of the time was spent discussing the weather prospects for the following day.

Hurricane Christina was steering a new course north of Cuba and would be passing much closer to the coast of Miami than anticipated earlier in the day. It might be that racing would be cancelled altogether. Mat was leaving for the airport the following morning anyway, but Marianne had decided to stay with Anthony and Sagradio for the rest of the Sunday events.

After dinner, they had a drink in the lounge and then went to bed. The yacht was now shifting heavily on the water. As they lay in bed, Mat once more tried to put his arm around Marianne and draw her toward him. But she was stiff and cold.

"Are you angry about something?" Mat asked, sensing her tension.

"Yes, and if you don't know that, you don't understand me at all."

"Why? Sagradio's pregnancy?"

"No, it's not her pregnancy. I'm thrilled for her. It's just that you don't think about me. You don't think how I might feel hearing the news. I didn't treat it as a joke you know."

"I know. I didn't suggest you did," he replied. "Can't we have a pleasant time anyway. It would be foolish to let someone else's good news cause our unhappiness."

"I'm happy for them. I'm just not happy for me. Good night," she said and turned away.

Mat lay on his back and looked up at the ceiling. He was sad that he couldn't get through to Marianne and he wished he had never agreed to come on this damn weekend in the first place; things were bound to go wrong. He would try to talk to her properly once they were back at home and had time together. In a cabin on board the Elliotts' yacht was neither the time nor the place to discuss their future.

At just after one o'clock, Mat awoke. He had been dreaming: he had been going to a meeting at Oxytec with the others in the pitch team and he had been turned away by a security guard at the door because he did not have his attaché case. In the dream he had said over and over again, "There must be some mistake," and the security guard at the door had also repeatedly said, "I'm sorry sir but you can't come in without your briefcase. It's company policy."

So when he awoke he couldn't get the attaché case out of his mind. He had to find it. Yet he couldn't think where it was. He could recall bringing it on board the *Espresso* the previous evening but after that he couldn't remember seeing it. Still a little confused by sleep, Mat got up and looked around the cabin. It was nowhere to be seen. He put on a robe and went through to the lounge, determined to find the case.

The boat was now shifting from side to side in the wind and Mat could hear something hitting the roof of the lounge. He put the light on and looked around the lounge. There was still no sign of the case. The banging on the roof was getting louder, an insistent thump, thump as though some giant hand was hammering on the roof, trying to get in. However ridiculous it sounds now, Mat thought that the thumping on the roof was a sign that something was trying to communicate to him, draw him outside.

Mat moved forward to bar area and looked out of one of the rear windows. The rain was falling heavily on the glass and he could see the dim shape of white-tipped waves in the bay beyond the marina.

His mind turned back to the thumping noise on the roof. Was it telling him something? Maybe he'd left the attaché case in the hold to the right of the steps onto the yacht? It was pretty foolish to go out and look in this weather but Mat felt he had to know where his attaché case was. He slid open the door onto the deck.The wind and rain hit him full force. It forced him backwards. He bent his head a little and stepped out.

The boat was rolling and tossing. From the light in the bar area, he could see the narrow passage to the hold and the steps onto the yacht. The rain and spray blew into his face; his robe was soaking wet. If he was going to find that damn attaché case, he'd have to do so quickly. He moved forward on the deck, holding on firmly to a wooden rail at his side.

The yacht gave another sudden heave on the water. Suddenly the light in the bar area went out, plunging him into darkness. He stood for a moment and then heard the thump, thump on the roof of the cabin areas behind him. He turned round in the dark to see if he could see what was making the noise.

He took another step forward and from the corner of his eye he saw the dark shape of the boom swinging around at him. In that fraction of a second, he probably saved his life. For he ducked just an inch or two and the boom struck him with a glancing blow on the side of the temple. If he had not moved, it would have hit him with full force and knocked him into the water. As it was, the boom hit him and sent him sprawling on the wet deck, unconscious.

He may have been unconscious for no more than a few seconds, but when Mat came round he felt groggy and freezing cold. He got to his knees slowly. The boat was thrashing about in the water. He needed to get inside; he kept telling himself: "Get inside, now." He pulled himself up in the dark and started to inch toward the door to the cabin area. He reached forward and felt his hand run across something sharp. He drew his hand away quickly. The palm of his hand felt strange. The rain was falling on his face and his hair. He wiped his hand across his face and eyes and moved another step to the door.

At that moment, the light in the cabin doors went on. He could see Marianne standing in the doorway. He stretched out his hand to her. She started to scream. She screamed and screamed. A moment later, Anthony was also at the door, he pushed it open and helped Mat inside.

They lay him down on one of the sofas in the lounge. Mat had blood smeared across his eyes and forehead. His hand was bleeding from a gash across the palm and there was a large bump on the side of his head. Anthony told him to lie still until he could get something to clean up the cut on his hand.

He lay there looking up at Marianne.

Later she was to say that as she looked out from the cabin door at the deck, she thought she had seen a dead man walking.

The missing attaché case

Four hours later, Mat was packing for the evening flight to Frankfurt to join the team on the Oxytec site for the pre-analysis. The bump on the side of his head was sore but had subsided and the cut to his hand was now neatly bandaged thanks to some help from Sagradio Elliott. The weather, too, was improving; Christina had passed back out to sea and the skies had cleared.

The bad news was that he didn't have his attaché case. He'd searched for it again but still couldn't find it inside the Elliotts' yacht. Fortunately, he'd kept his passport in his coat pocket – one of the things he'd learned from his car hijacking experiences was to always keep your papers and cards and ID in different places. Nevertheless, he was worried about the case. First, it was a present from Marianne; and second, all his work papers were inside that case. Confidential papers.

Anthony and Sagradio had promised they would carry on looking for the case and would call Marianne if they found it. Even so it wasn't like Mat to make a mistake like that. He was losing it, literally. The whole weekend on the yacht had unnerved him, heightened his sense that he was a pawn in somebody else's game. What's more he was still very upset by the news from Anneka and felt he was letting her down by not being there. For now though he couldn't do anything for her. He would just have to sit back and relax. He'd had virtually no sleep the night before and was feeling drained.

He put his seat into recline, pulled the mask over his eyes, and shut out the world.

Old Germany

Twelve hours later Mat was stepping off a plane in Erfurt where he was due to meet up with the team.

Erfurt is right at the center of the German land mass and, although it's known as "the green heart of Germany," spring had definitely come late. There was a harsh bite to the air, a stark contrast to the shirt-sleeve warmth of Miami. It was also a time shift away from Florida – and I don't mean just the few lunar hours. Erfurt belonged to another age. It was the capital of ancient Thuringia, complete with renaissance buildings, half-timbered houses, and heraldic motifs above archways recalling the days of the Knights of Thuringia. Around the Krämerbrücke area where the team had their hotel, it felt like stepping back into medieval Europe.

There were reminders of other times, too: the hotel had apparently been used by the Stasi police during the communist era. Erfurt was heartland East Germany.

The Oxytec plant was about six miles from the center of town and dominated the landscape. The site was vast, covering some 100 acres of metal and buildings. For Mat, this was like entering the heat of the furnace; on a pre-analysis with three of Tactilis's old pros: Eric, Katz, and Nancy. This was where he was going to find the truth about the unforgiving five minutes.

Eric, Katz, and Nancy worked well together; they did not necessarily like one another but they each trusted the other and shared a passion to get the job done. Although this was the first stage in what would be an intense few weeks of analysis of Oxytec operations, they were already finding the basic structures of the business. Just as a language has basic, invisible building blocks, which create meaning, so does a business.

They started with the very simplest elements of the business and built from there.

Some of the attitudes they were uncovering showed how far they had to go. One of the managers who had been brought in from a large company in Munich, blamed the poor performance on these "Ost Deutschen."

"The quickest way to turn this place around," he'd said, "would be to replace the East Germans with some talented managers. The East Germans just find it impossible to improve. They've spent too long in the old ways."

The Tactilis team liked this because they knew that if they could get this manager to be more pragmatic and get the most out of his team instead of denigrating them, then there would be real improvement to be had.

The team was also evaluating where the company was going and how it planned to get there. They were breaking the business down into all the component processes and systems that made up the whole. They were understanding the relationships between departments, looking for informal power groups and decision structures as well as getting a handle on values custom and practice and norms around how people behaved with each other.

In short, they were getting into the flow of the business. They were discovering how one department related to another and how one set of personalities and people related to another. They could see where departments were protecting their own turf. Different support functions (like personnel or engineering) were operating almost independently of the rest of the organization. Key tasks weren't being done in a synchronized way. In fact, different departments were even doing things that were contradictory or even obstructive.

It all boiled down to the simple truths like accountability and responsibility. They recognized in the Erfurt plant all the classic signs of lack of a clear sense of purpose or direction. People and departments did things because they were easy or because they matched their view of what was right, rather than because they were important to the company achieving its goals. So every department was working as hard as they could and putting in all the effort they could and yet still not making the right contribution to the business as a whole. The saddest part is that they didn't know this was happening. They had simply lost a sense of focus on their common goal and each was plowing their own furrow.

Mat enjoyed the ease with which the rest of the team was able to identify these inconsistencies within the organization so rapidly. He was struck by a great example Eric had given from his first project.

"I was assigned to the Research & Development group in an assembly plant and one of the first things I did was to get the designers I was working with to spend half an hour with me on the assembly line to see how it was. They were horrified when they saw line operators with saws trying to make pre-cut pieces to fit into the final product and asked why. The reply they got was, 'We told the drawing office that the specs they had were wrong and that the pieces should be cut differently.' The designers went away thinking, 'Oh, if the drawing office knows then something will be done.' I knew differently.

"I went back to the line operator and asked him how often this sort of problem happened. 'Oh, three or four times a day.' Then I asked who it was in the drawing office that he told and he gave me a name. I went to the drawing office and asked to see the man whose name I had been given. He was a young guy and had been there about 18 months. At first, he was a bit sheepish but then he went into a filing cabinet and said 'Ah! You're talking about the change notices. I'm glad you came. I've got a drawer full of them and don't know what to do with them!' So I took the drawer full back to the designers, who approved the changes in a couple of days and fed them into the appropriate departments and suddenly assembly beat its record for units assembled. I was quite a hero!"

So simple, such ordinary sense, Mat thought, and yet he could also see exactly how it would improve efficiency and save costs. For that reason maybe, although Mat was impressed by Eric, Katz, and Nancy's approach, he couldn't help thinking that with a bit of time he would have the same insights and make the same findings. There was nothing remarkable about it.

But it was what happened next that changed his opinion.

The meaning of measurement

Mat and the team were sitting in the project office late on the Wednesday evening going through data they gathered.

"What gets measured gets done," said Eric, in what seemed like an almost throwaway remark as he was going through some analysis charts.

He was observing the meaning of the charts he was working on, but he was also commenting on the whole nature of business and organizations. Mat was also collating some data and at first, because his mind was elsewhere, didn't respond to Eric's observation. But his mind replayed it: "What gets measured gets done."

What a simple way to shape the direction of a company: control what gets measured. Measurement gave facts, hard data. Data was the key to shaping behaviors. And behaviors were the most profound component to the success of a business. Here was a simple line that Mat could see, and it lead all the way from the CEO's office to the supervisor's actions between 12.40 and 12.45.

"True enough, but it isn't the only glue," replied Katz as if Eric had started off some game.

"It's like when I play Scrabble. The scores don't determine results, they only record them. I'm constantly amazed at the way new words form around existing ones. And how the game is every time different and every time the same like it's the laws behind the game that make it happen, the deep laws."

"Hey the Scrabble Kid's getting profound," said Nancy. "Did you hear that Eric? The deep laws..." she ended with a chuckle. "Those Scrabble tournaments, they must be wild..."

"OK wiseguys, laugh if you like but there are laws out there which make things happen right. Why do fish shoal? How does a flock of birds know how and when to turn? Why do similar people and activities cluster into groups and neighborhoods? How do cities take on characteristics? All of these have a law that shapes them. It's called emergence."

"So we can all marvel at nature, but how does that get us to win the game?" asked Eric.

"The answer is feedback, that's what the law of organizations is controlled by. In Scrabble, it's the relationship of letters and words which create connections. In companies, its feedback which creates connections."

"Measurement, you mean?" said Eric, agreement in his tone.

"Sort of, but a bit more than measurement alone. I mean the whole idea of feedback loops. Creating feedback loops which feed into other loops and which join all parts of a company. A state where the feedback is constant. That's how you get intelligence into a swarm of bees or a shoal of herring. It's feedback about local conditions which makes the group smart."

"I like that," said Eric. "I mean that's what we're seeing everyday, or rather its reverse: we see how organizations lose direction because they only listen to words of the so-called smartest cats around."

"Exactly. Only it's not about leadership or lack of it; it's about creating connections which go beyond leadership."

Mat was now listening with total focus. What was happening here, as it seemed to Mat, was that these three old campaigners were uncovering the core mystery of their craft. They were describing a level beyond organizational effectiveness, how you get departments to operate, or how you make sure the right co-operations take place. No, these three were going further and simpler. They were talking about the flow in business. How to get the flow to work.

"One of the things we put in place on every project is a Management Control and Reporting System," said Katz. "We look at how it works today, how they plan and control reports internally. Then we get them to focus on getting these structures right. It's amazing how even sophisticated companies simply don't know the reality of their business.

"The brilliant thing about an internal reporting system is that it forms the basis of a common language for everyone. An engineer's education is different from the education of a planner or a manager and as a result they learn subtly different languages. Simple words mean different things. A planner uses 'output' in a different sense to a production manager, for example. We help people to establish a common language, through which everybody understands what is being talked about."

Katz continued, "Once you've established this common language around what the numbers are – What is the base? Where are we improving from? What is the plan? What are we setting out to achieve? How are we actually doing? – then everything becomes clear. It creates an effective, useful, and *live* feedback system within the company. It gives a company coherence like a shoal of fish has coherence. No one needs to tell them where to go, because they are all acting with one mind. So the CEO doesn't set the direction, he is effectively wired into the direction."

"And, as I said, that's about measurement," added Eric. "We identify what needs to be measured, the key performance indicators, and then we deliver that information out to the people who actually create the data."

"Sure," said Katz, "but it goes further than that. It's not enough just to give people an MCRS and say here's the measurement system that's the answer to your prayers. You actually have to install that MCRS, install it *physically* like you would a pump or valve. You do it live, real time, with people. In meeting after meeting. You set up the rules and you do that so that you create the environment for feedback. It's no good just wanting feedback, you have to make sure it happens – physically happens, I mean."

"So the way we set up meetings is kind of crucial," said Nancy. "I think that, too. It's such an easy win for us but the discipline of action logs works every time. 'Never ever have a meeting without it being directed to actions, which are measurable and which are assigned to people.' I must have said that a thousand times and it's worked each one."

"Action logs are the muscle but they're not the nervous

system," continued Katz. "The nervous system is the other support ware. Like insisting on consistent data so that feedback loops can build across the company, almost of their own volition. If the data's consistent you don't just get feedback across that group in the meeting room, but across all the other groups they individually come into contact with. That's one element, but it's also things like insisting that meetings start on time and that no one's late and that everyone is there who should be there and never allowing an atmosphere to develop where people can show up late or just not show up at all."

"Yeah that drives me mad when people show up late," said Eric as though he was about to hit his fist on the table. "They miss out on information and they also fail to provide information on topics which have already been discussed. So everything's incomplete."

"OK I can see where you're at," said Nancy. "It's all the small things that happen around meetings, like our ground rules."

"That's it, as I said, our fundamental laws, like making sure that KPIs are made available before the meeting to all, that everyone's on time, everyone's prepared, each attendee can express views openly, all discussions are based on facts not hearsay, all cell phones are switched off, all communication is open and straightforward. It's this live stuff that makes feedback happen across a business."

"OK, all right, Scrabble Kid, I guess you're right," said Nancy. "Now can we get back to the DILO you did of that supervisor in the fermentation unit please?"

The conversation moved on. It felt to Mat as though he'd been overhearing a couple of craftsmen talk about the mysteries of their art, or painters sharing notes on how to get perspective to bring a picture to life.

But in this case what Mat had been listening to was how to get flow into a business. Not just data flow, although that was a critical part of it, but also energy flow. They were talking about how to connect people into a single coherent organization. The answer is through the ordinary everyday actions like making sure everyone's in a meeting who is supposed to be there. So simple, it's hard to argue with. But how many meetings actually start on time, with all the participants present and all the data distributed beforehand? Fewer than most of us would admit.

You can get all your Harvard MBAs working on a strategy for the next decade, but I bet they can't get everyone into a meeting room at the same time and then get them to base their discussions on facts.

Everyday knowledge, such as how to get meetings to run effectively so that everybody is given the opportunity to express their views openly – this is what drives basic success in a company.

When you stop to think about these ground rules, how simple they sound and yet how difficult they are to *actually* implement, then you begin to see how obvious it is that some organizations don't work. They have not got the fundamental laws right. The rules which shape behavior and without which feedback doesn't happen. The laws which allow local intelligence to make the organization smart. It's so simple, it's ridiculous. I could laugh out loud.

Letter from Marianne

Dear Mat,

I am FedExing your attaché case to you. Sagradio found it in our cabin;, somehow it had slipped down between the chest of drawers and the wardrobe. No wonder you couldn't find it. I hope it hasn't arrived too late for you to work on.

Perhaps I was wrong to insist that we spent the weekend with the Elliotts when you were obviously against it – for whatever reason. However, certain things became clear to me over the weekend and as a result I am beginning to see how different the two of us really are. I feel you don't understand me or respect my needs. I have to feel respected in order to feel loved. Right now I feel neither, and that is an unhappy position from which to plan a future.

I think it's best if we give one another a break for a while. I have been asked to go to Europe for some clients to source some pictures and I have agreed. It will allow me time to decide what to do for the best.

Call me if you need to. Hope your poor head and hand are healing.

Love,

Marianne X.

A sign

Mat read the letter from Marianne with a mixture of sadness and anger. How could she say he didn't respect her! That simply wasn't true. It was her way of looking for an excuse to treat him badly.

Well, if that's what she wants to do, fine. Let her have her space. He was too busy right now to deal with her. When this pitch was done he would make the decision about their future together. Perhaps they really were moving apart; she wanted the old safe surroundings, he wanted something new and real. So he would not act now. He would explain later what had been going on in his head over the previous few months. He would tell her about his father – because by then the pitch would have sorted out his life for him. In fact it would have given him back his life. Whichever way the pitch went, that was the direction his life would take.

Mat opened his attaché case.

On top of his papers was a tiny fragment of natural sponge.

It was from the deep waters; the time when their relationship had been good.

A night on the town

The first pre-analysis stage had gone well. The Tactilis team had covered a lot of ground in a very short space of time. They'd taken some first steps toward a desired or new organizational structure, and a plan for how that organization might be put in place at Erfurt. They had identified a number of the plant's key performance indicators and also that – not untypically – many departments were simply unaware of these indicators.

They had also set out the very basics of the management reporting system on a huge long roll of brown paper. The brown paper stretched for several meters around their project office and was littered with yellow Post-its, with notes scrawled on them in long hand, in order that they could all very quickly and directly contribute to building the picture of the actual, real interfaces in the plant and how they worked.

So things had gone well. They were already beginning to feel better about the pitch (maybe they really could beat Hardings this time) and everyone was getting more used to having Mat on the team. Perhaps things weren't so dire after all. Time to celebrate on a Thursday night. They planned an evening out in Erfurt.

Mat was still hurting from the letter he'd got from Marianne. After so long together, didn't he at least deserve a phone call!

He was angry and tired. He deserved a break from the grind of analysis.

So far the team had either eaten in at the hotel or got some food from the plant canteen. Now they were going to get a meal at a local restaurant. Nancy had asked at the desk and the concierge had recommended a place in the medieval quarter of town, just a short walk from the hotel.

It's one of the great truisms of life, but people who work extremely hard also tend to play hard. Eric, Katz, and Nancy were no exception. For all their grumbling about being away from home for so long, they liked life on the road. They liked the variety and the buzz of going to new places, so as they all walked to the restaurant together, they were laughing and happy.

The restaurant was called Zum Weissen Pferd and had a great iron door as an entrance. There was no one around on the streets outside and the building looked deserted, such that they wondered whether they had been directed to the right place.

Katz pushed the iron door open and they walked in. To their surprise, the inside opened up into a long vaulted room. There was a bar down one whole side of the room with barrels stacked behind it. The floor was paved with large flagstones and there were heraldic banners hanging from the ceiling. And the place was packed out with people. Tables of men and women having a riotous time, fuelled by the huge *Steins* of frothy beer being ferried from the bar to the tables by waiters in long white aprons.

It was such a surprise to see a restaurant this busy in the heart of Erfurt that it heightened the good mood among the team even further. Next they were ordering large *Steins* of beer along with the locals and having a fine time. And then pretty soon after that they were into stories about life on the road.

"You remember doing that analysis up in Utah," said Eric to Katz, "and we were staying in this motel – nothing in a hundred miles but gas and dinosaur bones. And they had this dance on the Tuesday night and a friend of one of the waitresses shows up and the waitress says to her: 'Your hair looks real different tonight,' and the friend says, 'Yeah, I washed it earlier…'"

By the time Eric got to the end of this anecdote he and Katz were in hysterics of laughter.

"And you remember that cappuccino machine? Some clever salesman had sold the motel a kaahpooocheeeno machine," said Katz, exaggerating every vowel, "and of course these tough trucker types up there they didn't take to it…said it was a faggot's drink and then we show up…and God knows what they thought we were, 'cos in the four weeks we were there we drank so much coffee we broke the machine – but not before we'd got every trucker in the state hooked on kaahpooocheeeno. All that cream and chocolate stuck to their macho moustaches…"

As the evening wore on, each of the old team told their favorite tales of horrible hotels and restaurants from hell, of union officials called Jabba-the-Hut, of Green River, Wyoming, and cement plants in Alabama. They laughed at the eccentricities of Robot 167 and how PowerPoint presentations had a mind of their own and a nasty desire to put slides out of order. They laughed about colleagues getting locked out of offices and rental cars and hotel rooms. They laughed about their job. And Mat couldn't remember having had such a good time since – well, since he was on a beach in Grand Turk listening to diving tales, sitting by a fire.

From the Zum Weissen Pferd the group then made their way to a club called BeeBop. Like the restaurant it was well-hidden and the team would not have found it without directions from Gretchen, one of the waitresses at Zum Weissen Pferd.

She said that she might join them later if her shift finished OK.

The BeeBop was really just a long thin room with a stage at one end and a small bar halfway down the right-hand side. But it was adequately full and there was a real atmosphere inside. The music was good, too. There was a small jazz band with a female singer. She had dark hair, cut just above her shoulders, and wore a white and black polka dot dress. She was young, perhaps in her late twenties but had a mature, rich jazz voice.

She mixed the numbers she sang – combining traditional jazz tunes like *One for My Baby* and *My Funny Valentine* with material from Kurt Weill. It was an odd mix perhaps, but at that stage in the evening it worked well enough at least for the group from Tactilis who were standing by the bar ordering drinks whenever they felt they needed one.

"Hey, look who's here," said Katz. "It's our friend from the restaurant. Hi there, Gretchen, can we buy you a drink?"

"Hello, again," said Gretchen. "Yes, that would be nice. A beer please."

Gretchen had changed out of her traditional waitress uniform and was now wearing a low-cut V-neck sweater and jeans. Out of uniform she looked a completely different person, young, chic, and self-assured. In the restaurant she had worn her blonde hair tied in a bun behind her head. Now it hung free about her shoulders. She wore small blue drop-earrings and, in her right ear, a tiny diamond stud as well. It might not have been diamond, of course.

"So you found the place all right?" she said to Mat.

"Yeah. Your directions were excellent. No trouble finding it," he replied.

"And what do you think?"

"Great place," said Mat. "The singer's really good."

"Yes that's Susie. She works at the university during the day and sings here most nights. She does it because it's her passion. It sets her free," said Gretchen.

"Everyone should have a passion, that's for sure," said Mat.

"I agree. What's yours?"

"Collecting sponges from the bottom of the deep blue sea," said Mat.

"Sponges?" said Gretchen. "Why sponges?"

"Because they're beautiful and also because they regenerate all by themselves."

"And if you collect sponges that must mean you like diving."

"Absolutely. My number one pastime. If I wasn't here, that's what I would be doing with my time."

"I like dancing," said Gretchen. "That's my passion."

"Do you feel like dancing now?" asked Mat.

"Why else would I be here?" said Gretchen, smiling.

Mat took her hand and they walked to a small spot of polished wooden floor in front of the band where one or two other couples were also dancing. When Gretchen arrived, Susie smiled down at her and gave her a little wave of acknowledgment.

Katz, Eric, and Nancy carried on drinking at the bar. Mat danced with Gretchen. She danced well, her body lithe and supple.

Somewhere around 1.30 Eric, Nancy, and Katz waved goodbye to Mat, saying they were turning in. Mat said he would follow them in a few minutes. He would just have one more dance with Gretchen.

Around 2.30, they closed the BeeBop and Mat asked Gretchen if she would like a drink. She said yes.

The only place where Mat could get a drink at that time of night was back in the hotel. They walked back to the hotel together. It was cold in the early morning and the mist ran through the medieval streets of Erfurt. They stopped on a corner, in the streets of cobblestones, and kissed, fully and passionately. He held her body close and felt her. He wanted her. She wanted him. He slipped his hands under her leather jacket and found her breasts. She felt so new, so different from Marianne.

At 6.30, Mat awoke in his bed. He turned over to stroke Gretchen's hair. She was gone. Yet the bed smelled of her perfume. Did he wake or sleep?

Complications

Mat was back in the US. He'd had a hard week, with no let up to the next. But he wasn't complaining. He was now part of the team and he was also close to an understanding; to the closure he had sought since that evening in Pittsburgh.

As he traveled back to see his sister, he thought of Marianne and what she would be doing right now. He felt distant from her and he was unhappy with that. He was sailing away from Marianne. Was that right?

Gretchen had been the perfect stranger. Like *Lovely Rita* in the Beatles song. But Marianne was altogether different; she came from different, deeper waters. He couldn't work out whether this was because he had got used to her company or whether there was a real connection between them. And everything that had happened to him in recent months, only made him feel more confused. He just didn't have the right frame of mind to make a decision. What's more he was becoming preoccupied with the upcoming pitch to Oxytec.

The incident over the case still worried him. Sagradio had had it sent back to Marianne. But should he say anything to Max and the others in the team about it? There were confidential papers inside. He was convinced Anthony wouldn't have looked at the papers, but nevertheless did he need to let the team know? Something in him said that was the right course of action, but then who was going to find out?

Mat felt like he was being pulled in all directions: by the pitch, by Marianne, and by Anneka's illness.

True to his word, Anthony had telephoned his contact at MGH and secured an introduction to a senior surgeon. Mat could meet the surgeon early on Monday morning before flying to the team's next pre-analysis meetings in Pittsburgh as well as on to his own meeting with Peter Smith's executive assistant, Shakira Price.

Anthony's contact at MGH was Shandra Singh, one of the most eminent surgeons at the hospital and a member of Harvard Med teaching staff. He had kindly agreed to see Mat at 8.00 before his day started in earnest – as long as nothing else had come up that was urgent.

Mat went in to see Anneka at around 7.30. She was sitting up, just like the last time he had seen her. Only this time a little more light had gone from her eyes and she looked thinner and more pale.

"Look, there's really no need for you to fuss about me," she said. "They haven't pronounced me dead yet you know."

"But they don't seem to have pronounced very much at all," replied Mat. "And that's just my worry. You have been in and out for tests for a couple of weeks now and the situation seems to be getting worse not better."

He looked at her thin face forcing on a smile.

"It's difficult for them. First of all they thought it could have been gallstones. Then they dismissed that idea and started looking for other indications. Now they think it's my pancreas playing up, but they won't be sure until they've done an exploratory operation."

"Well that's why I'm here, professor. I want to make sure that you get the very best surgeon on the case. Taking a look in at your pancreas, that's a serious business."

"By the way," he continued. "Why did they start to think it's your pancreas that's causing the problem?"

"Partly, I guess, because of the level of pain I'm in. They also asked me about Dad and his diagnosis and, well, I guess they're worried I may have the same thing."

Mat tensed. He had known deep down that this was exactly why they had changed prognosis; they were worried that Anneka had inherited the same pancreatic condition as their father.

Prepping up and the power of practice

Mat met Shandra Singh on the dot of eight o'clock in his office at the teaching wing of MGH. The office was bright and open. There were no photographs or pictures inside, but very large piles of journals and papers. It felt like its only decoration was dedication.

Shandra Singh had asked him in cordially and they had got straight to the matter.

"I am here because my sister has been admitted to MGH and naturally I'm worried about her and I want to see what I can do to make sure that she gets the best surgical treatment available."

"Of course," Shandra replied. There was no hint of reproach in his voice. He believed Mat had every right to do his best and seek out the best. "I understand your concern and while I have to say I think that Anneka is in excellent hands, I will be delighted to help you in whatever way I can."

"Well, what I really need is – and I hope this doesn't sound too ungrateful to the people who are looking after Anneka right now – for her to be treated by the best."

"That of course depends on how you define the best," replied Shandra. "If I'm going to be as open with you as I'm sure you would like, then I would have to tell you that at MGH we believe in practice not just talent."

Practice, doctor! Where on earth did that idea come from? We commit ourselves to you in the belief that as a profession you're supremely capable and highly trained and now you're telling us it's about practice. Heavens!

"There have been many studies over the years" Shandra continued, "on elite performers. Of course, one can define such persons in a number of ways, but let us say that typically one might select at the more cerebral end of performance – people such as concert musicians, chess Grand Masters, mathematicians, and so on. And correlating the results of these studies, the picture that's beginning to emerge is that the biggest difference between the top performers and the others is the amount they practise.

"Furthermore, we talk about gifted people, but the most important gift may be the talent to practise. The inner strength and desire to keep practising on and on. That's something you can't teach.

"These days I find that I am more and more influenced by surgeons who have this inner resilience and conscientiousness rather than those who are most obviously academically gifted."

Mat thought for a moment. He was here because he wanted to do the best for his sister, but he'd been caught by the intensity and originality of Shandra's observations. It was a fascinating premise that talent was ultimately about the ability to practise. All that talent myth he'd lived through at HBS and Hardings, how did all that stack up now? If it all came down to the determination to perform an act over and over again.

"And has your own experience borne out this research? I mean do people get better through practice in activities where the room for failure is minimal?" asked Mat.

"What we have found," said Shandra, "is that people who practise in teams become more accomplished faster than those who work alone. Learning is best done together. Certainly learning in operating is a team affair: surgeons, nurses, anesthetists all need to learn new roles when performing a new operation. And practice on its own does not make perfect.

"We gathered some data recently about different teams performing the same operation with the same training. We found that the determining factor was how the team practised. The best team for example was led by a relatively inexperienced surgeon who picked team members with whom he had worked before, kept them together for at least 15 cases before admitting new members, got the teams to do dry runs before the real thing, and ensured that they were doing six cases a week so there was an intensity about the whole experience. He wasn't autocratic either, he was willing to be a partner in the whole process."

Mat, like most of us, had the notion that a surgeon led his team much like a general did his troops.

"The simple truth about being a talented performer," said Shandra, "is that you learn by doing. Only by doing. We have found in hospital that performance improves dramatically if your team are deliberate about learning and practising and also measuring their progress."

"So where does that leave me right now? I still want to know what's best or indeed who's best for my sister."

"Well, I can give you my own personal views, and they are simply that, personal. Based on what I've just told you of course, I would recommend Aman Denton. He probably won't impress you immediately with his authority and bearing. That's because he's quite literally not out to impress you. So, for example, he won't tell you how difficult the operation is or how advanced the technology is. He's modest, unassuming, and probably comes across as a little anxious. When you first meet him you'll notice that he has a slight stutter and this puts a lot of people off. Interestingly this stutter disappears completely in the operating room. But if you're after a surgeon who delivers results he's your man – the stats would prove it."

"Of course my definition of a surgeon is framed around results, what else would people choose a surgeon on?" asked Mat, genuinely surprised that people might not select on results.

"You'd be surprised. People look for all kinds of things from surgeons – confidence for one. They might be convinced by a surgeon's reputation for technical mastery. Interestingly, most don't ask about – or possibly don't even want to know about – the data we have. Even when they have the data I have known some people ignore it altogether and, strange as it may seem, I can understand that. Remember this is real, living medicine – a world where information at any moment is never complete and the science is often ambiguous. It's a world where our knowledge and abilities, because they are human, can never be perfect. Sometimes it's hard not to be taken in by factors other than results."

"Thank you for your time and patience," said Mat.

"Anthony is a good friend," said Shandra. "I am delighted if I have been of any help."

Executive code

Mat had agreed to meet Shakira Price at the conference center next door to the Westin Hotel in Pittsburgh.

He hadn't been back to Pittsburgh since the week he'd been hijacked and left on the ice. Now he had come back to the place where the rivers met. But as a new person, with a different eye.

It was early summer and the waters of the rivers flowed freely. Sunlight glinted on the Ohio River as the road emerged from the splendidly theatrical Fort Pitt Tunnel, opening up onto dramatic views of the city, with its mix of modern and Victorian architecture. It was a city with stories to tell.

Mat had arrived a little early for the meeting and to pass the time, decided to take a walk to the Strip District, which was only a few minutes along Pennsylvania Avenue.

Mat walked under a heavy traffic bridge and the environment changed. From busy streets where people passed one another in mutual silence, here the atmosphere was one of relaxed animation. It had the feeling of a market. Individual shops lined the sidewalk: Wholey's, the Pennsylvania Macaroni Company, the Pittsburgh Candy Store, as well as numerous pottery stores, cafés, and restaurants. Inside the stores, the same market stall atmosphere pervaded, with shop assistants shouting out customer numbers, or the day's fresh catch, or their unbeatable special offers. Here you could buy a fish sandwich or sushi from a stall. Here, Native Americans sold knitwear on trestle tables. And elsewhere, there were the blackened windows of the Voodoo Lounge, where nothing moved before noon.

The Strip is literally that, a thin strip of land which runs alongside the Ohio River. It has a character all of its own, formed by the generations of people who have worked here, worked the barges along the river. Mat thought of all the generations who had loaded and unloaded goods from up and down the river. They had left their impression like a hand in soft concrete. Not just in the buildings and warehouses, but in the spirit of the place. Towns and cities were fashioned by what people did, not what they thought. Actions left tracks in the road.

Mat walked slowly back to the conference center and got ready to meet Shakira. It was likely to be one of those conversations where you had to listen for what *wasn't* said, for the codified messages, the inference of a smile. Mat understood that the choice of an off-site location for the meeting, away from Oxytec sites, was a significant one. This would be a more off-the-record version of the facts – and of course nothing would remain of the conversation.

Shakira was a tall, young black woman from the educated middle-class, Southern society. Mat guessed her parents could have been teachers at an all-black high school. She was smart in every sense, very alert, and without armor. Mat was reminded of another young black woman who had said to him "We don't all have deprivation narratives, you know."

They talked briefly about the flights they'd each had and then Shakira moved into first gear, thanking Mat for taking the trouble to meet her here. "I had a couple of meetings in downtown Pittsburgh today and it just worked out better for my schedule. Hope that was OK for you?" she said.

"Of course," replied Mat and they moved very quickly into the briefing game.

"Peter thought it would be better if I had an initial talk with you. He didn't want, I think, to influence your approach too early in the process."

This was a signal that he was looking for something different from Tactilis. He knew what he would be getting from Hardings: pure thoroughbred thought. But Tactilis, they might surprise him.

Shakira went on, "Every now and then we recognize that we need to look further afield. There's value in difference – to change a famous saying, one should never be too confident or too comfortable."

This was code for we're not sure which direction to take.

Throughout the conversation, Shakira would qualify her remarks with a gentle "don't take this as fact, we're always looking for fresh thinking" or the constant refrain "but I wouldn't want to lead you or direct your ideas in any way." It was a masterclass in showing you one route out and then withdrawing it just as fast.

They talked around Oxytec's geographic spread and its move into new markets in Asia, they discussed the role of life sciences and biotech in society – "we're a company that has a responsibility to improve lives" she said – and they had also talked about Peter Smith himself.

"Peter's a remarkable person, you know. A very gifted manager and a man with profound vision. People don't always see this side to him; they see him as a man who delivers numbers and who can be relied on to hit targets. We perhaps need to make people aware of his wider perspective.

"He has almost been too successful, set up too many expectations. Success itself is a challenge. How does one deal with its assumptions? Reality is not easy, it is complicated and even messy."

This was code that Oxytec wasn't going to continue to grow in the way that the markets and analysts expected. Peter had looked at the numbers and he just couldn't see where the big change was going to come from. And when you're a big league chief exec, and you've made the headlines with some spectacular gains, anything less next time is seen as a failure. There can be no extenuating circumstances, the graph just has to keep going up, the CV just has to become ever more fascinating. The "career" CEO, the brilliant mind who moves from company to company, may not cultivate celebrity status, but it will soon find him. And it will use him.

"Peter," she went on, "sometimes gets so frustrated. He knows which course he wants to set but, with such a huge vessel, how does he get people to steer in the same direction? How does he get everyone across the organization to do what he wants?"

Shakira was moving in and out of the shadows, giving Mat glimpses of the problems.

"Ours is a relatively large company and it's often difficult to see what's going on at ground level. We're like a lot of *Fortune* 100 firms where the pressure is on to think in macro-economic terms – terms which may not adequately describe the reality."

The "reality" word again. Mat's antennae picked up. Shakira was getting closer to the core.

"Our situation reminds me of descriptions of the early days of the Vietnam war, when the officers in the field were reporting heavy losses but the generals could only see victory. Victory was inevitable, how could they lose?"

Mat was being told about an organization with a huge reputation that was in big trouble. Information wasn't getting through the organization properly; the senior management were beginning to feel powerless to effect big changes and the middle management weren't sure whether to go on reporting heavy losses or simply ask for reinforcements.

And in the midst of it all, Peter Smith knew that he had a brilliant organization full of great potential that just wasn't delivering. Peter Smith had sensed that the main job was to deal with the reality. There was nothing inherently wrong with the business; it just wasn't performing as it should. They needed to cut out the non-value-added, increase efficiency, leverage the world-class reputation Oxytec undoubtedly had. Did they need new strategic thinking? Well, as Shakira would say, "I wouldn't want to lead you or direct your ideas in any way...."

The meeting lasted a little over an hour and a half and at the end Shakira and Mat shook hands cordially. There had been a meeting of minds; not necessarily the complete download but a partial steer nonetheless. Mat was pleased, very pleased. Tactilis did have a very good opportunity here. The pitch was not a foregone conclusion. In fact, Mat could see a way to win. The message was: concentrate on the tangible, focus on the reality.

The unexpected consequences of honesty

Mat called Max from his cell phone on the way to meet up with Katz, Nancy, and Eric. He was driving on the main route out of town.

"Max," he said. "It's Mat here and I have just finished a very useful meeting with Shakira Price. Impressive, smart woman, classic diplomat. We got on well and I got a very good steer. We have definitely got a chance to take this pitch from Hardings. No doubt about it."

"Good news, Mat," said Max. "I knew you'd get on with her. We can talk more when I get into Pittsburgh tomorrow."

"Fine," said Mat, "There is one other item I wanted to mention to you. It's rather embarrassing, really. But, as you may or may not know, Marianne, my partner is a good friend of Sagradio Elliott, Anthony Elliott's wife. We were invited a weekend ago to spend some time on their yacht."

"Sounds fun," said Max. "Just don't tell Eric. He'd be hopping mad about it, accuse you of handing over all sorts of confidences to Anthony Elliott."

"Actually something did happen… I managed to leave my attaché case behind. It had a number of papers inside but I am sure it was OK."

"What sort of papers?" asked Max.

"All the material that Eric and I had gathered from Alanstown. Plus your original notes."

"That's pretty serious, you know, Mat. If Hardings did read that material they would have a very good idea of what approach we were going to take," said Max.

"Yes, I know, but I am convinced that Anthony Elliott wouldn't have looked in the case."

"Me too," replied Max, "But I can't take that call on my own. I have to ask the rest of the team what they think about it. It's their pitch, too. I'll have a word with them and get back to you."

Mat put his cell phone down and turned the car into the side of the road. He was parked at the edge of the bridge and from the window of the car he could see out across the Ohio River.

A little while later Max phoned back. He had talked with the team and agreed that it would be best if Mat sat this one out. That was the way it was – unfortunate circumstances, but there was no way around it.

In the space of 20 minutes or so, Mat had thought he had found a way to win the pitch for Tactilis and then had found a way to get himself taken off the team.

His world had just come tumbling down.

At the water's edge

Mat couldn't remember the route he'd taken to get to Wentworth's that night. And in the sunshine of a May day everything looked very different. But he felt sure that if he started out, his sense of direction would lead him where he needed to go.

He headed west out of the city center, keeping the river on his right. He drove through the edge of the commercial district and then into small suburban streets. Always with the river on his right, he drove on, guided by instinct.

He took a turn nearer the river and then onto a road that went alongside it. He kept on for about a mile or so and then, on the far side of the stream, he saw the outline of Wentworth's disused buildings.

Then he saw a track leading down to the water's edge. He got out of the car and walked to the lip of the river. This must have been the place where they had forced him out on to the ice. He looked out across the river, the deep, fast-flowing river. He felt the volume of water. He would have drowned in seconds – they would have found him washed up in the next state.

He picked up a piece of driftwood from the bank and threw it into the water. He watched as it bobbed in the stream, halting for an instant before gathering pace with the river.

Should he do the same? Should he throw himself into the water? He stepped forward to within an inch or two of the edge. It would be so easy to step in and wash downstream like a piece of driftwood.

He looked down at his reflection in the water, with the blue sky above. He felt tears rise in his eyes.

He stood there sobbing, openly and without any sense of self-consciousness. He cried for many minutes, letting the thoughts of what he'd been through in recent months and the anguish and hurt all take their effect. As though for the first time he had allowed himself to recognize the damage done.

What if there was no force behind him? He'd just taken a series of wrong decisions which had cost him his job, his girlfriend, and his future. What a fool.

The tears ran down his face.

Slowly he stopped sobbing. His breathing settled from deep gulps of air to a more normal pattern.

Deep inside, Mat knew he had been driven to this point. He hadn't simply imagined his father or Brad's accident or that night on the boat. They had been real for him and they meant something.

Beyond all his experiences with ghosts and supernatural forces, which were true for him if not others, there lay actual, tangible proof. The discoveries he'd made about business were true and real. To him that was undeniable.

He took a pace back.

He couldn't give up the pitch. It was still his only way to show he'd been right. So why had he been taken off it now? He'd missed something, or rather there was a dimension still to uncover.

He would not give up. He would call Max and if necessary Katz, Eric, and Nancy and force them to take him back onto the team.

Mat turned and made his way back to the car. As he reached to open the door, he heard his cell phone ringing. It had to be Max saying he'd reconsidered.

"Hello Max…" said Mat.

"Do I sound like Max?" said the voice. "Because, good God, if that's so, I'll have to do something about it." The voice had a broad Irish accent.

"This is Danny O'Connor calling. Eric Stadler said you wanted to talk to me. Something about trying to make a connection."

The legendary salesman

Some people know things, other people know people. I have found that it is very often the latter who have proved to have an impact on my life. They are particular spirits whose role it is – whatever their actual job may be – to put people in touch with one another. To make those simple but vital connections.

"Why don't you have a word with so-and-so? He's an interesting guy," they say. Suddenly you can find yourself on a whole new path.

That was what Danny O'Connor, legendary Tactilis salesman and free spirit, did for Mat Durer.

Mat had arranged to call Danny back later in the afternoon on a landline and they had a long talk. Mat went through all the things he'd picked up in recent weeks and especially his excitement over discovering the five-minute snapshot and getting in the flow and how measurement and feedback pulled a company together and set it into action. What he was after now, he said, was some way of tying these ideas together. It wasn't that they didn't fit – they did. They were all part of the same picture, or rather the same explanation. He just felt there was some other element missing, as though he had the sentence idea, but not the subject.

He asked Danny if anyone else in Tactilis had thought through these ideas and whether they had come to any sort of formulation.

"Not that I know of," said Danny. "The sort of things you're describing, they're of course central to what we do. But I don't think they've been collated before – not in the way you've described any how."

He hesitated for a moment.

"But, look, there is a guy I met recently. He lives in New Orleans. He's an ex-Marine colonel. Very together. He has been making some interesting speeches about military strategy and the way it's changing in the modern world. May seem strange but it sounds to me like you two are talking about a lot of the same things. Why don't you speak to him? You'd like him anyway. His name is Warren Gable. If you want, I can find his number."

Magic is alive and thriving on our mystical streets

The following day, Mat was on a flight to New Orleans. He had called Warren on the phone and they had agreed that it would be easier to discuss matters face to face.

Before he left, Mat had also called in to the hospital to speak to Anneka. She had met with Aman Denton and had liked him. They had agreed that he would undertake exploratory surgery on Thursday. Mat just had time to get down to New Orleans, have his meeting in the evening, and then fly back East if he was needed.

Warren had suggested that they meet in a restaurant named Vever in the Old French Quarter around eight o'clock.

What Warren had failed to tell Mat was that this was Voodoo Week and the whole area was bursting with people in masks and costumes. Some had skeletons painted on their bodies, others had grotesque images painted to their faces and everywhere there was taped Voodoo music. It was a fairly corny sort of a sound, but nevertheless it gave the streets a definite atmosphere that night.

As Mat made his way through the busy streets he'd catch a different sound or rhythm in each doorway. It was like the world had just broken out into music, all speaking in tongues.

Mat arrived at the Vever and looked around. The restaurant took its name from a voodoo ritual symbol and Mat noticed there were strange markings on the floor and walls around the bar.

He looked across the restaurant. There was only one man seated alone, listening intently to the Cajun band who were playing. Mat walked over to him. The man remained intensely focused on the music that was rippling through the dancers on the small area of floor in front of the band.

The man turned round.

"Wild music, eh?" he said with a big grin.

"Certainly is."

"Man those Louisiana boys can play! That's just fine music," he said, foot tapping to the frantic dance rhythm.

"My name is Mat Durer. I'm looking for Colonel Warren Gable."

The man stood up. He was well over six feet, slim, and with the build of an athlete. He had a big, bowed chest and a grip like iron.

"Pleased to meet you, Mat," he said shaking Mat's hand. "Warren Gable. Please take a seat."

Mat sat down opposite.

"What are you going to have to drink?" asked Warren.

"What do you recommend?" asked Mat.

"Chilli martinis, boy," said Warren, raising his glass of colorless mixture. "Chilli martinis. You've just got to try one."

Mat agreed and the two of them sat sipping martinis with a kick and listening to Cajun music.

"How do you like New Orleans, Mat?" asked Warren.

"Interesting. I hadn't realized it was going to be Voodoo Week down here with all these weirdos dressed and casting spells over people."

"Yeah, kind of crazy isn't it? But that's New Orleans for you. Always the unexpected."

Neither spoke much more until the band had finished its set and the group of frantic dancers had retaken their seats.

"Now, I know we spoke a little on the phone," said Warren,

"and you explained to me what you were after and that my good friend Danny O'Connor had suggested that we talk. But that's about as far as I remember."

"That's a good enough résumé. What Danny said to me was that you had made some interesting speeches recently about military strategy in the new world. That's what I wanted to talk to you about."

"Very good, very good," said Warren. "I'll be delighted to tell you what little I know. Once we've ordered, wouldn't you say? They do some very interesting things here. Not quite Cajun sushi or samurai sushi, but highly unusual nonetheless."

The menu was long with specials such as blackened catfish, crawfish *étouffée*, file gumbo, red beans and rice, alligator sausage, bread pudding with Cajun meat pies, crabmeat ravioli aurora and, of course, *cochon au lait* with *macque choux* salad.

Mat chose the andouille gumbo made from the chef's own andouille sausage, then the blackened twin beef tenders – *petits filets* seasoned and blackened in a cast iron skillet served up with a black sauce. Warren started with the crabmeat ravioli followed by duck and shrimp dulac – tender duck breast with shrimps, leeks, sun-dried tomatoes, mushrooms, and a duck glaze. And, of course, some more chilli martinis.

Warren relaxed into his monologue as the food started to arrive. He'd been a colonel in the US Marines, recently retired but his body was still taut and upright and he kept moving in his chair as he talked.

"The thing is that warfare has changed," he said. "In the past, the idea of war was predicated on a model of symmetrical confrontation. In fact this model ran right the way through the Cold War. Essentially, the idea is that you have two armies of more or less equal competence ranged against one another – in symmetrical confrontation. They fight until one of them achieved an asymmetry – by that I mean there are more of my side alive and fighting than yours. Then the war was over. Well, you know what? That whole symmetry model is now over, finished."

"So what's taking over in its place?" asked Mat.

"Well, what it led to was a military doctrine of building larger forces and smarter weapons that would prove victorious in the struggle for asymmetry. You and I would probably call that the doctrine of 'overwhelming force.' Now we're entering an age where there are no armies to fight. Or, if there are, they never amass on a battlefield. We've entered the new age of fractured, sporadic contact, where the enemy may be as small as a unit, as a single individual. That requires a whole new way of thinking and it's what I have been talking about."

"Yes I can see that," said Mat "So where does it lead us?"

"Into a idea that was first put about by a defence strategist under the Clinton Administration, named Larry K. Smith," continued Warren. "He said that overwhelming force implies almost by definition a lack of precision. That won't work now. 'What we're going to need,' he said, 'is a much greater emphasis on the concentrated application of street smarts.' Smith called these sort of operations 'Closework.'"

Mat heard the word and everything came together. He had never felt the physical "hit" of an idea in this way before. It was almost literally uplifting.

"OK," said Warren, "I can see from the body language that you've either taken a very large slug of chilli martini or the idea appeals to you."

"The chilli martinis are good, but Closework's better," said Mat. "You know how sometimes you hear a word or an idea and it's like a revelation, an epiphany? I just had that experience. It was almost like I got religion."

"Good, we'll make you into a good Southern boy yet!" said Warren. "Closework cleared up a lot of things in my mind, too. It made me see that what we were going to need in future was extremely precise missions formed around the very highest standards of intelligence training, preparation, timing, and execution."

"So," he went on, "what Closework really means is that we will never again apply generalized solutions. Every combat from now on will depend on intimate, exact local knowledge, often inside knowledge, about the whole range of circumstances. About climate, terrain, the culture of the people we're engaging. Every local detail."

Already Mat was thinking in terms of the five-minute snapshots and how they cohered into a single workable vision of a business through the steady, continuous flow of local information and feedback. Closework was the description of all that he'd witnessed with Tactilis over the past weeks.

"Some other ideas occur to me in all this," continued Warren. "Principal among them is that often, because of the nature of intelligence gathering, we're not going to be able to acknowledge the heroes of the future. In fact, in a lot of cases we may not even know there has been an incident until some time later – if at all. So a new kind of hero is going to emerge, or at least a new understanding of heroism. Not the stand-out kind but the kind you never see."

Mat was thinking about Eric's comments and the people he'd met. And about humility.

"And I think we can also apply Closework to an understanding of how conflicts begin," said Warren. "I've read some interesting material about civil wars and how in the real world people don't sign up for one side in a great clash of civilizations, they join the guys they think are going to come out on top. If we're trying to stop enemy groups from forming in the Middle East – or in any change situation where we are trying to win hearts and minds – then we should approach it from the position of gaining as much local information as possible and even use local subcontractors to convince people. You could say that this was a retail approach, conducted down to an individual level."

Mat was ahead of him. He was thinking about the way all of this connected to his insights at Tactilis. Closework was about reality not assumptions, about verifiable facts not inference, it suggested a whole new set of behaviors and a whole new breed of heroes. It was about the CEO and the supervisor being in the same loop system. It was about dealing with how things *really* worked, rather than how they should work. It was not a strategy. It was not thinking. It was doing. It was a way of life.

Mat was also thinking about how Closework applied to the pitch. The careful consideration of appropriate evidence in a pitch situation would of course be a perfect example of Closework.

As they got up to go, Mat wanted to grab Warren by the arm and thank him for the revelation of Closework. But he was a little more restrained and simply shook his hand.

"Don't mention it," replied Warren. "Glad to be of help to you. Oh, and by the way, here's a small keepsake to remind you of New Orleans."

Warren handed over a small bag. It was a gris-gris bag. Inside there were charms.

Mat looked up at Warren.

"That's very kind of you," he said.

"Good, I hope they help you find what you're looking for," said Warren in a mock serious voice.

He paused and then added: "I bought them from a stall down the road for $1.99!"

Bursting out laughing, he headed home.

Taxi Driver No. 68772 and MGH

The following morning Mat traveled back to Boston. He went straight from the airport to the hospital by taxi.

His driver was a huge black guy called Maxine. On the way they entered part of the Big Dig tunnel system, the vast construction project across Boston that was aimed at taking much of the traffic underground. Maxine took up position in the outside lane and started to accelerate. As he passed by another cab, a younger black driver motioned to him to slow down with what looked like a coded hand signal.

Even though there was no sign of a police car or speed trap, Maxine dutifully took his foot off the gas and glided into the middle lane.

"Any problems?" asked Mat.

"No sir," replied Maxine. "Only you don't ignore the voice of a brother driver, even if you think you're right and there are no police around."

They arrived at the hospital and Mat made his way straight to his sister's room. When he arrived, he found her asleep. He subsequently spoke to one of the care team looking after her.

"She's fine," said the nurse. "Everything went very well and Dr Denton was very pleased."

"Did he discover the cause of the problem?" asked Mat, not wanting to hear the answer.

"Yes. It was a gallstone, which had become lodged in her bile duct. They're very hard to pick out on any of the scans and really the only way to be sure is to take a look," said the nurse. "They also give much the same symptoms apparently as inflammation of the pancreas. Anyway he removed the gallstone and she should be right as rain very soon."

Relief flowed through Mat's body, as though someone had given him a shot of morphine right there. Since he'd last spoken to Anneka, deep down he'd been terrified that they would find out that her problem was the same pancreatic condition that had caused their father's death. It was only now that she was clear that he could admit this to himself.

Mat took one more look in at his sleeping sister. He felt like giving her a big hug. He also felt like doing the same to Aman Denton, the practitioner surgeon. The man who saved lives by practising his art.

Old ground

From MGH, Mat took the T to Harvard. It was a slow journey and every now and again the guard would make an announcement about the fact that it had been a tough morning and they were all doing the best they could to cope with the conditions. He was being so honest about the problems it seemed the passengers didn't mind the wait. "Hey, look, guys. We all get bad days…"

Eventually the T pulled in to Harvard Square station.

Whenever Mat came back here it amused him to think that the station was almost directly under Harvard Square, under the original community that the first settlers had called New Towne. He walked toward the exit barriers; just to the right of the stairs was a Dunkin' Donuts franchise. Right underneath the hallowed ground of New Towne. Was this what the escape to a brave new world had been about?

Mat walked up the steps into Harvard Square and into bright sunlight. He crossed over J.F. Kennedy Street and walked to the Charles Hotel, where he'd booked a room for the night. The receptionist at the Charles was charm and professionalism embodied. She made him feel like they had been expecting him since they woke up that morning.

He took the lift to the third floor, along noiseless corridors hung with quilts fashioned by women in the late 19th century and now handsome works of art. His room was decorated with soft beige colors and fabrics. There was a large television, a CD player, and a Bose sound system. He lay down on the bed and fell asleep.

He awoke a little after one o'clock and for a brief moment wondered where he was. He got up and had a quick shower. He was hungry and took the elevator downstairs to Henrietta's Table. It was bustling as usual. There was a group of three men seated to his right. A fourth joined them and one of those seated stood up and introduced him as the mayor. They were all here for the cooking. "Fresh and Honest" – that's the motto printed on Henrietta's menu.

After lunch Mat took a stroll out into the streets beyond. It might seem like a strange place to choose as a retreat, one might imagine somewhere more isolated, more like Walden's log cabin, but this was where Mat felt he needed to be: staying in the comfort of the Charles with Harvard around him.

There are some places which are your spiritual home, to which you feel drawn and when there you feel different: calm, untroubled, in touch with deeper dimensions to your life. You may have little or no association with this place, little reason to be there. But once you arrive you sense the spirit of the place. It can happen anywhere, at the top of a mountain or in a restaurant, or an apartment building. For Mat it was here, in Harvard. Not because he'd been here at business school. It was just that he felt calm here, like he could see for miles.

He had been close to collapse when he stood at the water's edge in Pittsburgh. But the meeting in New Orleans, Anneka's recovery, and his own resilience had turned things around. He had regained, at last, his sense of direction.

He walked back past Harvard Square and the entrance to Harvard Yard and the First Unitarian Church. Then he stopped, at the Old Burying Ground at the edge of the Common. It was where the first new citizens had chosen to bury their dead. For Mat this small patch of ground had a real sense of history that many of the grander buildings lacked. Perhaps it was because there were real people buried here, and in the names on the plates one could read a simpler story: soldier, slave, wife.

Mat walked around the Common and then over to the Harvard Book Store on Massachusetts Avenue. He browsed around the bookshelves. Not allowing himself to think but simply being in the place he had chosen. He felt calm, focused even, but strangely not on any particular subject. He wandered from cookery shelves to poetry and picked up a copy of Robert Frost to read the lines: "But I have promises to keep, And miles to go before I sleep."

He went back out into the sunlight and walked over to the Charles. He had a sense that things had been decided within him and he should let them work. It was as if he were a computer, connected and online but with new software downloaded on to its hard disk. The new software wouldn't work unless you switched the system off and rebooted. You had to shut down, start up again, wait for the virus scan to run, then operate.

Mat spent the rest of the day in his room at the Charles Hotel, listening to music and reading the volume of Robert Frost poems that he had bought from the Harvard Book Store. He had a quiet supper at Henrietta's Table and went to bed early.

He woke several hours later. It was quiet and the room was slightly too warm. He looked at the clock. It was 2.30. He felt like he had been brought back from a dream he could feel but not remember. He felt different, changed. He tried to remember the dream but it was still distant, like a figure in the mist.

He got up and walked over to the mini bar and took out a bottle of water. He looked around and saw his attaché case lying on top of the desk. He opened it and reached for the fragment of sponge inside a pocket on the lid.

He felt the sponge and remembered the dream. He was diving with Marianne and they were swimming side by side. Without saying anything she reached out and held his hand. That was what he remembered: the two of them swimming together. That was good and true; it was her he missed. She had been the center of that dream.

Old acquaintances not forgot

"Hello Angela," Mat said to one of the three receptionists on duty at Hardings' peach colored head offices.

"Hello, Mr Durer, it's nice to see you."

"Thank you, Angela. I'm here unannounced I'm afraid. I just wondered whether Brad Johnson was available. I wanted a quick word with him."

"Of course, Mr Durer. I'll try his line now."

Fortunately, Brad was in the office and came down to greet Mat in one of the client meeting rooms.

"Mat, what a pleasant surprise. I thought you'd be hard at it with your pitch team, burrowing away through the research."

"Well, I know this is going to sound like I'm offering you a hollow victory, Brad, but I'm off the pitch team. So it's all over to you – to screw up without any help from me."

"Goodness, didn't you match up?" asked Brad.

"Something like that," said Mat.

"Well, probably all for the best. We've put together a real first-class team for this pitch and we both know that what Oxytec really need is some heavyweight support at the executive level. Peter made that pretty clear to Anthony when they met and I got the same impression from the guys at Bond & Co."

"Oh really, my reading was rather different," said Mat. "But that's immaterial now. I've come to ask for a favor. I need to get an introduction to Jim Bates. You worked with him on the Isotronics account and I thought you could put in a good word for me."

"Jim Bates," said Brad with genuine surprise. "Sure I know him, but I'd have thought *you* would know that he's just retired. Got a few non-exec positions, but effectively he's removed himself from front-line fighting for good. Wants to concentrate on writing his autobiography and growing wine – or so I've heard."

"Yes, I do know he's retired."

"So what possible good could he do you or your consulting firm, Mat? You do know that CEOs commission business and everyone else says yes don't you?" said Brad.

"Yes, I remember you telling me that some time ago."

"Well, obviously it didn't register, because Jim Bates is no longer a CEO. He's out of the picture, a person of no importance to the fee earner."

"Yes I know. I just want to talk to him. Get his advice about something."

"You mean how to become a celebrity CEO without really trying?"

"No, I want to ask him about Northern Utilities. I think he might have something interesting to say."

"That water outfit up in Michigan? He wasn't there for more than a year or so."

"Even so, I'm interested in speaking to him."

"OK. I'll call him. He lives out north of the city on some big farm by a lake – you know, Walden territory. He probably thinks it's his little log cabin where he can settle down to write."

Mat stared at him.

"OK enough," said Brad, smirking. "I'll call him and see what I can arrange. But you owe me one."

"I always did," said Mat.

"Too right. Oh, one other thing," said Brad as Mat stood up. "You did know that Peter Smith was a Hardings alumnus, didn't you? Left us in '87."

"Yes, I did know actually," said Mat.

"Makes the decision pretty much a foregone conclusion wouldn't you say?" said Brad.

"Probably," said Mat.

Brad was about to leave the room when he turned to Mat one last time.

"By the way," he said, "I'm meeting up with your good friend Marianne in a couple of days."

Mat stiffened. He hadn't spoken to Marianne since he'd received her letter along with his attaché case.

"Oh, really," said Mat, not wanting to let Brad know that he and Marianne hadn't been speaking, though by the smug look on Brad's face it seemed he suspected something.

"Yes, the afternoon after the pitch actually. You probably know Anthony has got her doing some work on the San Francisco offices," said Brad. "In fact, Anthony has been amazingly supportive of her since her business nearly went bust."

Astonished at this comment, Mat looked across at Brad.

"What do you mean nearly went bust?" he asked.

"That's right. While the two of you were on your romantic trip to the Turks, I gather. Her business partner walked out and she had no one running the show. Not only that, but he walked out with most of her money. Anthony helped her get in touch with some financiers that would give her a bridge until she came back. It didn't work out but she insisted on staying on the Islands to stick by you. Can't think why. She put her own business at risk, right down to the wire."

Mat looked at Brad, still stunned by the news.

"Anyway, I'm sure you knew all of that really," said Brad.

Mat mumbled something that sounded like "Absolutely." All he could think of was that evening at Mambo on the Turks, dancing with Marianne and the sound of sadness in Yolanda's voice. She had lied to protect him. He had sensed that then, but had not asked himself why.

"Well Marianne is one of the family now," continued Brad, sensing that the intended damage of his comments had been done. "And since it's the 20th anniversary of our operations in California, a few of us are flying down in the corporate jet to do a bit of PR and pressing the flesh over there. Anthony thought it might be fun if she joined us on the trip. Naturally, I agreed."

"Naturally," said Mat, turning to go and staring down at the floor. "Well be sure to have a good flight down there."

"We will," said Brad. "By then we'll have the Oxytec business to celebrate."

Getting back on the pitch

On his way out of Boston, Mat phoned Max. There was no reply from his cell phone. He left a message.

"Max, it's Mat Durer here. I wanted to speak to you about the Oxytec pitch. I appreciate that the team might think I have let them down, but I have discovered something that I think could really help. It will make all the difference. So please call me back. Thanks."

Interview at Jim Bates's house, Up Island, Martha's Vineyard

It was late afternoon in the garden at the rear of my house on Martha's Vineyard. But Mat was anything but relaxed. Rather, he had the look of someone who was about to walk into a boxing ring – for a title fight.

"If I have only got ten minutes then I'd better be direct," he said. "So excuse me if this sounds a bit abrupt. But you'll get the drift.

"First, I want to tell you about an idea called Closework."

He paused.

"Then I'm going to persuade you to pitch this idea to the board of Oxytec. Because when I've finished telling you about it, you'll believe in it as much as I do."

"You sound pretty confident. But then, so do all snake oil salesman," I said surprised at his bravado.

"I am confident," said Mat. "Very confident. And if you don't buy the idea in ten minutes, I'll finish my iced tea and walk out of here."

He clinked the ice cubes of his drink against the glass and raised it in a mock gesture of "cheers."

"Agreed?" he asked.

Probably because I wanted to get rid of the guy as quickly and as expeditiously as possible I said "agreed."

"Do you believe in ghosts?" he asked.

"No," I said, flatly.

"Fine, then I'll make a note to convince you of that, too. Though it might take a little longer."

The pitch

The Oxytec pitch took place at 2.30 p.m. at the company's corporate headquarters in New Jersey.

The steering committee who had been assembled to decide it were: Peter Smith CEO; Sarah Cummings, CFO; Sam Gordon, Group Counsel; Taylor Wilkes, Vice President Innovation; Philip Moore, President European Operations; John Lime, Bond & Co; Jim Breszinski, Bond & Co.

Tactilis were second up. Hardings had made their pitch in the morning. After lunch it was always that little bit more difficult to get the client to engage.

As the seven members of the steering committee filed into the room they found a sheet of white paper at each of their places. It was a confidentiality agreement. It required each of the committee to sign that they would keep the contents of the Tactilis presentation confidential.

That was going to make them sit up and take notice. You don't normally start off a meeting like this by making demands on your prospective clients.

At precisely 2.30 p.m., the Tactilis team walked into the room. It was a team of four: Max Larsen, Eric Stadler, Elias Katzonopolis, and Nancy Dearden. Mat and I followed a little way behind them. The front-line team entered the room looking very composed. Like they knew exactly what they were going to do over the next 40 minutes. Just before they had come in, Katz had reminded them of his tournament advice: "Stay focused, have ice for blood."

They took their seats.

Max introduced the team and briefly mentioned Mat and me – saying he would explain my presence a little later in the proceedings. He then thanked the members of the steering committee for signing the confidentiality paper. "I realize that this is a little unorthodox but we have one or two unusual elements to our presentation this afternoon and we need to have complete freedom to use them to their full potential."

Unusually indirect words from Max, but he was obviously wanting to keep his powder dry.

Then Max got Eric to start the presentation. Eric stood up and outlined the scope of the pre-analysis phase and how they had visited plants in Germany and the US. He talked about how they could make sustainable cuts to operating costs and significant improvements to asset utilization. He also outlined the real opportunities to improve organizational effectiveness through a new design.

"Overall," said Eric, "we are confident that we can take out $100 million from your costs within a period of 18 months."

A few of the steering committee members looked up from their papers. The words "million" and "hundred" always get the audience going.

"But of course you probably knew that already," said Eric.

Now Peter Smith was looking up.

"Anyone can make you a promise. What you want to know is can we deliver? Can we deliver significant, sustainable change?"

You could see right there from the glint in Smith's eyes and the way his CFO fidgeted with her pencil, that that was indeed exactly what they were after. This was the Holy Grail. This was stock price up ten digits. This was PE up by a couple of dollars. This was front cover *Business Week*.

Katz and Nancy got up. They both had a small stack of documents.

"In these pages," said Katz, holding one of the documents up, "you'll see the first-glance findings of our visits to your plants. You'll see where we have identified overlap and unnecessary management supervision."

"You'll also see our initial outline proposals for a new organizational design," added Nancy, "that will improve your internal processes, your management control systems, and the relationships between the departments we have scoped out."

Katz took over again.

"We've identified functional divisions, inefficient reporting structures, areas lacking in clearly defined responsibilities and ownership, high labor and indirect costs, and structures which result in fragmented activity and lack of focus.

"We have also, you'll be pleased to know, identified the areas where in our opinion you're reaching six sigma and performance is excellent."

Then he handed back to Nancy.

"Finally," she said, "you'll see in this proposal a provisional road map for how we would approach the project, together with a very simplified guide to some of the timescales and milestones we'd envision."

With that Katz and Nancy passed over copies of the Tactilis proposal to the seven members of the committee.

Eric stood up again and joined Katz and Nancy.

"We have put all our recommendations to you in that document. These are obviously initial recommendations, but we have tried to be as specific as possible. You may have a number of questions, which we would of course be glad to answer. But I come back to the basic questions you will have: Can they deliver? How will they deliver? Frankly, nothing else matters."

Now Max joined his team. His pro ball, hard ball champions.

"We can't convince you that our recommendations will work. Because right now those proposals are on paper. They are theory. Only words. And if you know anything about Tactilis you'll know that we are practitioners. We act. So we have this divide. We have to explain to you on paper what we know will only come alive through actions. It's how we get people to actually change behaviors that matters. And we do that through working with supervisors and maintenance men and customer services reps and production managers and secretaries and firemen and shift workers and everyone else we come into contact with. That delivers not just the sort of cost savings we've outlined in our document, but lasting sustainable change."

He moved toward the door and gave it a light tap.

"How do we bring to you the reality of change?" Max continued.

"Well, we're going to take a risk. We're going to ask you to listen to someone who's experienced this change first hand."

Max walked over to where I was sitting with Mat. I was wearing a blue suit with the neat tip of a white handkerchief just visible in my breast pocket, a powder-blue tie and black brogues. I was sharp, smart and didn't care who knew it.

It was about to be my turn on stage.

"Let me introduce at this point, Jim Bates," he said.

"Jim Bates is the former CEO of a number of major corporations which will be well known to you. He has very kindly agreed to join us and share his experiences of his time at Northern Utilities – a project we were also heavily involved in. Jim, thank you."

I stood up.

"Thank you, Max, and good afternoon ladies and gentlemen, Peter, Sarah," I said nodding to the members of the committee in friendly recognition.

"May I first say that, unfortunately, Tactilis have declined to offer me any incentive – financial or otherwise – to talk to you today. I'm here on my own time, so we had better make this quick." I was warming the audience up. They knew I didn't do much charity work.

"I'm here because a few days ago I was at home writing and I got a call from a young man," I turned and gestured toward Mat, "who said he needed my assistance and wanted to come to see me."

"I agreed. His name is Mat Durer and he works for Tactilis. He spent four hours at my home one afternoon getting very passionate about a set of discoveries he'd made about making business work. I was intrigued. I felt I had spent much of my life doing exactly the same thing. Some people have been kind enough to credit me with a good deal of success at this activity. But the reason I am here is because when Mat had finished getting all passionate about business, he then asked me to talk to you about failure. My failure."

There were looks of surprise from the committee. They'd been expecting a commercial not a confession.

"Yes, it's an original request isn't it?" I said, walking about the space at the end of the table.

"It's the reason why I have asked Tactilis to ensure that each of you signed a confidentiality agreement before this meeting started."

I stood in front of the committee.

"Why did I agree to this unusual request? Well, in part, because what Mat told me and what I knew from my own experiences at Northern Utilities compelled me to. Also, because I like a little theatre."

There was a chuckle from the audience; they were warming.

"Raymond Chandler once wrote 'When in doubt have a man come through the door with a gun in his hand.' Well I am that man, and the gun I have is the truth."

There was more low laughter.

"Here's the truth. The simplest strategy for any business is to have the best core technical operations possible. In other words do your core business brilliantly. The rest will take off itself. Why is this constantly ignored?" I asked.

I was really playing the room now, walking around the edge of the table, eyeballing the audience.

"Because ladies and gentlemen, it's so damn hard to do. It's hard work. Or rather, as I discovered from my conversations with Mat, it's Closework."

I turned and wrote CLOSEWORK in big letters on the flip chart board to the side of him.

Then I underlined the word with a flourish.

"Neat word, simple concept. I'll come back to that in a moment. But let me talk to you first a little about failure."

"Let me start with a story from NU. We were involved in a big IT program – a change program. One Friday, I got a call from the manager who was running it. He said he and the team were having a strategic meeting and wanted to share some important findings with me. He asked me if I could attend an offsite meeting that afternoon. I agreed – this change program was pretty much top of our agenda.

"Anyway, I get to the meeting and the manager and his peers sit me down in front of a screen and put up some figures. The figures were derived from the new IT systems we'd installed, which instead of measuring each individual business in its own unique way, applied a common data platform to all of them. I looked at the figures. And then I looked again. And I said to the guys, 'If these figures are right, we'll be bust in a few weeks.' And they said: 'They are right.' And I thought, 'Holy shit, we have a burning platform here.'

"I had no idea. I was the CEO of the group and I had no idea that we were on the edge of disaster. We'd been running the business on what you could call hearsay data, not facts. Quite simply, I had failed.

"How did this happen? Lots of ways. When you hear yourself talking about 'changing the culture of the company' and what you really mean is 'let's get the employees to change not us, we're fine'. That's failure.

"Or when you get to the point in your career when you think leadership is about throwing a ball over the fence and saying 'That's the plan, now go do it. Oh and by the way, don't make me look bad in the process.' That's failure, too.

"Failure comes when you're outside of the business. And at NU, I wasn't in the business and my managers weren't in the business. We worked extremely hard and very long hours, but we were outside the business. We thought that we were supposed to do the planning and strategy. But that just meant we were externalizing ourselves.

"So how did we put this right?" I said. This was my big theatrical moment. My chance to grab their minds.

I paused a little longer and looked down at the ground before speaking.

"OK here's what I learned from the NU turnaround. These points aren't in any exact order and some of them I've got to by talking through Mat's ideas on Closework. But here goes anyway."

I walked into the center of the room, maneuvering myself into a little extra space. This was a business aria that was about to happen so I needed a stage.

"First, forget about creating a chain of command in your company. What you're doing is creating a flow, a flow of energy and ideas and local information. This flow connects the mechanic to the boardroom. So instead of thinking about hierarchies think about rivers and streams, channels of energy.

"Flow also directs people. You only get people to go where you want by shaping the flow.

"Flow doesn't happen by cranking up the lines of responsibility. It's created by getting the interfaces between people right. By that I mean how people talk to one another, in meetings letting everyone have their say. Without that freedom there is no flow. Recognize that business only happens when people interact. So get your meetings right. Put in a system that compels people to meet often, but only ever discuss facts. Never opinions. At the end of each meeting make sure it leads to specific actions.

"Generate wins by focus, key down onto a very few items and constantly measure your performance in these areas. At NU, we aligned everything to fit with our focus on these core criteria.

"Encourage local informers. In fact only rely on local information. If guys on the ground say something isn't working, they're probably right. Ask them – often.

"You only know and learn by doing. In other words, action is the key to any success, not thinking. Get people to improve by encouraging practice, within a context that allows for mistakes. We had a lot of talented people at NU. They didn't pull us round as a business. It was the people who actually did things who made the difference. That wasn't something I'd expected. Reward performance.

"If part of your business isn't working. Go down and fix it. Yourself.

"Think also about creating a whole new cadre of employee: the fixers. Their role is to coach others on how to get through situations; they listen to problems, they have the social skills to bring the best out in people. These fixers are not managers – although if you had more fixers you might well need fewer managers. They should be paid very well.

"Get managers into the flow of work. How? We got them involved in gathering the data, not just reviewing it.

"There's no such thing as a Hollywood command in business. You know, when John Wayne says something like: 'That's an order, Kowalksi.' In business, everything is by negotiation. And all business is personal.

"Be very generous with facts. Give the facts to those who are actually generating your business. Give your customer service rep your customer facts. But also give them the facts about how well they're performing. Don't let managers be the only ones who review the data.

"Behaviors are the fundamental of your business. Recognize that the biggest influence on behaviors are facts.

"Create an unbreakable connection from action to measurement. What gets measured gets done. I repeat, what gets measured gets done.

"Believe in people. Ultimately, most of us would rather do a good job than a bad one. Optimism is why we're in business.

"Finally and here's the biggest surprise of all. Strategies grow out of performance and not the other way round. The best way to build a strategy is to measure your key performance indicators and then work out from those. That way you're always basing strategy on reality. Otherwise strategy may be no more than a wish list and based on unreliable data. This holistic strategy I'm suggesting will not give you a new direction so much as a new way to be. But isn't that what strategy is all about anyway?"

I had finished my speech. I thought it was a reasonable performance. For a moment I was sure that one of the guys from Bond & Co. had a bead of sweat on his brow.

I looked around at the seven people who were sitting on the other side of the table from me.

"That's what I learned from my time at NU," I said.

I turned back to the flip chart.

"It's what I would now call Closework," I said, underlining the word again.

I waited for another brief moment, holding their attention for emphasis.

"One final question, which I'm sure is on your minds," I said. "It certainly would be on mine – why did I agree to talk to you?

"When Mat came to see me, he talked about how he had experienced failure and how a business he'd worked on had subsequently closed. His story struck a chord with me. Because when I looked back I recognized that some of the successes I had taken credit for didn't last very long after I had left. At the time, I thought that I was the critical factor and that my leaving was the reason things didn't work out. The business world supported me in that assumption – all power to the CEO, right? But listening to Mat made me look at the pattern in a different way, from a Closework perspective. Maybe there was another story here, maybe I hadn't changed all that much in my companies. Sure, things had looked good for a while, but I hadn't altered performance deep down. I took the successes and moved on, but the companies I'd left still had their faults, their inherent weaknesses.

"I now realize that I had, at best, only limited success and that what matters is the deep down change, both in a company and personally. You can have the smartest strategies in town but if you haven't made the right changes deep down, those ideas will ultimately fail.

"That's what Mat discovered in Pittsburgh. It's what I am discovering now. And it's why the lessons of Closework are so persuasive for me – because they're about deep down change."

I was now looking straight at Peter Smith and his steering committee.

"You don't have to appoint these people. But I just wanted you to know the truth about the turnaround at NU and how it happened. When you go through their proposals you won't see Closework in the margin. But if you want to know how they're going to deliver – then I've just told you."

I had no more to say. I sat down.

Peter Smith looked about at his colleagues and then said:

"Well thank you, Jim. It's always a pleasure to see you and you've given us a lot to think about. Do you have any questions, anyone?" He looked down the line of his fellow steering committee members. One or two shook their heads, others smiled.

"And Max, do you have anything more to add?"

"No thank you, Peter. Our recommendations are all in those documents. We'd love to work with you and hope we have the chance. If you have any queries, please call me or one of the team: Eric, Katz, Nancy, or Mat."

The pitch over, the Tactilis team gathered their papers to leave.

As they were walking out of the door, Eric caught Mat's sleeve.

"That was a great show," said Eric. "But can you really do it? Can you perform?" It was his parting reminder of who was still boss in this pack.

Mat smiled. He walked over and thanked me for what I'd done in the meeting.

"I hope I gave a true account of what we discussed." I said.

"Absolutely," replied Mat, "Just spot on."

"Good, because I rather enjoyed it actually," I said. "Got me thinking about changing my autobiography – or maybe writing something else entirely."

"Well, I'm glad we've been some inspiration," said Mat and shook my hand.

The Tactilis group were leaving ahead of him and Max and I were getting back to talking when Peter Smith walked out of the conference room. He made his way over to Mat.

"Just one question," Peter said quietly to Mat. "How did you know that Jim had failed at NU when he'd been such a success everywhere else?"

"I talked to the guys on the ground," said Mat.

At the airport

Mat should have been feeling a huge sense of relief. The pitch was over. He had done everything he could to win it for Tactilis. His job was done. Now it was up to Peter Smith and his team to decide.

But Mat wasn't feeling relieved. Quite the opposite. The first thing he thought about once the pitch had concluded was the Hardings team taking off to California. Marianne was going with them. Of course he now knew that the real reason for the trip was to keep her company going and earn a large commission from Hardings, but nevertheless Mat was uncomfortable. He hated the idea of her flying off with Brad. Above all, it didn't feel right to Mat. He had that sense of premonition again, just like he'd had on the yacht in Miami. Something was about to happen.

For the first time in his life, Mat acted on impulse. He came out of the Oxytec offices, said goodbye to Eric, Katz and the others and got in a taxi to Laveau Airport, a private airport on the south side of town. He was going to stop Marianne from taking that flight.

Thirty minutes later Mat was standing at the front entrance to the Laveau.

Cars pulled up.

Anthony Elliott and Brad got out of one; other Hardings' colleagues out of the others.

"Mat," said Anthony, "What a pleasant surprise to see you again. Quite unexpected."

"Yes, I'm here to have a quick word with Marianne. She's been away in Europe and I haven't managed to catch up with her yet about plans for the weekend."

"How very gallant of you to come out all the way to the airport, rather than calling her on the phone," said Brad.

Anthony shot him a glance.

"Yes, how thoughtful of you," said Anthony. "Marianne has kindly agreed to help out with the redecoration of our San

Francisco offices and I thought it might be a good idea if we all traveled together."

"Sure," said Mat. "I just want to have a word with her before she goes."

"Very good. Well, we'll leave you to it. We'll go inside,"

Anthony, Brad, and the others pushed through the swing doors and entered into the VIP lounge.

Mat stood waiting outside. Other cars and taxis pulled up and Mat checked each one of them for Marianne. No sign. Mat waited another ten minutes. Perhaps she was already here.

Mat walked inside and made his way to the welcome desk.

"Do you know if a Miss Marianne Grover has checked in to the VIP suite yet?" he asked.

"Just one minute, sir," said the young woman on the desk. "I'll check for you."

She hit the keys on the terminal in front of her and waited a few seconds.

"No, sir. No one by that name has checked in yet," she said.

"Thank you so much," said Mat and walked back outside.

As he emerged, another taxi pulled up. He could see Marianne sitting in the back.

He opened the door for her.

"Hello Marianne, darling…"

"Mat, what on earth are you doing here?" she said, cutting him short.

"I needed to see you," he said. "I needed to talk to you."

"Not now," she said. "I'm taking a flight with Hardings over to San Francisco and I'm late already."

She handed over a few notes to the taxi driver and got out of the car.

"You could at least say you're pleased to see me," said Mat.

"Of course I'm pleased, it's just that this is the wrong time and the wrong place to have a heart to heart."

"I know that," said Mat. "I haven't just come to talk. I've come to stop you taking the flight."

"Don't be ridiculous," said Marianne, looking at him with a mix of anger and impatience. "I'm a guest of Anthony Elliott on the corporate jet. I'm not turning that invitation down thank you."

"But you must," said Mat, taking hold of her arm.

She shook his grip away angrily.

"Who the hell do you think you are?" she said. "You don't own me you know!"

"Yes, I know. But I can't let you get on that plane."

"If this is some absurd act of wounded male pride, you can forget it," said Marianne, picking up her bags and making to walk around Mat. "I'm on this flight for strictly business purposes. We can talk when I get back."

"No," said Mat firmly. "I can't let you leave."

"Jesus, Mat. What's come over you? You're acting like a madman. I thought there'd been something strange about you lately and now I'm sure. If you don't get out of my way this instant then we're over, finished. Do you understand?"

Mat held firm.

"Look, I know this is going to sound odd but I have a bad feeling about you going to San Francisco. I have had this kind of feeling before and it's proved right. So I have to believe it now, too. I can't let you go off to San Francisco."

"Bad feelings! What kind of an explanation is that? You're losing it, you know that, Mat? You're really losing it. No wonder you couldn't take it at Hardings any more."

Mat took hold of her arm once more and tightened his grip.

"I'm not losing it. Four months ago I saw the ghost of my dead father. Ever since then, I have been having premonitions. Getting signs about things. That's what's happening right now. I am being told you shouldn't go to San Francisco. Pure and simple."

"You're sick, Mat," she said, looking at him straight in the eyes. "Honestly, your father's ghost? You need help."

She pulled away from him again and walked toward the doors.

He turned swiftly and barred her way.

"All right, don't believe me. I don't blame you. But here's

something you have to believe. I love you. I want to marry you."

Marianne looked at him.

"I know now what you did for me on the Turks," he said. "I know all about what happened to your business and I know that you were prepared to sacrifice everything for me. You didn't talk about it. You did it. That makes all the difference."

She took a step forward and started beating her hands on his chest, tears streaming from her eyes.

"You bastard. Why now? You nearly ruined my whole life. I loved you and you wanted to ruin my life. Why now?"

He tried to clasp her arms but she was still striking out at him wildly.

"Because I didn't know right from wrong until today. Because I got confused between being somewhere new and being with someone new. Above all, because I've learned to stop thinking and start acting," he said and brought her into his arms. "That's my secret to life and I'm going to stick to it."

He held her for a moment and then kissed her eyes and face and lips.

"Do you mean it?" she asked, gasping between deep sobs.

"Yes I mean it," he said.

She tilted her head back and tried to wipe away her tears. Her hands were shaking, her shoulders convulsing slightly.

"I should leave you, you know," she said.

"No, you can't do that," he replied looking straight at her "You know you can't do that. Not when I love you."

She held him again as though now she would never let him go and kissed him.

"All right. If it means that much to you, I won't go. I'll just go and tell Anthony I can't come," said Marianne.

"No, you wait here," he said. "I'll tell them. Hang on to the taxi. Perhaps he can take us back into town and find a registry office or something."

"Maybe we should take a flight to Grand Turk instead," she said, smiling.

"Great idea. Hold that thought. I'll be back in a moment."

Mat walked inside and over to the welcome desk.

"Hello again," he said. "Could you tell Mr Elliott in the Hardings party that Ms Grover won't be taking the flight after all."

"So I can see," said the young woman, smiling and looking out at Marianne waiting by the taxi.

Mat smiled at her and went back out to join Marianne.

They got into the taxi together and set off into town. Seated on the back seat with their arms around one another, they felt closer than they ever had.

It was like being underwater.

"Sending me that fragment of sponge in my attaché case was a lovely thing to do," said Mat, leaning down and touching the case.

"What fragment of sponge?" she said. "I never put anything in your attaché case."

Reuters News Headlines

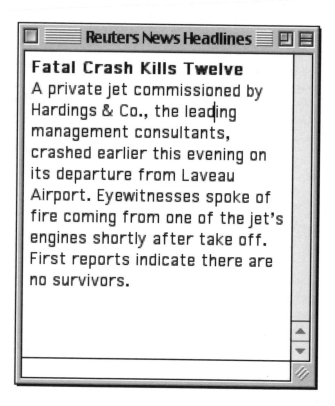

Reuters News Headlines

Fatal Crash Kills Twelve
A private jet commissioned by
Hardings & Co., the leading
management consultants,
crashed earlier this evening on
its departure from Laveau
Airport. Eyewitnesses spoke of
fire coming from one of the jet's
engines shortly after take off.
First reports indicate there are
no survivors.

Coda

It was a warm, spring afternoon on Martha's Vineyard. The trees were coming into leaf and the garden was beginning to regain its color and shape.

I was sitting on the bench beneath the American oak, just as I had been when I had first met Mat those months before. The sunlight flickered on the fresh green leaves above and a soft breeze blew in from the ocean. It was hard not to feel uplifted by the sense of life burgeoning all around.

My thoughts turned to the tragic events some months before.

For me, the world changed that day of the crash. I had taken little direct part in the actions; I was an observer, yet nevertheless I was profoundly influenced. Obviously, I was distressed on a personal level at the loss. But it would be true to say that I was also deeply affected professionally. The tragedy had for me signalled the passing of an age.

The hegemony had passed from the people who relied on ideas. In particular, there had been the belief that a business, or indeed a life, could be improved by ideas and intellect; that thinking was all that ultimately counted and that talent determined success and career. With the crash, all that passed.

I knew Anthony would have been persuaded by what Mat had told me and what I said at the pitch, even though Hardings as a business has since continued. I knew he would have seen the truth of Closework and even he, the Grand Master, would have recognized that the torch had passed from "thinking" to "doing."

Indeed, on that warm afternoon, with the lush world of natural life on the big upswing to Spring, I thought how the Grand Master would have smiled at the sudden reversal of his play, would have realized he had walked into check mate.

At that moment, I had the strong feeling that he was sitting there on the bench with me. He was still wearing that elegant suit from Huntsman of Savile Row.

He smiled.

"Don't worry, Jim, everything is quite all right. I just thought you might need a little jog. The game is not done. You have one more move to make."

"What do you mean?" I asked.

"Closework," he said. "It's not quite complete. You've avoided giving me a resolution."

"Yes, I have been thinking about that too," I said. "And I have felt here, now, in the garden, that Closework is about building the DNA of doing. At its most elemental, Closework says there is a DNA of doing."

"What, you mean the basic, simple building blocks of all the complexities of life are just four little letters: ATCG – that sort of thing?" remarked Anthony.

"Yes," I replied. "However complex the activity, it comes down to the repetition of simple basic blocks. You can only discover these building blocks through experience. Once discovered, you then have to connect them and you have to let them grow. Then these small, unremarkable actions will grow into a strategy more brilliant than any idea. Equally, of course, the secret of long-term, sustainable business is getting the right simple blocks in place."

I felt excited, elated that Anthony had pushed me to a final understanding.

"And you can apply this to a single activity or a whole company," I said. "If you want to turn around a company or a life, you have to start with the building blocks, the DNA of doing, of individual actions."

"The DNA of doing," said Anthony with a wry smile. "Yes I like that. That will do fine."

I looked out to sea and he was gone.

Why and how this book happened

Why are most business books so similar in their approach? Why does the world of business feel compelled to be so damn academic? After all business takes place in the real world; it's about people coming together to solve problems. These simple, everyday truths seem so often to get passed over in the search for the next all-powerful theory. It's as if the words "big business" mean we have to stop thinking about reality and ascend to a different world where credibility can only be achieved through the use of abstract language.

This book came about through our meeting Celerant Consulting. They are a company with a radically different approach to business. They combine a hard-nosed focus on delivering quantifiable results with a profoundly optimistic belief in people and a willingness to engage with such intangibles as motivation and desire. Corny as it may sound, they believe that people actually want to improve, that they come to work *wanting to do better*. Their track record of successful and sustainable change in business performance is built on this assumption. Although they wouldn't put it like this, they have a philosophy of business as profound and intellectually robust as their more cerebral competitors.

As writers we were intrigued: how do you communicate this kind of vision? The standard consulting firm device – a fact-based argument (often citing the same "usual suspects") leading to a theoretical hypothesis – seemed totally inappropriate here. The traditionally impersonal style of business literature felt just that, too impersonal, to do justice to what they do.

The more we talked, the more we realized that fiction was the best way of exploring these views. A novel, with its world of characters, experiences, and events together with its narrative drive, would allow the reader to literally "feel" the difference in Celerant's approach to business. The kind of change they have brought about in hundreds of companies over the past 20 years needs to be lived to be believed. Its powerful and challenging intellectual underpinning needs to be understood *during and after* the experience not *instead or outside* of it.

All business stories are human stories.

Acknowledgments

We are grateful to the people of Celerant and in particular to its CEO and founder Ian Clarkson for their commitment and involvement. We would also like to thank those individuals in Celerant's client companies who shared their experiences with us. Needless to say, all the characters in the book are fictional and there are no representations of any particular company or any specific situation. Tactilis as a consulting firm shares many values with Celerant but it is not Celerant.

We have incorporated a number of other people's thinking into the argument of the book, and where appropriate, made this explicit in the text. We are, obviously, indebted to Joe Klein for his article "Closework" that appeared in the *New Yorker*. We found Atul Gawande's book *Complications* an inspiration, and were taken, in particular, with his discussion on the importance of practice. We enjoyed Malcolm Gladwell's *New Yorker* article "The Talent Myth" and cover some of the same ground. We would like to thank a number of divers who have shared their world with us.

We want to thank those who commented on early versions of the book – Jill Burnett, Benedicte Clarkson, Claire Crocker, Dwight Gertz, Catherine Reynolds, and Rob Reynolds.

Thanks are also due to those who helped make the book a reality – Kevin Foong, Malcolm Glyn, and Helen Blake at Celerant; Martin Liu, Rob Andrews, and especially Pom Somkabcharti at Cyan Communications.

AL & SG

About the authors

Adam Lury spent 20 highly successful years in advertising and management consulting and then re-invented himself as an author. He teamed up with Simon Gibson to write the acclaimed *Dangerous Data* and its follow-up *Blood Data*, introducing a new cybersleuth, Arthur C. Dogg.

Simon Gibson has been a writer since giving up a highly flawed career as a teacher in Spain. He has worked as a speechwriter for a number of the leading companies in Europe and the United States. He has also worked on award-winning scripts for documentary films and television and contributed to the *Financial Times* and *The Times*. He now writes books with Adam Lury.